Using Microsoft® and IBM® BASIC

THE PWS-KENT SERIES IN COMPUTER SCIENCE

Using Microsoft® and IBM® BASIC
AN INTRODUCTION TO COMPUTER PROGRAMMING

Julien Hennefeld
BROOKLYN COLLEGE, CUNY

PWS-KENT PUBLISHING COMPANY
BOSTON

PWS-KENT
Publishing Company

20 Park Plaza
Boston, Massachusetts 02116

PWS-KENT Publishing Company is a division of Wadsworth, Inc.

Library of Congress Cataloging-in-Publication Data

Hennefeld, Julien O.
  Using Microsoft and IBM BASIC.

  Includes index.
  1. BASIC (Computer program language)   I. Title.
QA76.73.B3H47   1987   005.13'3   86-25489
ISBN 0-87150-087-6

Printed in the United States of America

     89 90 91 — 10 9 8 7 6 5 4 3

Sponsoring Editor: Robert Prior
Production Coordinator and Cover Designer: Robine Storm van Leeuwen
Production: Editing, Design & Production, Inc.
Cover Photo: © Eric Carle, New York/Stock, Boston
Typesetting: Maryland Composition
Cover Printing: Phoenix Color Corp.
Printing and Binding: The Maple-Vail Book Manufacturing Group

to
my parents, Lillian and Edmund,
and
Marianne, Daniel, and Maggie

Preface

Using Microsoft and IBM BASIC: An Introduction to Computer Programming is intended for a first course in computer programming and requires no previous computer experience. It is written specifically for the Microsoft and IBM dialects of BASIC. Reflecting a modern, structured programming style, the use of meaningful variable names is illustrated and encouraged. FOR-NEXT loops and WHILE loops are used almost exclusively, with handmade loops relegated to a brief chapter that cautions the reader about their shortcomings.

In this book, I also place great emphasis on having the students learn to use pseudocode and stepwise refinement as tools in writing their programs. Consequently, for many of the programming illustrations, the solution is arrived at in stages by the use of these techniques.

Using Microsoft and IBM BASIC is written to be read and enjoyed. A good textbook should do more than present the material thoroughly, it should also teach the material so that the reader can genuinely assimilate it. This text employs a number of novel pedagogical devices that make it especially readable. There are many short programs whose printouts the reader is asked to determine before reading on. For some of the more complicated programs, the reader, informed of what the program is to accomplish, must fill in one or two blank program lines. Most importantly, when introducing a new topic, this book gives a working understanding of the concepts before moving on to more technical details.

The program examples are not only lively and interesting, but they also give the reader the flavor of more complicated programs from the real world. Examples range from simpler programs, such as campaign letter, automatic teller, and psychotherapy programs, to more complex programs, such as the membership file maintenance program in Chapter 27 and the artificial intelligence program in Chapter 28.

Note to the Instructor

There is a well-balanced exercise set for each chapter. The exercises range from some that closely parallel the programs in the chapter to others that are quite challenging. In an elementary course, instructors should base the programming assignments primarily on the unstarred exercises. In a more challenging course, instructors could move quickly through the initial chapters and utilize the starred and double-starred exercises and also the more mathematical exercises in Appendix B.

The short, bite-sized chapters increase the book's flexibility, so that the topics need not be covered in the order given. For example, while the command, PRINT #, is introduced in Chapter 26, entitled Sequential Files, what is needed from this chapter to direct output to the screen or printer can be covered earlier in the course.

Acknowledgments

I am especially grateful to Donald Brusca, not only for extensive proof-reading but also for more substantive, creative help in the development of this book. I am greatly indebted to Paul Johns for the significant improvements he helped me to make. The following reviewers have contributed many helpful comments: David Berry, Xavier University; John Castek, University of Wisconsin—La Crosse; Thomas Falconi, Columbus Technical Institute; Paul Johns, Lansing Community College; and Meredith Stewart, PTC Career Institute.

I would like to thank Nancy Buck for typing earlier drafts of the manuscript. Robine Storm van Leeuwen, the production coordinator at PWS, and the staff of EDP have also made excellent contributions to the book. Finally, I wish to thank Bob Prior, my editor at PWS Publishers, for his superb guidance.

Contents

Introduction

Brief History

Computers have become so pervasive in today's world that it is easy to forget what a recent development they are. The first general-purpose, purely electronic digital computer, called ENIAC, was not built until 1946. ENIAC was a large, cumbersome device that contained 18,000 vacuum tubes, occupied a space of 50 feet by 30 feet, and weighed 30 tons. ENIAC was built for the U.S. Army to make calculations for weather predictions and ballistics tables. UNIVAC I, the first real commercial computer, was introduced in 1951.

Since those early days, there have been enormous advances in electronics technology. Perhaps the most remarkable breakthrough involved the miniaturization of electronic circuits, allowing a circuit containing hundreds of thousands of switches to be etched onto a silicon chip the size of a fingernail. Today a computer that sits on a desktop and costs under $1000 has more computing power than did earlier computers that filled an entire room and cost several hundred thousand dollars.

Computer Programs and the Language, BASIC

In order to have a computer accomplish something useful, such as solve a problem or process information, the computer must be given a precise list of instructions. This list of instructions is called a *program*. The program must be written in a form that the computer "understands," that is, in one of the computer languages. All the programs in this book will be written in the language BASIC, which stands for Beginner's All-purpose Symbolic Instruction Code. Of all the general-purpose computer languages (some others are FORTRAN, Pascal, COBOL, and PL/1), BASIC is the easiest to learn.

Input-Process-Output

The running of a computer program can be subdivided into three types of operations: (1) information is input into the computer (2) the information is processed (3) the results are output. Here is a pictorial representation of these operations.

For example, when you use a bank's automatic teller machine, you must first *input* your account number and desired transaction. The transaction must then be *processed* by being added or subtracted to your balance, and finally the receipt for the transaction and your new balance is printed as *output* for you.

Physical Components of a Computer

Hardware. Hardware is a fancy term for the physical components of a computer system. There are five basic types of hardware: (1) input devices (2) output devices (3) Central Processing Unit (4) internal computer memory (5) external storage devices.
Let us consider each of these in greater detail:

Input Devices. How do you communicate your program and data to the computer? Do you write them down on a piece of paper and hold it up to the computer? Of course not. For microcomputers you input your program and data by typing it at the computer *keyboard*. (Other input devices are a *mouse* and a *joystick*.)

Output Devices. The two main output devices are the video screen and the line printer.

CPU. The Central Processing Unit, or CPU, can be considered the brain of

The IBM personal computer. (Photo courtesy of IBM)

the computer. The CPU contains the arithmetic and logical circuitry and is responsible for all the actual processing of the data.

Internal Computer Memory.   When your program and its data are input to the computer, they are stored in the computer's internal memory. In running a program, the CPU processes and manipulates what is in its internal memory.

Capacity of a Computer's Internal Memory.   All information in memory is represented in a series of bits (binary digits, 0's and 1's). A **byte** contains eights bits. For example, 01001011 is a typical byte. Since *one* byte can store a very limited amount of information (i.e., a single letter or a number no greater than 255), the storage capacity of a computer is discussed in terms of **kilobytes** or **K**. A kilobyte is approximately 1000 bytes. Typically, a microcomputer will have 64, 128, 256, or 512 K of internal memory in which to store its information. Additional memory can usually be added.

ROM versus RAM.   ROM stands for Read Only Memory. ROM is permanent memory; its contents are fixed by the manufacturer and cannot be altered by your programs. ROM contains information that helps guide the CPU in its internal functioning. It is not available for storing your programs.

   The part of internal memory that is used as workspace to store your current program and its results is called RAM, which stands for Random Access Memory. RAM is not permanent. In fact, whenever the computer is turned off, the contents of RAM are completely erased.

External Storage Devices.   Suppose that you have just typed a program into the computer. How do you save this program for future use? Recall that when the computer is turned off, your program will be completely erased from internal memory. The answer is that you can save the program on an external storage device. Microcomputers generally use a **disk drive** and **diskette** for that purpose. A **diskette** is a plastic disk on which information can be stored in magnetically coded form. The **disk drive** functions like a cassette recorder—programs can be stored and retrieved in much the same way as music can be recorded and played back using a cassette recorder.

Getting Started with Microcomputers

Booting Up.   Although **booting up** is easy to do, many beginners are a little confused about what this phrase means. Roughly speaking, booting up is the way to turn on the computer so that it can run and save your programs. More precisely, booting up is the process of loading the disk operating system (which acts like a traffic cop for the system as a whole) into the computer's memory.

   To boot up the computer, you simply place a master diskette (which contains a copy of the computer's disk operating system) into the computer's primary disk drive and then turn on the power switch.

Formatting or Initializing Diskettes.   Before a *new* diskette can be used to store your programs, it must have a network of tracks and sectors written onto it. This process of making a *new* diskette ready to store your programs is called **formatting** (or initializing) the diskette. Consult your manual for the procedure for formatting a diskette on your particular system. (For the IBM-PC with two disk drives, you put the Master Diskette in drive A and the new diskette in drive B and type FORMAT B:/S.) You must be careful to format only new diskettes or those no longer needed, since formatting *erases* everything previously on the diskette.

Machine Language versus Higher-Level Languages

The mother tongue for a computer is **machine language**. In machine language all instructions consist of sequences of 0's and 1's. For example, a typical instruction in machine language might be

0100 1010 0101 0011

In the early days, all computer programs were written in machine language. Now, however, much programming is done in higher-level languages such as BASIC. These languages resemble ordinary English. A typical instruction might be PRINT "HELLO."

How does the computer understand your programs written in BASIC, considering that its mother language is machine language? The answer is that the computer must be supplied with a translating program (either an *interpreter* or *compiler*) that will convert your program from BASIC into machine language. Do not worry, this translating program works automatically; it is either part of the computer's ROM or is loaded into RAM when you boot up.

Can Computers Think?

Computers cannot think. Computers are incredibly fast (millions of operations per second) and accurate, but they are also very dumb. Computers can only do what they are *explicitly told* to do. Moreover, they have no ability to recognize what you must have meant when you make a slight mistake in communicating with them. For example, if you were to type PRINNT instead of PRINT the computer would have no idea what you meant.

Knowing How to Solve the Problem.   In order to write a program to solve a particular problem, you must know how to solve the problem yourself. You, *not the computer*, must devise a *step-by-step* procedure for solving the problem.

Beginners often ask, "Then what good is the computer, if you are the one who really has to solve the problem?" To understand the answer to this question, you must realize what an asset a speed of millions of operations per second is. There are many tasks of a repetitive nature that would be very tedious and time-consuming for people but that can be done easily and quickly by a computer. As one example, consider the task of alphabetizing the following list of 50 names: Hall, Bond, Smith, Jones, Boole, Black, Kay, Jahr, Halley, Smyth, Snell, Simon, Tell, Blaine, Payne, Fay, Katt, Pell, Hart, Hill, Spock, Toole, Ames, Bold, Block, Faye, Catt, Lott, Mott, Heller, Cobb,

Hayes, Polk, Cott, Kant, Cato, Holt, Mann, Yuen, Chan, Kite, Alou, Foy, Kent, Allen, Dent, Alt, Dean, Ard, Chen. It is possible to write a short computer program that will alphabetize this list in a *fraction of a second*. Can you alphabetize this list in under one second? Of course not. You probably cannot even do it in 200 seconds. Try it.

Artificial Intelligence.   As we have already mentioned, a computer can only do what it has been explicitly programmed to do by a human. So, in this sense, a computer cannot think. Nevertheless, there is a branch of computer research, called **artificial intelligence**, that is devoted to programming the computer to perform tasks that would seem to require real "intelligence." Results in artificial intelligence (for example, chess-playing programs, language translation programs, and expert systems such as computer medical diagnoses) have been quite impressive. Although there is no general agreement among computer scientists concerning the significance of these results, clearly the distinction between human thought and what a computer can achieve is not as cut and dried as once believed.

CHAPTER

1

Practice with LET and PRINT Statements

A computer program consists of a sequence of instructions to the computer. All the programs in this book will be in the computer language BASIC. Of course, in order to understand and write programs in BASIC, you must learn the commands and rules of BASIC. In this chapter we present just enough of the elements of BASIC to be able to give some simple programs.

1.1 Running a Program

Let us suppose that you are at a computer. To run a program in BASIC you must do three things: (1) get into BASIC, (2) type your program, and (3) type the word RUN on a separate line and press the RETURN key (the ENTER key on some systems). What the computer types back is called the **printout**.

1.2 Assigning Values to Variables

Numeric Variables. A variable represents a quantity that may assume different values during the running of a program. Each of the 26 letters of the alphabet is a valid numeric variable name. For example, A, B, and X are valid numeric variable names. Microsoft BASIC and IBM BASIC also allow longer variable names that begin with a letter and are composed entirely of letters and digits. Thus, SUM, PROFIT, and TAX1987 would all be valid

1

variable names. Generally, it is a good idea to use *meaningful* variable names. Not only will this help you in writing your programs, but it will also make it easier for others to understand them.

LET Statements. One way to assign a value to a variable is by the use of a LET statement. For example, the statement LET A=3 assigns the value 3 to the variable A.

A Simple Program. Each LET statement assigns a value to the variable on the left side of the equal sign. This program computes the sum of two numbers.

```
10   LET  A=3
20   LET  B=5
30   LET  SUM=A+B
40   PRINT  SUM
50   END
RUN
```

After you type this program and then type RUN and press the RETURN key, the printout will be ⬚8⬚. Line 10 assigns the value 3 to A. Line 20 assigns the value 5 to B. Line 30 assigns the sum of the values of A and B to SUM. Line 40 causes the computer to print the value of SUM. Line 50 terminates execution.

Line Numbering. Every line in a BASIC program must begin with a line number. On most microcomputers, a line number must be an integer between 1 and 32767. It is a good idea to number lines in tens to allow for the insertion of additional lines (if the program needs to be revised). System commands like RUN are typed without line numbers.

READ, DATA Statements. Another way to assign values to variables uses READ and DATA statements.

```
10   DATA  5,9
20   READ  A,B
30   LET  SUM=A+B
40   PRINT  SUM
50   END
RUN
```

The values in the DATA statement are assigned respectively to the variables in the READ statement.

When this program is run, the printout will be ⬚14⬚. Here is why: Line 10 supplies the data. Line 20 assigns the values 5 and 9 to A and B, respectively.

Line 30 assigns the value 14 to SUM. Line 40 causes the computer to print the value of SUM.

NOTE: A DATA statement may be placed anywhere in a program. Usually, it is at the beginning or the end.

QUESTION   What will the printouts be for the following two programs?

(a)
```
10  READ A,B
20  LET AVG=(A+B)/2
30  PRINT AVG
40  PRINT B
50  DATA 9,5
60  END
RUN
```

(b)
```
10  READ A,B,PROFIT
20  PRINT A
30  PRINT PROFIT
40  DATA 5,8,4
50  END
RUN
```

ANSWER   **(a)** The printout in program (a) will be $\begin{array}{c}7\\5\end{array}$ because in line 20, AVG is assigned the value (9 + 5)/2, which equals 7. In line 30 the value of AVG is printed. In line 40 the value of B is printed.

(b) In program (b), the printout will be $\begin{array}{c}5\\4\end{array}$. Note that in line 10, A becomes 5, B becomes 8, and PROFIT becomes 4. In line 20, the value of A is printed. In line 30, the value of PROFIT is printed. The value of B is not printed at all.

1.3 Change in Variable Value

PRINT Statement and Current Value.   Sometimes during the running of a program the value of a variable changes. Any PRINT statement uses the current value for each variable involved.

```
10  DATA 3,5
20  READ A,NUMBER
30  PRINT A
40  LET A=9
50  PRINT A
60  PRINT NUMBER
70  END
RUN
```

The printout is

$$\begin{array}{c}3\\9\\5\end{array}$$

In line 20, A is assigned the value 3; and NUMBER the value 5. In line 30, 3 is printed. In line 40, A becomes 9. Then in line 50, the current value of A (9) is printed. Finally, in line 60, the value of NUMBER is printed (5).

LET and Value of Variable on Left.   The left side of a LET statement must consist of a single variable. A LET statement assigns a new value to this variable; namely, the value prescribed by the right side. For example,

LET C = D + 2   assigns a value to C, namely D + 2
LET F = G + A   assigns a value to F, namely G + A

The variable of the left side sometimes appears also on the right. In this case, its current value is used in prescribing its new value.

LET A = A + 1   increases the value of A by 1.
LET BALANCE = BALANCE − 5   decreases the value of BALANCE by 5.
LET SUM = SUM + X   increases the value of SUM by X.

We should emphasize that a LET statement only affects the variable of the left side. Thus, LET SUM = SUM + X does not change the value of X.

QUESTION   Suppose that at a certain point in a program, T is 5 and Y is 7. What values will T and Y have after LET T = T + Y?

ANSWER   T will become 12. Y will remain equal to 7.

Memory Boxes.   You may find it helpful to think of each variable in your program as the name of a memory box. The contents of that memory box will be the current value of the variable. When a variable receives a new value, the old value is erased and replaced by the new one.

EXAMPLE

```
10 DATA 3,7
20 READ A,B
30 LET A=A+1
40 PRINT A
50 LET A=A+1
60 PRINT A
70 LET A=A+B
80 PRINT A
90 END
```

The printout is
```
4
5
12
```

In line 20, A becomes 3 and B becomes 7. In line 30, A becomes 4. In line 40, the current value of A is printed. In line 50, A becomes 5. In line 60, 5 is printed. In line 70, A becomes its most recent value plus the current value of B. Thus, A becomes 5 + 7, which is 12.

Multiplication and Division Symbols.   The symbol for multiplication is the asterisk, *, and the symbol for division is the slash, /.

QUESTION   What will be the printouts for these two programs?

(a)
```
10  DATA 3,6
20  READ A,B
30  LET A=A+1
40  LET PRODUCT=A*B
50  PRINT PRODUCT
60  PRINT A
70  END
```

(b)
```
10  READ A,B
20  LET B=A+1
30  PRINT B
40  LET B=A+B
50  PRINT B
60  PRINT A
70  DATA 2,9
80  END
```

ANSWER   (a) In program (a) the printout is

```
24
4
```

because line 30 gives a new value to A, (4—the old value plus 1). In line 40, the value of PRODUCT becomes 4 times 6.

(b) In program (b) the printout is

```
3
5
2
```

In line 10, A is assigned the value 2, and B the value 9. In line 20, B becomes 3. In line 30, the current value of B is printed. In line 40, B becomes 5 (the value of A plus the old value of B). In line 50, the new value of B is printed. In line 60, the current value of A is printed.

A Line-by-Line Table for Values of Variables.   One way to keep track (line-by-line) of the values of variables in a program is by using a table, with a column for each of the variables and an additional column to show whatever is printed. The following illustrates this type of table for the right-hand program from the previous question.

Line #	A	B	Anything Printed
10	2	9	
20	2	3	
30	2	3	3
40	2	5	
50	2	5	5
60	2	5	2

Note that lines 70 and 80 are not included, because they did not print anything or change the value of any variables.

Optionality of Word LET.   The word LET can be omitted from LET statements. For example the statement LET A = A + 1 and the statement A = A + 1 have exactly the same effect. Both of these assignment statements increase the value of A by 1. Later in the book we will usually omit the word LET from assignment statements. (The word LET is used to underscore the fact that the equal sign does not mean mathematical equality. Rather the equal sign means that the variable on the left side will be assigned the value given by the right side.)

Some Legal and Illegal LET Statements
LET A + B = C   is illegal (left-hand side must be single variable)
LET 2∗A = 4   is illegal (left-hand side must be single variable)
LET A = A + B + 1 is legal
LET C = 2∗C   is legal
LET 4 = 2 + A   is illegal (left-hand side must be a variable)

1.4 More on PRINT Statements

Material in Quotes.   In BASIC, when the computer executes a statement like PRINT A, it will print the current value of A. However, when the computer executes a statement like PRINT "HOWDY", it will print exactly what is inside the quotation marks—in this case HOWDY.

QUESTION   What will the printouts be?

(a)
```
10  DATA  2,6
20  READ  A,B
30  PRINT  "B"
40  PRINT  "HOWDY"
50  PRINT  A
60  END
```

(b)
```
10  DATA  -3,8
20  READ  A,B
30  LET  B=A+7
40  PRINT  A
50  PRINT  "B"
60  PRINT  B
70  END
```

ANSWER   (a) In program (a) the printout is

```
  B
  HOWDY
*   2
```

Note that when line 30 is executed, the computer prints the letter B rather than the value of the variable B, which is 6.

(b) In program (b) the printout is

```
 -3
  B
   4
```

The first value of B is 8, but by the time line 60 is executed, B is 4.

QUESTION   What will the printouts be?

(a)
```
10  DATA  3,5,7
20  READ  X,A,B
30  PRINT  A
40  PRINT  A+B
50  PRINT  X
60  END
```

(b)
```
10  DATA  3,6
20  READ  A,B
30  PRINT  A*B
40  PRINT  A+1
50  PRINT  "A+1"
60  END
```

* The number 2 is not aligned with B and HOWDY, but instead indented one space. The space has been left for a possible minus sign. The number 4 is indented one space in the next printout for the same reason.

ANSWER **(a)**

```
5
12
3
```

(b)

```
18
4
A+1
```

Semicolons in PRINT Statements. A semicolon separating items in a PRINT statement causes the computer to print the items close together on the same line. (Anything in quotes is printed verbatim.)

```
10  DATA 2,5
20  READ A,B
30  PRINT A;B
40  PRINT "A EQUALS";A
50  END
```

The printout is

```
2   5
A EQUALS 2
```

QUESTION What will the printouts be?

(a)

```
10  DATA 4,6
20  READ A,B
30  PRINT A;B
40  PRINT "B EQUALS";B
50  END
```

(b)

```
10  DATA 4,7
20  READ F,G
30  PRINT F
40  PRINT "F+G=";F+G
50  END
```

ANSWER **(a)**

```
4   6
B EQUALS 6
```

(b)

```
4
F+G= 11
```

Note that anything in quotes was printed verbatim.

EXAMPLE **Feet to Inches** So far, all the programs have been drill. Let us now consider a program that performs a useful calculation.

```
10  DATA 4
20  READ FT
30  LET IN=12*FT
40  PRINT FT;"FEET EQUALS";IN;"INCHES"
50  END
```

The printout is

```
4 FEET EQUALS 48 INCHES
```

What would the printout be if line 10 were replaced by 10 DATA 6?

ANSWER

```
6 FEET EQUALS 72 INCHES
```

1.5 String Variables

So far, all variables have had numeric values. However, there are also variables that can have as their values **strings**—that is, words or even arbitrary sequences of characters. Such variables are called **string variables**; string variable names must end with a dollar sign. A$, N$, and FIRST$ are all valid names for string variables. An assignment statement like LET A$ = "JOE" would assign the value JOE to the variable A$. Just as with numeric variables, A$ could be visualized as a memory box.

What will the printouts be for the following programs?

(a)

```
10  LET FIRST$="JANE"
20  LET LAST$="SMITH"
30  PRINT LAST$
40  PRINT FIRST$
50  END
```

(b)

```
10  DATA "JANE","SMITH"
20  READ FIRST$,LAST$,
30  PRINT LAST$
40  PRINT FIRST$
50  END
```

ANSWER Both programs will produce the same printout, namely,

```
SMITH
JANE
```

No Space between Consecutive Strings. In executing a PRINT statement with two strings separated by a semicolon the computer will not leave any space between the strings.

```
10  LET X$="JACK"
20  PRINT "HELLO";X$
30  PRINT "HELLO ";X$
```

The printout is

```
HELLOJACK
HELLO JACK
```

Note that the method used to cause the computer to leave a space when printing material in quotes followed by a string variable is *insertion of a blank space within the quotation marks.*

Mixed READ Statements.   In the next program, note that the READ statement contains both a string variable and a numeric variable.

QUESTION   Fill in line 30 so that the printout will be ⌈JOHN IS 23 ⌉. Make sure your PRINT statement uses the variables NAM$ and AGE.*

```
10  DATA "JOHN",23
20  READ NAM$,AGE
30  PRINT _____
40  END
```

ANSWER   Line 30 should be PRINT NAM$;" IS";AGE. Note the space between the quotation mark and the I of IS.

Exercises

1. What will the printouts be?

(a)

```
10  DATA 5,7
20  READ A,B
30  LET A=A+1
40  LET B=A+B
50  PRINT A
60  PRINT B
70  END
```

(b)

```
10  DATA 3,9
20  READ X,A
30  LET X=X+2
40  LET PROD=A*X
50  PRINT PROD
60  PRINT "A EQUALS";A
70  END
```

* NAM$ is used instead of NAME$ because, as we shall see, NAME is a reserved word.

(c)

```
10  DATA 3,8
20  READ C,B
30  PRINT C
40  LET C=B+1
50  PRINT B
60  PRINT C
70  END
```

(d)

```
10  DATA 4,7,11
20  READ A,B,X
30  LET A=A+1
40  PRINT "A"
50  LET X=A*X
60  PRINT X
70  END
```

2. What will the printouts be?

(a)

```
10  DATA 10,5
20  READ HRS,RATE
30  RATE=RATE+1
40  PAY=HRS*RATE
50  PRINT "PAY $";PAY
60  END
```

(b)

```
10  DATA 10,5
20  READ HRS,RATE
30  PAY=HRS*RATE
40  RATE=RATE+1
50  PRINT "PAY $";PAY
60  END
```

3. For the program below:
   (a) Use a line-by-line table to keep track of the various values for the variables A and C, and of anything that is printed.
   (b) What will the printout be?

```
10   DATA 5,3
20   READ A,C
30   LET A=A+C
40   LET A=A+1
50   LET C=C+A
60   PRINT C
70   LET C=C+5
80   PRINT C
90   PRINT A
100  END
```

4. What will the printouts be?

(a)

```
10  DATA 3,6
20  READ A,B
30  A=A*A
40  B=A
50  A=B+1
60  PRINT A+3
70  END
```

(b)

```
10  LET D=0
20  LET D=D+1
30  LET D=D+2
40  LET D=D+3
50  LET D=D+4
60  PRINT D
70  END
```

(c)

```
10  LET  A=3
20  PRINT  "A  EQUALS;A"
30  END
```

(d)

```
10  LET  A=3 .
20  PRINT  "A  EQUALS";A
30  END
```

5. Identify the mistake in each of the following.
   (If correct, just write "correct".)
   (a) LET A+B=A+C   (c) LET A EQUAL B
   (b) LET 2*A=4   (d) A=A+2

6. What will the printout be?

(a)

```
10  DATA  7,9
20  READ  D,HOWDY
30  PRINT  "HOWDY"
40  PRINT  HOWDY
50  PRINT  D+HOWDY
60  END
```

(b)

```
10  COUNT=0
20  COUNT=COUNT+1
30  COUNT=COUNT+1
40  COUNT=COUNT+1
50  PRINT  COUNT
60  END
```

7. What will the printout be?

```
10  LET  NAM$="JONES"
20  PRINT  "SO  LONG";NAM$
30  PRINT  "SO  LONG  ";NAM$
40  END
```

8.

```
10  DATA  "SMITH",95
20  READ  X$,G
30  PRINT  _____
40  END
```

Complete this program so that for the given DATA the printout will be:

```
SMITH  EXAM  SCORE  95
```

9. Give the printout.

```
10  DATA  "SMITH","JOHN"
20  READ  LAST$,FIRST$
30  PRINT  FIRST$;LAST$
40  PRINT  FIRST$;" ";LAST$
50  END
```

2
Writing and Running Programs

In this chapter we take a more detailed look at what is involved in writing programs. We also discuss some issues related to the typing and running of programs on the computer.

2.1 Writing a Program

Who Does What. The computer can only do what it is instructed to do by the programmer. Therefore, in writing a program to solve a particular problem, you do not merely describe the problem to the computer and then say, "Go solve it." You must do much more. You, *not the computer*, must devise a procedure or process for solving the problem. That procedure should be unambiguous and should communicate step by step what must be done.

Concept of Algorithm. A step-by-step procedure that can be used to solve a particular kind of problem is called an **algorithm**. In writing a program, you are faced with *two* somewhat separate tasks: devising an appropriate algorithm and then coding the algorithm in a particular computer language.

Input-Process-Output. Input, output, and process are the three main subdivisions of a program. When you start to write a program, you should ask yourself: what data will be Input; what form will the Output take; and then—the most difficult question of all—what is a Process (or algorithm) for converting input to the desired output.

13

Some Elementary Problems.   Although programming exercises will become more complicated in later chapters, *in this chapter* the process for converting input to output will simply be a formula. In this chapter the programs that you will be asked to write can be constructed by following three steps.

1. Select variable names (they should remind you of what they stand for).
2. Figure out the formula for converting input to output (work out a specific problem with actual numbers, if you are stuck).
3. Write the full program. The first few lines should read in the data; the next line should be a LET statement expressing the output variable in terms of the input variable(s); finally, there should be a PRINT statement and an END statement.

PROBLEM   Write a program that converts yards into inches. For DATA 2 the printout would be

```
2 YARDS EQUALS 72 INCHES
```

PROGRAM IDEAS

Select variable names YDS for yards and INS for inches. What is the formula for expressing the output variable INS in terms of YDS? Use a statement of the form LET INS = _____.

QUESTION   Fill in lines 30 and 40 of the program. If you are having trouble with line 30, ask yourself how to figure out the number of inches in 2 yards.

```
10   DATA 2
20   READ YDS
30   LET INS=_____
40   PRINT_____
50   END
```

ANSWER   Line 30 should be LET INS = 36*YDS; and line 40 should be PRINT YDS;"YARDS EQUALS";INS;"INCHES"

What Goes in Quotes.   Let us consider again the printout from the previous program.

```
2 YARDS EQUALS 72 INCHES
```

Which parts of that printout will result from material in quotes? Let us underline the verbatim material and circle the numbers that will result from values of variables:

②   YARDS EQUALS ⑦⑫ INCHES

To construct the print statement, put quotes around the verbatim material, and replace the numbers 2 and 72 by the appropriate variables.

PROBLEM   Write a program that converts Fahrenheit degrees into Celsius degrees. Use 59° Fahrenheit as data.

PROGRAM IDEAS

Select variable names. FAHR for Fahrenheit, CELS for Celsius. Since CELS is the output variable, you need a statement of the form LET CELS = _____. If you do not know the formula for converting Fahrenheit to Celsius, you will not be able to write the program. The formula is LET CELS = (FAHR − 32)*5/9. Now can you write the program? Here it is:

```
10   DATA 59
20   READ FAHR
30   LET CELS=(FAHR-32)*5/9
40   PRINT FAHR;"FAHRENHEIT EQUALS";CELS;"CELSIUS"
50   END
```

The printout will be

59 FAHRENHEIT EQUALS 15 CELSIUS

2.2 Rerunning a Program with Different Data

Suppose that you have just run the previous program, which converted 59 degrees Fahrenheit into degrees Celsius, and now you want to convert 77 degrees Fahrenheit into degrees Celsius. It is not necessary to retype the entire program. Your program is still in the computer's memory. You simply type the new DATA line, 10 DATA 77, on a line by itself. This automatically replaces the old line 10 in your program by the new one. Then you type RUN on a separate line and press the RETURN key. The new printout will be

```
77 FAHRENHEIT EQUALS 25 CELSIUS
```

The previous program was designed so that it will produce the correct Celsius output for *any* Fahrenheit data.

2.3 REM Statements

You may insert explanatory remarks within a program to make the program more understandable to you and to others who may look at it. REM statements are used for this purpose. During the execution of a program, whenever the computer comes to a REM statement, it ignores the statement and moves on to the next line.

PROBLEM   Write a program that converts two DATA numbers, representing a number of quarters and nickels, respectively, into a total amount. For example, for DATA 3,2 the printout should be

```
3 QUARTERS AND 2 NICKELS EQUALS 85 CENTS
```

PROGRAM IDEAS

Let us use QTRS for quarters and NKLS for nickels; these are both input variables. Let TOT, for total, be the output variable. To help clarify features of the program let us also use three REM statements. Here is the start of the program:

```
5    REM FIND TOTAL FROM QUARTERS AND NICKELS
6    REM *****
10   DATA 3,2
20   READ QTRS,NKLS
30   REM HERE IS THE CONVERSION FORMULA
```

Can you finish the program? Line 40, the conversion formula, should be a statement of the form LET TOT = _____. Here is the entire program:

```
5    REM FIND TOTAL FROM QUARTERS AND NICKELS
6    REM *****
10   DATA 3,2
20   READ QTRS,NKLS
30   REM HERE IS THE CONVERSION FORMULA
40   LET TOT=(25*QTRS)+(5*NKLS)
50   PRINT QTRS;"QUARTERS AND";NKLS;"NICKELS EQUALS";TOT;"CENTS"
60   END
```

This program would also have been correct if the REM statements had been omitted. To repeat: In executing a program, the computer ignores all REM statements. Their purpose is to help *humans* write or read a program.

2.4   Typing and Running Programs

Numbers 1 and 0.   The number 1 is not a lowercase L, and zero is not the letter O. The numerals are separate keys, usually on the top row of the keyboard.

LIST.   LIST is a command to the BASIC interpreter. If you type LIST on a line by itself (without a line number) and press the RETURN key, the computer will type back your program as it stands in the computer's memory. This command is especially useful if, in typing a program, you have made corrections and insertions and want to see a clean copy of your program in proper line number order.

Program Execution.   When the computer follows the instruction given in a line of your program, it is said to **execute** that line of your program. The computer does *not* execute the lines of your program as you type them; rather, it stores them sequentially in its memory and does not begin executing your program until you type RUN (without a line number) and press the RETURN key.

Order of Numbered Lines.   If you were to type and run the following program:

```
20   PRINT "HI"
10   PRINT "JOE"
30   END
RUN
```

The printout would be

```
JOE
HI
```

You should note that JOE is printed before HI. As you type in a program, the computer stores it in memory with the lines automatically arranged in increasing numerical order. Note that sometimes there is a discrepancy between what currently appears on the screen and what would be displayed if you were to type LIST. If you were to type LIST, either *before* or *after* running the previous program, the program listing would be

```
10  PRINT  "JOE"
20  PRINT  "HI"
30  END
```

AUTO Mode.   The easiest way to type a program is to have the computer automatically type the line numbers for you.

Suppose you are ready to start typing in a program. Type the command AUTO (for automatic line numbering) and press the RETURN key. The computer will respond with

```
10
```

It has typed the first line number for you. When you finish typing line 10, press the RETURN key. The computer will drop down to the next line and also type in the line number 20 for you.

You continue in this fashion until you have entered the END line. You need to type RUN on a line by itself without a line number. To do this you must first *break out of the AUTO mode* by pressing down the CTRL and BREAK keys. (On some systems you press down the CTRL key and the letter C.) Now you can type RUN. Here is an example showing what would appear on the screen:

```
10  PRINT  "HELLO"
20  PRINT  "GOODBYE"
30  END
40
RUN
```

← At this point you break out of the AUTO mode.

The general form of the AUTO command is AUTO n,m. The number n gives the starting line number and the number m gives the increment. Thus, AUTO 100,5 would start with line 100 and go up by fives.

Inserting Additional Lines.   For most simple programs, it is a good idea to do the line numbering in tens, making it possible to add lines between two lines in a program already typed. Suppose you have just typed the following program to multiply two numbers. Note that a statement to PRINT PROD has been omitted.

```
10   DATA 146,192
20   READ A,B
30   LET PROD=A*B
40   END
```

To rectify this, you do not need to retype the whole program. You simply select a line number between 30 and 40, such as 35, and type, on a line by itself, 35 PRINT PROD. The computer will insert this line between lines 30 and 40. When the program is run, it will compute and print the desired product. (If you are in the AUTO mode, you must get out of AUTO before you can type in line 35.)

Correcting a Line.

1. If you discover a typing mistake before you have entered that line (i.e., you have not pressed the RETURN or ENTER key yet), you can correct it by using the backspacing method. Backspace to the mistake farthest left on that line and then retype the remainder of the line correctly.

2. If you have already entered a line, you can replace that line at any time by typing its line number followed by the desired version. In Chapter 3 we discuss the EDIT commands that allow us to make changes in a line without retyping the entire line.

Deletions.   To delete a line from a program without replacing it, type the line number and press the ENTER key. To delete a block of lines, say 50 through 90, you would type DELETE 50–90.

Erasing Programs.   When you are finished with a program and are ready to type a new one, it is advisable to erase the old program. (Failure to do so can lead to errors, because lines from your previous program might be unintentionally included in the new program.) To erase a program type the system command NEW on a line by itself without a line number and press the RETURN key.

NOTE: Do not enter the NEW command until you no longer need the old program, since that command will completely erase your program. If you wish to start a new program without losing the old one, you should SAVE the old program on disk first.

Saving Programs. You should learn the procedure for saving (on an external storage medium such as a diskette) programs you have typed and want to save for your personal library. Type the word SAVE, followed by a space, and then type the name of your program in quotes. For example, SAVE "DEGREES" would save the current program under the name DEGREES.

Retrieving Saved Programs. To retrieve a saved program named "DEGREES" so that a copy will be in the computer's current memory, you would type LOAD "DEGREES".

2.5 Printing Listings and Output on Paper: LLIST and LPRINT

LLIST versus LIST. The command LIST will cause the computer to list your current program only on the video screen, whereas LLIST will cause the computer to print a copy of your program only on paper. (The extra L in LLIST stands for Line Printer.)

LPRINT versus PRINT. Unfortunately there is *no* command LRUN that would print the program printout on paper. Instead, to obtain your printout on paper, you must change *each* PRINT statement to an LPRINT statement and then type RUN. (A PRINT statement directs its printout to the video screen, whereas an LPRINT statement directs its printout to the line printer. The capital L in LPRINT stands for line printer.)

```
10  LET  A=9          10  LET  A=9
20  PRINT  A*A        20  LPRINT  A*A
30  END               30  END
```

When you type RUN the left-hand program would produce 81 on the video screen, whereas the right-hand program would print 81 on paper.

So far the only way you have learned to change a PRINT statement to an LPRINT statement is by retyping the entire line. In Chapter 4 we will see an easier method using the INSERT command.

PrtSc Key on the IBM-PC.   On the IBM-PC you can use the PrtSc key to make a printed copy of whatever is currently on the screen. To do so you hold down the shift key and press the PrtSc key.

For short programs and printouts this method of making a printed copy may prove easier than the LLIST and LPRINT method.

Print #.   Section 7 of Chapter 26 provides a method of allowing the programmer to specify at the top of the program whether the printout should be directed to the screen or to the line printer. With this method, the programmer is enabled to run the program on the screen first. When the program works satisfactorily, the top line can be changed to direct the printout to the printer.

2.6   Errors and Error Messages

In the course of learning to program, you will write many programs that contain errors. Errors can be subdivided into two general categories: (1) errors that produce an error message and (2) program logic errors.

Error Messages.   Certain types of errors cause a program to terminate prematurely with an **error message**. You should not be demoralized by an error message; instead view it as information designed to help you perfect your program. For now, we will only consider SYNTAX ERROR and TYPE MISMATCH error messages. Later in the book we will discuss other error messages.

SYNTAX ERROR Message.   A syntax error is a violation of the BASIC grammar. Syntax errors generally arise from misspelling a keyword, using an illegal variable name, or using an incorrect format. In the example below, the syntax error is the misspelling of the keyword LET.

```
10  PRINT "HI"
20  LOT A=4
30  PRINT A*A
40  END
```

When this program is run, the computer will stop execution in line 20. The output will be

```
HI
SYNTAX ERROR IN LINE 20
```

TYPE MISMATCH Error Message.   A type mismatch error message usually means that the computer has been asked to assign a string value to a numeric variable or vice versa.

Programs Containing More Than One Error

```
10    LET NAM=" JOE "
20    LET A=25
30    PRRNT NAM$; "  IS"; A
40    END
```

This program has two errors. However, when this program is run, it will produce only one error message because execution stops when the first error is reached. It will stop with the message TYPE MISMATCH IN LINE 10, since it cannot assign a string value to the numeric variable NAM. If you were to correct line 10 by changing it to LET NAM$="JOE" and rerun the program, line 30 would then produce an error message because of the misspelling of PRINT.

Other Error Messages.   Later in this book we also discuss other error messages such as DIVISION BY ZERO, OUT OF DATA, UNDEFINED LINE NUMBER, and ILLEGAL FUNCTION CALL.

Program Logic Errors.   An error in program logic is often difficult to detect. Although the output will be incorrect, no error message will appear. For example, the following program will not give an error message. Can you find the mistake that produces the obviously incorrect output of a 60 average for exam scores of 92 and 88?

```
5     REM LOGIC ERROR
6     REM ****
10    DATA 92,88
20    READ A,B
30    PRINT  "AVERAGE" ; (A+B)/3
40    END
```

Printout

```
AVERAGE 60
```

NOTE: The average should be computed by $(A+B)/2$.

At the Computer.   Do not compose your programs at the computer. Write them down in advance on a piece of paper. Also, be considerate of other users about how long you try to correct faulty programs while you are actually on the computer.

Exercises

Remember, the number 1 is not typed as a lowercase L and 0 is not the letter O. Also, don't forget to press the ENTER key after you have typed RUN.

1. We want a program that converts yards to feet, so that for DATA 7 the printout has the form

```
7 YARDS EQUALS 21 FEET
```

   (a) For the above printout, underline whatever is quote material and circle what comes from variables.
   (b) Write and run the program with DATA 7.
   (c) Run it again, this time using DATA 9. Remember that you do not need to retype the entire program. Then rerun it using DATA 13.

2. Write a program that converts degrees Celsius to degrees Fahrenheit. Run it four times, first using CELS = 25; then with CELS = 100, 40, and 18. (*Hint:* Here is the formula: FAHR = (CELS*9/5) + 32.)

3. Write a program that converts two DATA numbers representing yards and feet, respectively, into inches. For example, for DATA 1,2 the printout should be

```
1 YARDS AND 2 FEET EQUALS 60 INCHES
```

4. Write a program that will find the average of three DATA numbers. Run it first with DATA 8,23,14. Run it again with DATA 5,10,3.

5. Which of the following will appear on your screen if you use the AUTO mode?

   (a)
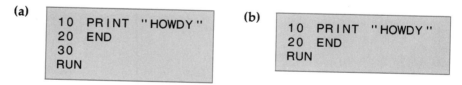
```
10  PRINT  "HOWDY"
20  END
30
RUN
```

   (b)
```
10  PRINT  "HOWDY"
20  END
RUN
```

6. Suppose the computer is hooked up to a printer. What will the printout be? (If there will be two printouts, explain what they are.)

```
10  PRINT  "HELLO"
20  LPRINT  "SO LONG"
30  END
```

7. (a) What is the purpose of LIST?
   (b) How do you delete a line in a program?
   (c) What is the purpose of a REM statement?

8. For your system how do you
   (a) erase an entire program?
   (b) delete lines 50 through 90?
   (c) save a program for your personal library?
   (d) have the computer automatically type line numbers 5, 10, 15, 20, 25, and so on?

9. What will the printout be for the following program? (Note the line numbers)

```
20  PRINT  "GOOD EVENING"
10  PRINT  "KAREN"
15  PRINT  "SMITH"
30  END
```

10. What will the printout be?

```
10  REM PRINT  "HOME"
20  PRINT  "JAMES"
30  END
```

★ 11. Write a program that converts hours and minutes into minutes only. For example, for DATA 2,15 the printout should be

```
2 HOURS AND 15 MINUTES EQUALS 135 MINUTES
```

(*Note:* Do you need two or three variables?)

---

* Those problems marked with a star (★) are more difficult than the unmarked ones.

CHAPTER
3
Editing

In Chapter 2, the only method given for correcting a line already entered was retyping the entire line. Editing techniques provide a more convenient way to make corrections.

Since IBM Editing and MBASIC Editing are quite different, we discuss them in separate sections.

3.1 IBM Editing

Changing Mistyped Characters. Suppose you have already typed this program

```
10   PRIGT  "HAWDY"
20   PRINT  "SO LONG"
30   END
```
← Line 10 has two mistakes.

To correct line 10, first you type EDIT 10. The computer responds with

```
10   PRIGT  "HAWDY"
```
← The cursor is a blinking dash under the 1.

Use the right-arrow key to position the cursor under the G.

```
10   PRIGT  "HAWDY"
```

25

Type N, and the G will be *replaced* by an N. Next keep pressing the right-arrow key until the cursor is at the A of HAWDY. Then type O. Since no further corrections are needed, press the ENTER key.

Inserting. Suppose that you have entered

Line 20 is missing an RI in PRINT and a T in COMPUTER.

To insert the missing letters, first type EDIT 20, and then, by pressing the right-arrow key, position the cursor under the N.

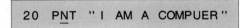

Then press the Insert key. The blinking dash becomes a blinking square.

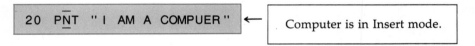

Computer is in Insert mode.

Then type RI. Next move the cursor so that it is under the E—in position for the next insertion. *Pressing the right-arrow key has gotten you out of the Insert mode.* Press the Insert key and then type T. Finally, press the ENTER key.
In general, to insert in IBM editing you must

1. type the EDIT command and hit ENTER.
2. use the right arrow key to position the cursor.
3. hit the insert key
4. type the material to insert.
5. repeat steps (2) through (4) if necessary.
6. hit the ENTER key.

Mixed-Inserting and Changing on Same Line. Suppose you have entered

10 PRINY "WHAT ISYOUR NAME"

This line has two mistakes: (1) The Y of PRINY must be changed to a T. (2) A blank space must be inserted to separate IS from YOUR.

To make these corrections, first type EDIT 10. Then position the cursor under the first Y and type T. Next position the cursor under the second Y, press the Insert key and type one blank (space bar).

Deleting.   Deleting is similar to changing. When the blinking dash is beneath the character you wish to delete, press the Delete key.

Making PRINT Statements Into LPRINT Statements.   This should be done by Inserting an L. After you have typed EDIT (line #), position the blinking dash under the P of PRINT. Then press the Insert key and type an L.

3.2 MBASIC Editing

Editing in MBASIC is more complicated than in IBM BASIC.

Changing One Character at a Time.   Suppose you have already typed this program

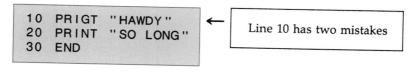

Line 10 has two mistakes

```
10  PRIGT  "HAWDY"
20  PRINT  "SO LONG"
30  END
```

To correct line 10, first you type EDIT 10. The computer responds with

```
10  ■
```

Each time you press the space bar, the computer will reveal another character from line 10. Keep pressing the space bar until the screen displays

```
10  PRI■
```

Now type the letter C to put the computer in the Change mode. Then type the letter N. The screen will display

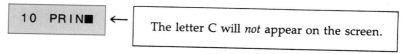

```
10  PRIN■
```

The letter C will *not* appear on the screen.

Next, to correct the A, you must keep pressing the space bar until the screen displays

```
10  PRINT  "H■
```

Then proceed as before. When you have changed the A to an O, you can press the ENTER key.

Changing Several Consecutive Characters.   Suppose you have entered 10 PRUMG "HAVE A GOOD DAY". To change the UMG to INT, first type EDIT 10 and position the cursor to the right of the R. Then type 3C (this informs the computer that 3 *consecutive* characters will be replaced) and type INT. Of course, 3C will not appear on the screen.

Obtaining Copy of Line To Be Corrected.   Let us consider again the first example from Section 3.2. Suppose you want a copy of line 10 directly above. *Type EDIT 10, press the ENTER key, and then type L.* The screen will display

```
10  PRIGT  "HAWDY"
10  ■
```

Now you can make the appropriate changes under the original line.

Inserting.   Suppose you have entered

```
20  PINT  " I  AM  A  COMPUER "     ←
```
Line 20 is missing an R in PRINT and a T in COMPUTER.

Type EDIT 20 and press the space bar until the screen displays

```
20  P■
```

Next type I for Insert. Then type the missing R (the I for Insert will not appear on the screen).
    The next step is very important. Before you can move the cursor to the next mistake, *you must get out of the Insert mode by hitting the ESCape key.* Then you again use the space bar until you have

```
20  PRINT  " I  AM  A  COMPU■
```

Now type I for Insert and the missing T. Finally, since there are no further corrections, press the ENTER key.

In general, to insert in MBASIC editing you must.

1. type the EDIT command and hit ENTER.
2. use the space bar to position the cursor.
3. type I for Insert.
4. type the material to insert.
5. hit the ESCape key.
6. repeat steps (2) through (5) if necessary.
7. hit the ENTER key.

Deleting.   Suppose you have entered

```
20  PRINGT  "HOWDY"
```

To delete the unwanted G, type EDIT 20 and move the space bar until the screen displays

```
20  PRIN█
```

Then type D (for Delete). The screen will display

```
20  PRIN\G\
```

The backslashes around the letter G indicate that it has been deleted in the computer's memory. Now you can press the ENTER key. If you need to delete several consecutive characters, you type a D for each character to be deleted.

Mixed-Changing: Inserting and Deleting on Same Line.   In making different types of corrections on the same line, the main thing to remember is that *after each Insertion you must press the* ESC*ape key* before moving the cursor *into position for the next correction.*

Changing PRINT Statements into LPRINT Statements.   You do this by inserting an L when the cursor is covering the P from PRINT. For example, suppose you have entered

```
20  PRINT A
```

To change this to LPRINT A, first type EDIT 20. Then all you need are *three* keystrokes—I, L, ENTER key. Note that it was not necessary to use the space bar because the effect of EDIT 20 was

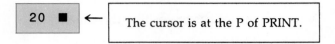

20 ■ ← The cursor is at the P of PRINT.

Exercises

1. In IBM editing
   (a) where is the cursor situated when you type EDIT 10 to change the line 10 PRIN X?
   (b) which key should you press to move the cursor along before changing anything?
2. Answer Exercise #1 with respect to MBASIC editing. (Do this only if you have MBASIC.)
3. Type in the following program as is (and get a hard copy):

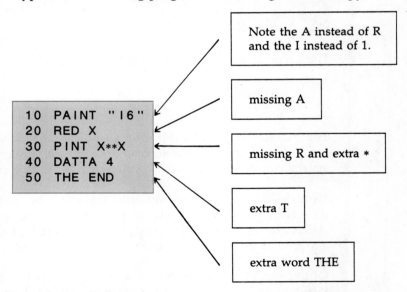

```
10  PAINT  "I6"
20  RED  X
30  PINT  X**X
40  DATTA  4
50  THE  END
```

Note the A instead of R and the I instead of 1.

missing A

missing R and extra *

extra T

extra word THE

Use editing to correct the program, and RUN it so that its printout is

```
16
16
```

4

INPUT Statement

The INPUT Statement provides another way of entering data. With the READ/DATA combination all the data are entered *before* the word RUN is typed. By contrast, the INPUT statement allows the user to enter data *during* the running of the program. Thus, the INPUT statement allows interaction between the human user and the computer—in fact, the user can have "conversations" with the computer.

4.1 INPUT Statement

Suppose you have typed the following program:

```
10   INPUT  N
20   PRINT  N; "SQUARED  IS"; N*N
30   END
```

When you type RUN and hit the RETURN key, the computer will begin executing your program. It executes the statement INPUT N by typing a question mark and then stopping.

```
RUN
?
```

The computer is waiting for you to type a number in response to the question mark. This value will be assigned to N and then the computer will resume executing your program. Suppose you typed 5 after the question mark *and hit the RETURN key*. Here is what the complete printout on the screen would look like:

```
RUN
?5
5 SQUARED IS 25
```

If you wished to rerun the above program for a different input number, you would type RUN again and then respond to the question mark by typing your new input number.

Use of Prompting Messages.   In writing programs, it is generally advisable to include a **prompting message** (in quotes) within INPUT statements. A prompting message will indicate to the user what should be entered in response to the question mark. For example

```
10   INPUT "ENTER A NUMBER OF FEET";F
20   PRINT F;"FEET EQUALS";F*12;"INCHES"
30   END
```

After you type RUN (and hit the RETURN key) the computer will type back

```
ENTER A NUMBER OF FEET?
```

and then wait for your response. Suppose you type 6 after the question mark, and *hit the RETURN key*. Then the computer would resume execution. the complete printout on the screen would be

```
ENTER A NUMBER OF FEET? 6
6 FEET EQUALS 72 INCHES
```

We have underlined the 6 to emphasize that it is typed by the user and not by the computer.

4.2 INPUT Statements with More Than One Variable

In an INPUT statement containing a list of two or more variables, commas must be used to separate the variables (for example, INPUT A,B or INPUT "ENTER THREE NUMBERS";X,Y,Z). In response to an INPUT statement, the user must type the appropriate number of numbers separated by commas. Thus, in response to the question mark from INPUT A,B the user might type 8,13.

PROBLEM   Write a program so that when the user types RUN, the computer, before halting, will print

```
PICK TWO NUMBERS?
```

and then if the user types the two numbers 7,9 (and hits the RETURN key) the total printout would be

```
PICK TWO NUMBERS? 7,9
7 TIMES 9 IS 63
```

ANSWER: Here is the program:

```
10  INPUT "PICK TWO NUMBERS";NUM1,NUM2
20  PROD=NUM1*NUM2
30  PRINT NUM1;"TIMES";NUM2;"IS";PROD
40  END
```

4.3 INPUT Statements with String Variables

```
10  INPUT "WHAT IS YOUR NAME";NAM$
20  PRINT "HELLO ";NAM$;" NICE TO MEET/YOU"
30  END
```

A typical printout is

```
RUN
WHAT IS YOUR NAME? GEORGE
HELLO GEORGE NICE TO MEET YOU
```

We have underlined the name GEORGE to indicate that it is typed by the user after the computer halts with a question mark. (Do not forget that the user must also hit the RETURN key after typing GEORGE.)

REMARKS
1. In line 20, note the space after the O of HELLO and before the N of NICE.
2. It is not necessary to put quotation marks around a string value entered in response to an INPUT statement. (The only exception to this is if the string contains a comma or semicolon. For example SMITH, JOHN would have to be entered as "SMITH, JOHN".)

4.4 Program with More Than One INPUT Statement

In executing a program, the computer will halt after each INPUT statement until you type an appropriate input and hit the RETURN key. For the program below, suppose you input the name HARRY and the age 19. What will appear on the video screen at the time of *each* halt for an input and what will appear on the screen by the end of the RUN?

```
10  INPUT "WHAT IS YOUR NAME " ; NAM$
20  PRINT "HELLO " ; NAM$
30  INPUT "WHAT IS YOUR AGE " ; AGE
40  PRINT "YOU ARE VERY MATURE. YOU LOOK AT LEAST" ; AGE+5
50  END
```

ANSWER
```
WHAT IS YOUR NAME?
```

After you type HARRY and hit the RETURN key, the following output will appear on the screen when the computer halts again:

```
WHAT IS YOUR NAME? HARRY
HELLO HARRY
WHAT IS YOUR AGE?
```

By the end of the RUN, the screen will contain

```
WHAT  IS  YOUR  NAME?  HARRY
HELLO  HARRY
WHAT  IS  YOUR  AGE?  19
YOU  ARE  VERY  MATURE.  YOU  LOOK  AT  LEAST  24
```

4.5   INPUT versus READ/DATA

We introduced the READ/DATA combination before the INPUT statement because READ/DATA is easier for beginners to understand. As we have seen, however, the INPUT statement allows for interaction between the user and the computer. In the next few chapters we rely exclusively on the INPUT statement.

In general the INPUT statement is the better method when only a few items of data are needed or when it is essential for data to be entered interactively. On the other hand, READ/DATA is the preferred method when long lists of data need to be processed, especially with the use of loops. (Examples of this are in Chapters 8–11.)

In actual applications, when the lists are much longer, files would generally be used. The READ/DATA method provides preparation for handling data manipulation through files.

Rerunning a Program: INPUT vesus READ/DATA.   To rerun a program in which the data are supplied by an INPUT statement, type RUN again, and then supply the new data when the computer halts with a question mark. By contrast, to rerun a program in which the data is supplied by the READ/ DATA combination you must give the new data *before* you type RUN; you do so by replacing each old DATA line with a new one.

4.6   INPUT Message and Values Not Printed on Paper

Unfortunately, prompting messages within INPUT statements and also input values will *only* appear on the screen.

For example, suppose that when the following program is run (with the printer turned on) the user inputs 59:

```
10   INPUT  "DEGREES FAHRENHEIT";FAHR
20   CELS=(FAHR-32)*5/9
30   LPRINT  "IS";CELS;"DEGREES CELSIUS"
40   END
```

The only printout on paper will be

```
IS 15 DEGREES CELSIUS
```

The input value will not be immediately obvious to someone reading this printout on paper. There are two possible ways around this difficulty:

Method 1.   Modify line 30 so that the input value will appear in the LPRINT statement. Thus, we would replace line 30 by

```
30   LPRINT FAHR;"FAHR. IS";CELS;"DEGREES CELSIUS"
```

Method 2—Include an Echo LPRINT Statement.   If you wished the copy printed on paper to contain the prompting message and the input value, you can use an **echo LPRINT statement**, such as that in line 15 below.

```
10   INPUT  "DEGREES FAHRENHEIT";FAHR
15   LPRINT  "DEGREES FAHRENHEIT";FAHR
20   CELS=(FAHR-32)*5/9
30   LPRINT  "IS";CELS;"DEGREES CELSIUS"
40   END
```

It should be noted that line 15 will not print a question mark at the end of the prompt. (If you wish the question mark to appear you must include it within the quotation marks in line 15.)

4.7   User Need Not Understand Programming

Frequently, the user of a program is *not* the person who has written the program. This fact is largely responsible for the widespread use of computers in a whole variety of business activities, since it means that complex programs written by experts can be used by people who, perhaps, know nothing about programming. Thus, an airline clerk can enter new information into a master ticketing file by running an interactive program. Such a program might contain the following fragment:

```
400  INPUT  "TYPE FLIGHT NUMBER, NUMBER OF TICKETS";FLT,TKTS
410  INPUT  "TYPE DATE GIVING MONTH,DAY,YEAR";MON,DAY,YR
```

Note that line 410 of the program expects three *numerical* responses. This is determined by the type of variables used. For example, JUNE 25, 1985 should be entered as: 6,25,1985. If the clerk accidentally types the word JUNE instead of 6, an error message will appear.

It should be noted that the above program fragment forms part of a much longer program also containing *file handling* lines that transfer the input data from the computer's memory to the master file. However, the clerk need not know anything about file handling instructions, since the clerk's task is to enter the input and read the output—not to understand the inner workings of the program.

4.8 PRINT Statements Preceding INPUT Statement

Part of the prompt for an INPUT statement can be provided by a separate PRINT Statement.

QUESTION Write a program that would halt for the user to input two numbers and would produce as printout

```
WILL COMPUTE PRODUCTS
PICK TWO NUMBERS? 7,9
7 TIMES 9 IS 63
```

ANSWER

```
10  PRINT "WILL COMPUTE PRODUCTS"
20  INPUT "PICK TWO NUMBERS";A,B
30  PRINT A;"TIMES";B;"IS";A*B
40  END
```

It is illegal for an INPUT statement to contain variables other than the one(s) to be supplied values. For example, in the fragment below, line 20 is illegal.

```
10   INPUT "WHAT IS YOUR FIRST NAME";FIRST$
20   INPUT "WELL, ";FIRST$;" WHAT IS YOUR LAST NAME";LAST$
```

In Exercise 9, you are asked to rewrite the illegal two lines above as three lines.

Exercises

In the exercises below (unless otherwise stated) printout means the printout that would appear on the screen.

1. Write a program in which a number of yards is input, and the computer outputs the equivalent in inches. A typical printout would be

```
ENTER NUMBER OF YARDS? 2
2 YARDS EQUALS 72 INCHES
```

Rerun your program for 5 yards. Then rerun for 7 yards.

2. Run a program in which two numbers are INPUT and the computer prints back their sum. Include a prompting statement in your program. A typical printout might be

```
TYPE TWO NUMBERS? 5,12
THE SUM OF 5 AND 12 IS 17
```

3. The following INPUT statement has an error in it. Explain the error.

```
10   INPUT "ENTER NUMBER OF FEET";5
```

4. Write a program in which three numbers are INPUT, representing the number of dimes, nickels, and pennies, respectively. The computer should print back the total number of cents. A typical printout might be

```
TYPE NUMBER OF DIMES, NICKELS AND PENNIES? 4,3,3
4 DIMES 3 NICKELS 3 PENNIES EQUALS 58 CENTS
```

5. Write a program that will compute a person's yearly income from an input of his weekly income. A typical printout might be

```
TYPE  WEEKLY  INCOME?  200
YEARLY  INCOME  10400
```

6. Run a program in which degrees in Celsius is INPUT, and the computer prints back the Fahrenheit equivalent. Run it for 35 degrees celsius then for 50. Use the formula FAHR = 32 + CELS*9/5.

7. If you enter the input JOE, what will be the printout for the following? (Beware of the faulty spacing in the printout.)

```
10   INPUT  "WHAT  IS  YOUR  NAME " ; NAM$
20   PRINT  "HELLO" ; NAM$
30   END
```

8. (a)
```
10   INPUT  "YARDS " ; YARDS
20   LPRINT  " IS" ; YARDS*36; " INCHES "
30   END
```

What will be printed *on paper*, if the number 5 is input when this program is run?
(b) How would you modify line 20, so that the input value for YARDS is printed on paper?

9. Answer the question from Section 4.8.

10. Write a program that computes the depreciation of a machine from the formula

$$\text{depreciation} = \frac{\text{cost} - \text{scrap value}}{\text{life}}$$

INPUT the values of cost, scrap, and life respectively. Run the program inputting the values 700,100,3. Rerun it with the values 500,100,7.

11. (a) Write a program to convert yards to inches. Use echo LPRINT statements so that if the user inputs the value 2, the complete printout *on paper* will be

```
ENTER  NUMBER  OF  YARDS  2
2 YARDS  EQUALS  72  INCHES
```

(b) Modify the program so that the printout on a page would include a question mark after the words YARDS.

12. Write a program using separate variables for the last and first names, so that if the user input DOE,JOHN the total printout on the screen would be

```
WHAT IS YOUR NAME. TYPE LAST, FIRST? DOE,JOHN
SO YOUR LAST NAME IS DOE
HELLO JOHN DOE
```

13. (a) Write a program so that if the user inputs JOE and 15 respectively, the final printout will be

```
WHAT IS YOUR NAME? JOE
WHAT IS YOUR AGE? 15
HELLO JOE
YOU ARE MATURE, JOE. YOU LOOK AT LEAST 25
```

★   (b) Insert the necessary statements so that the questions and input responses would also be printed on paper.

14. Also see Appendix C, Exercises 1 and 2, for some income tax programs.

CHAPTER 5

Expressions and Notation

There are some differences between the way certain arithmetic expressions are written in ordinary notation and the way they are written in BASIC. One difference already noted is the use of the asterisk symbol for multiplication. For example, it is illegal in BASIC to write 2A; instead it would be written as 2*A. In this chapter, we discuss further the correct way to write arithmetic expressions in BASIC.

5.1 Rules of Priority

Consider the expression $2 + 3*4$. Is it equal to 20, since $(2 + 3)*4 = 5*4 = 20$? Or is it equal to 14, since $2 + (3*4) = 2 + 12 = 14$? Answer: It equals 14, as determined by the following rules of priority:

Priority	Operation	Symbol
highest	exponentiation	$\wedge$ ($\uparrow$ on some systems)
second highest	multiplication, division	*, /
lowest	addition, subtraction	+, −

Exponentiation is performed before multiplication or division; multiplication and division are performed before addition or subtraction.

41

EXAMPLE   Thus, in BASIC, $2+3*4$ is not ambiguous. It will be viewed by the computer as 2 plus (3*4), since multiplication has a higher priority than addition. It equals 14. Also, $2+1/2$ equals 2.5 since division has a higher priority than addition.

QUESTION   What is $5*3/\!\!\wedge 2+1$?

ANSWER   It equals 46 because exponentiation has the highest priority. Thus, the expression $5*3/\!\!\wedge 2+1 = 5*9+1 = 45+1$, which is 46.

QUESTION   What is $1+2*3+4$?

ANSWER   It equals 11, because it is the same as $1+(2*3)+4$.

Expressions with Operations of Same Priority.   When an expression with *no* parentheses contains two operations of the same priority, the computer performs first whichever occurs first (from left to right).

QUESTION   Is $2/3*4$ equal to 1/6 or 8/3?

ANSWER   It equals 8/3 since the computer first divides 2 by 3; then it multiplies by 4. Note that 8/3 will be printed as the decimal 2.66667 rather than as a fraction.

Parentheses Take Precedence.   Arithmetic operations within parentheses are always performed first. Thus, if you want the computer to multiply the sum $A+B$ by C, you would write $(A+B)*C$. Note $2+3*4 = 14$, but $(2+3)*4 = 20$.

QUESTION   How do you write $\dfrac{1+2}{3+4}$ in BASIC? (Note that $1+2/3+4$, which equals $1+\frac{2}{3}+4$, is not the answer.)

ANSWER $(1+2)/(3+4)$.

▬▬▬ 5.2 Large Numbers and Exponential Notation

In BASIC, commas are never used in representing numbers. The number 44,253 is written 44253 without the comma—44,253 would be considered two separate numbers, namely 44 and 253. Furthermore, any number beyond a certain size (at least one million for some systems, ten million for others) must be expressed using a special exponential notation.

EXAMPLE   In BASIC, the number 750,000,000 or 7.5 times 10^8 is written as 7.5E + 8. The E + 8 means that 7.5 is multiplied by 10^8.

Here is a method for determining the exponent. Consider 750,000,000. Count how many places you must move the decimal point to the left to place it between the 7 and the 5. The answer is 8; thus the BASIC notation is 7.5E + 8.

QUESTION   Express 1,376,000,000 in BASIC.

ANSWER   Consider 1,376,000,000. Count how many places you must move the decimal point to place it between the 1 and the 3. The answer is 1.376E + 9. The computer will always place the decimal point after the first significant (non-zero) digit.

QUESTION   Consider 1,376,000,000; the same number as in the previous example. It can also be written as .1376E + (?). What is the correct exponent?

ANSWER   10; that is, this number can be written as .1376E + 10. You simply count how many places the decimal point is moved until it comes before the 1.

Negative Exponents.   Negative exponents are used in representing small fractional or decimal numbers.

EXAMPLE   In exponential notation, .0025 is written as 2.5E-3. The E-3 means that 2.5 is divided by 10^3. To find the exponent, count how many places to the right you must move the decimal point to place it between the 2 and the 5.

QUESTION   Express .000001 in BASIC exponential notation.

ANSWER   To find the answer count how many places you must move the decimal point to the right to go from .000001 to 1.0. Thus, the answer is 1.0E-6.

5.3 More on Variable Names

Here is a list of the rules related to making up variable names. (Some of these rules were already mentioned.)

1. A variable name must start with a letter of the alphabet. Its other characters must *all* be letters, digits, or the period. The maximum number of characters in a name is 40. For typing convenience, we will use short variable names—often only a single letter.

2. Blank spaces are not allowed in a variable name—the period may be used instead to make a "two word" variable name easier to read. For example, while VOTECOUNT and VOTE.COUNT are both legal names, the version with the period is preferable.

3. Keywords such as END, LIST, DATA, and NAME cannot be used as variable names. Similarly END$, LIST$, DATA$, and NAME$ are also illegal—a type declaration symbol such as $ cannot be added to a keyword.

4. The dollar sign is a type declaration for a string variable. Other type delaration symbols are % for integer variable, ! for single precision (with a precision of seven decimal digits) and # for double precision (with a precision of 17 decimal digits).

5.4 Immediate Mode

If you type a PRINT statement *without a line number* and then strike the RETURN key, the statement will be executed immediately. Two major applications of the immediate mode are

1. Calculations can be performed without having to run a program. For example, typing PRINT 79*31 and hitting the ENTER key will output the result, and

2. The immediate mode can be helpful in debugging a program that has *just* been run. A statement such as PRINT C will print the value of C at the end of the run.

5.5 INT Function

INT(X) is equal to the largest integer that does not exceed X.

Examples with X Positive.   For X positive, INT(X) truncates the fractional part:

$$INT(4.9) = 4 \qquad INT(4.1) = 4 \qquad INT(9.5) = 9$$

Examples with X Negative.   For X negative, INT(X) drops down to the negative integer just below X:

$$INT(-4.9) = -5 \qquad INT(-4.1) = -5 \qquad INT(-9.5) = -10$$

Use the immediate mode to check each of the above results.

▬ 5.6 SQR Function

The function SQR(X) gives the square root of X. For example, LET A = SQR(2) assigns to A the value 1.41421, which is the square root of 2 (to 6 places).

The variable or expression to which you are applying the INT or SQR function must be enclosed in parentheses. Thus, INT(X) and SQR(A + 7) are valid expressions, whereas INTX and SQR4 are invalid. If the computer is asked to execute a statement containing the square root of a negative number, such as SQR(−4), the program will terminate execution with an error message. (Other functions are discussed in Chapter 18 and in Appendix A.)

▬ 5.7 Integer Operators: MOD and BACKSLASH \

These operators should be used only with integers or with variables having integer values.*

MOD. A MOD B gives the remainder when A is divided by B. Thus, 9 MOD 2 equals 1. 37 MOD 8 equals 5.

Backslash \. A\B gives the same result as INT(A/B). That is, A\B is equal to the largest number of times the integer B goes into A. For example:

15\4 equals 3   9\2 equals 4
15/4 equals 3.75 9/2 equals 4.5

EXAMPLE Converting Inches into Feet and Inches

```
10  INPUT "HEIGHT IN INCHES";INS
20  PRINT INS;" INCHES TALL IS SAME AS"
30  PRINT INS\12;"FOOT";INS MOD 12
```

For an input of 74, the output would be

```
HEIGHT IN INCHES? 74
74 INCHES TALL IS SAME AS
6 FOOT 2
```

* If A or B is not an integer, the computer truncates the fractional part(s) before performing A MOD B or A\B.

■ 5.8 Variables without Assigned Values

Numeric Variables. What will the computer do if a PRINT statement contains a variable that has not been assigned a value? Similarly, what will happen if the right side of an assignment statement contains such a variable? The answer is that any numeric variable not already assigned a value by the program will automatically have the value 0. For example, the programs

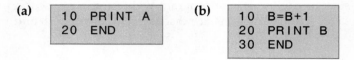

(a)
```
10  PRINT A
20  END
```
(b)
```
10  B=B+1
20  PRINT B
30  END
```

Will have printouts

(a)
```
0
```
(b)
```
1
```

Note that in program (b), line 10 increases the old value of B by 1. The old value is automatically considered as 0.

String Variables. A string variable that has not been assigned a value will automatically be given the value of the **null string**—that is, the string consisting of no characters. The null string is different from a string consisting of one blank character. Consider the following example:

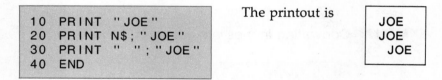

```
10  PRINT  "JOE"
20  PRINT N$; "JOE"
30  PRINT  " "; "JOE"
40  END
```

The printout is

```
JOE
JOE
 JOE
```

The null string can be represented as two consecutive quotation marks with no blanks between them ("").

■ 5.9 Numerical Difficulties

Computers do not perform all arithmetic calculations with absolute precision; instead, they give only an approximate answer for certain calculations. That is, every computer has some degree of "numerical difficulty."

These are some of the causes of numerical difficulty:

1. The computer performs calculations using the binary system (base 2). However, many fractions and decimals do not have exact representations in base 2. thus, PRINT 33*.3 gives the output 9.900001, although the correct answer is 9.9.

2. In raising integers to higher powers the computer uses logarithms. For some computers PRINT 2/\13 gives a noninteger even though the correct answer is an integer.

3. The computer's ordinary mode for performing arithmetic calculations is with a precision of seven digits (single precision). This may not be sufficiently precise for certain types of problems. A double precision mode (precision of 17 digits) is also available.

Exercises

1. What does each of these BASIC expressions equal? (Check by using the immediate mode.)
   - (a) 2*3+4
   - (b) 2+3*4+5
   - (c) 5+1/2
   - (d) (2+1)/3
   - (e) 2*2+3*3
   - (f) 3/4*8
   - (g) 2*3/\2+1
   - (h) 32/4/2*(4+1)

2. Write in BASIC each of the following:
   - (a) $\dfrac{A+B}{2}$
   - (b) $5A^2+B$
   - (c) $\dfrac{A+B}{C+D}$
   - (d) $(A \cdot A)+(C \cdot D)$
   - (e) $\dfrac{X1+A+B}{2}$

3. Write in BASIC using the special exponential notation:
   - (a) 53,000,000
   - (b) 792,000,000
   - (c) .0000000134
   - (d) .000256897

4. Write each of the following using ordinary decimal notation:
   - (a) 4.72157E+2
   - (b) 5.81334E+6
   - (c) 5.31461E−1
   - (d) 9.14567E−3
   - (e) .345678E+3
   - (f) 3.45678E+2

5. Determine whether each of the following variable names is legal. If not, explain why.
   - (a) X
   - (b) PHONE#
   - (c) 2X
   - (d) NAME$
   - (e) NAM$
   - (f) EXAM SCORE
   - (g) EXAM.ONE
   - (h) X COUNT

6. What does each of the following equal?
   (a) INT(3.6)   (e) SQR(INT(4.5))
   (b) INT(4)   (f) INT(8/9)
   (c) INT(3*3 + 1/2)   (g) INT(150/60)
   (d) SQR(3)   (h) INT(37/10)

7. Write in BASIC:
   (a) $\sqrt{A^2 + B^2}$ (c) $(\sqrt{A^2 + B^2})/2$
   (b) $\sqrt{A} + \sqrt{A1}$

8. (a) What is 4/5 expressed as a percent? What is 2/3?
   (b) Write a formula in BASIC that expresses A/B as a percent.
   (c) Write a program so that for DATA 4,5 the printout is

   ```
   4 OUT OF 5 EQUALS 80 PERCENT
   ```

   Rerun it using DATA 1,3.

9. If A = 5, B = 9, and C = 27 find
   (a) A MOD A   (e) C/A
   (b) B MOD A   (f) A/B
   (c) A\B   (g) B\A
   (d) C MOD B   (h) C\A

10. Also see Appendix B, Exercise 1.

6

Two-Way Selection and Transfer of Control

In the programs considered so far, the computer has been used much like a hand calculator. A single program has not had the flexibility to employ different types of calculations for different classes of input.

IF-THEN-ELSE gives a computer program the capacity to take the course of action appropriate to the particular input. As a simple example, suppose baseballs are priced at $7 each if fewer than 10 are purchased and at $6.50 each if at least 10 are purchased. To compute the cost for a purchase, the computer must be able to test whether fewer than 10 were purchased in order to decide which of two formulas to use.

6.1 IF-THEN (Action Statement)

The IF-THEN (Action Statement) is used when you want the computer to perform some action or calculation conditionally; that is, *only* when a certain condition is true.

The general form is

IF (condition) THEN (action statement)

If the condition is true, the computer executes the action statement and then proceeds to the next line of the program. If the condition is false, the computer proceeds directly to the next line of the program.

For example, the following are permissible:

IF AGE>=21 THEN PRINT "OF AGE"
IF X>Y THEN C=C+1
IF A+B>C THEN PRINT "OK"

Conditions.   There are six condition symbols available. There are the usual mathematical symbols:

> means greater than
< means less than
= means equal to

There are also the following symbols typed as *two* keystrokes:

>= means greater than or equal to (i.e., at least)
<= means less than or equal to (i.e., no more than)
<> means not equal to

QUESTION   For each given value of A what will the printout be for the following fragment? **(a)** A = 25 **(b)** A = 14

```
40  IF A>=21 THEN PRINT "OF AGE"
50  PRINT "GOOD LUCK"
```

ANSWER   **(a)**
```
OF AGE
GOOD LUCK
```
(b)
```
GOOD LUCK
```

Note that when the condition is not satisfied, the computer skips the THEN branch.

QUESTION   Suppose X = 5, and C = 31 at the start of line 70. What will the printout be?

```
70  IF X>8 THEN C=C+1
80  PRINT C
```

ANSWER
```
31
```

One-Way Selection.   One-Way Selection is another name for a line consisting solely of an IF-THEN (action statement). In one-way selection, the computer tests whether or not to execute the THEN branch before proceeding to the next line. In the next section, we consider *two-way selection*, in which the computer decides which of *two* branches to execute.

6.2 IF-THEN-ELSE

EXAMPLE   **Pass-Fail Program**   In order to pass you must receive a grade of at least 65. In this program the computer will print out either YOU PASS or YOU FAIL , depending on whether or not the input number is at least 65.

```
10   INPUT "ENTER GRADE" ; G
20   IF G>=65 THEN PRINT "YOU PASS" ELSE PRINT "YOU FAIL"
30   END
```

For an input of 83, the printout would be YOU PASS . For an input of 62, the printout would be YOU FAIL . The computer executes either the THEN branch or the ELSE branch. It *never* executes both.

The general form of IF-THEN-ELSE for two-way selection is:

IF (condition) THEN (branch A) ELSE (branch B)

If the condition is true, the computer will execute branch A and then proceed to the next numbered line; if the condition is false, the computer will execute branch B and then proceed to the next numbered line.

QUESTION   For the fragment given below **(a)** What would the printout be if in line 50, $Y = 14$; **(b)** same question if $Y = 5$ in line 50.

```
50   IF Y>9 THEN PRINT "HI" ELSE PRINT "BYE"
60   PRINT "SO LONG"
```

ANSWER   **(a)**
```
HI
SO LONG
```
(b)
```
BYE
SO LONG
```

(a)   Since $Y>9$, the computer executes the THEN branch, which is to PRINT "HI", and then continues to line 60.

(b) Here, Y<=9, so the computer executes the ELSE branch, which is to PRINT "BYE", and then continues to line 60.

QUESTION Fill in the blank in the following program so that if the input IQ is greater than 75 the printout is HIRED , whereas if the input is less than or equal to 75 the printout is NOT HIRED .

```
10  INPUT "YOUR IQ";IQ
20  IF IQ>75 _____
30  END
```

ANSWER Line 20 will read: IF IQ>75 THEN PRINT "HIRED" ELSE PRINT "NOT HIRED"

Typing ELSE Branch on Unnumbered Line. It improves readability to type the ELSE branch on its own unnumbered line so that ELSE is aligned with THEN. For example, the following is equivalent to the previous job hiring program:

```
10  INPUT "YOUR IQ";IQ
20  IF IQ>75 THEN PRINT "HIRED"
            ELSE PRINT "NOT HIRED"
30  END
```

NOTE: Line 20, which is displayed over two lines on the screen, is to be a single line in the computer's memory. Thus, you should not press the RETURN key after typing "HIRED". Instead you should drop down to the next line after "HIRED" by holding the CTRL key and striking the J key. Then you should use the space bar until the cursor is positioned directly below the T of THEN. (Some systems have a single *Line Feed* key that performs the same function as the CTRL/J combination.)

QUESTION Write a program in which you are asked to input an M if you are male, and an F if you are female. The printout will be either YOU ARE MALE or YOU ARE FEMALE . Write this program putting the ELSE branch below the THEN branch. Of course, it could also be written with both the THEN and ELSE branches on the same line.

ANSWER
```
10  INPUT "ENTER M IF MALE, F IF FEMALE";S$
20  IF S$="M" THEN PRINT "YOU ARE MALE"
             ELSE PRINT "YOU ARE FEMALE"
30  END
```

Did you remember to use a string variable for the sex, M or F? Did you remember that the ELSE branch line does not receive a new line number?

Investigate Your System.   In typing an ELSE branch under the THEN branch, how do you drop the cursor down to the next line? Describe here _____

PROBLEM   Dress shirts are priced at $24 each if fewer than five are purchased. They are $22 each if at least five are purchased. Fill in the blanks in the following program to print the total cost for an input number of shirts.

```
5    REM DRESS SHIRT PRICES
6    REM *****
10   INPUT "NUMBER OF SHIRTS";NUM
20   IF NUM<5 THEN _____
               ELSE _____
30   PRINT NUM;"SHIRTS COST $";COST
40   END
```

ANSWER   The first blank is the calculation when NUM<5. Since the shirts cost $24 each when fewer than 5 are purchased, the first blank is COST=NUM*24. The second blank is COST=NUM*22, since in this case each shirt costs $22.

PROBLEM   Team jackets cost $30 each if at least 8 are purchased, and $32 each if fewer than 8 are purchased. Write a program with a single PRINT statement to print out the total cost for an input number of jackets.

ANSWER
```
5    REM JACKET PRICES
6    REM *****
10   INPUT "NUMBER OF JACKETS";NUM
20   IF NUM>=8 THEN COST=NUM*30
                ELSE COST=NUM*32
30   PRINT NUM;"JACKETS COST $";COST
40   END
```

You also could have used the test IF NUM<8 with the *appropriate* THEN and ELSE branches.

PROBLEM   **Overtime Wage Program**   An employee receives $4 per hour for working 40 hours or less. An employee who works over 40 hours receives $4 per hour for the first 40 hours and $6 per hour for each hour over 40 hours.

For example, someone working 40 hours would earn $160. Someone working 30 hours would earn $120. However, someone working 42 hours would earn $172—$160 for the first 40 hours and an extra $12 for the two hours of overtime.

Fill in the blank lines in the following program:

```
 5    REM  WAGE
 6    REM *****
10    INPUT  "ENTER  HOURS" ; HRS
20    IF  HRS<40  THEN  WAGE=_____
                  ELSE  WAGE=160+_____
30    PRINT  HRS; "HRS  WAGE  $" ; WAGE
40    END
```

ANSWER   In the THEN branch WAGE = HRS*4, because the pay rate is a straight $4 per hour. In the ELSE branch WAGE = 160 + (HRS − 40)*6 because the pay is $160 for the first 40 hours and the number of hours over 40 is equal to HRS − 40.

6.3   AND, OR, NOT

Now we consider IF tests that involve compound conditions AND, OR, and NOT.

For example, the following are valid:

IF 2< = B AND B< = 9 THEN PRINT "BETWEEN 2 AND 9"

IF A>10 OR B>10 THEN PRINT "AT LEAST ONE EXCEEDS TEN"

IF X = 1 AND Y>0 THEN PRINT "YES"
                                 ELSE PRINT "REJECT"

IF NOT (A = 0 AND B = 0) THEN PRINT "A AND B ARE NOT BOTH ZERO"

AND.   In an IF (condition) AND (condition) THEN statement, the computer executes the THEN branch only if both conditions are true.

QUESTION

```
30  IF  X=1  AND  Y>2  THEN  PRINT  "YES"
40  PRINT  "SO LONG"
```

(a) What printout will this produce if X = 1 and Y = 5?

(b) What printout will this produce if X = 1 and Y = 1?

ANSWER **(a)**
```
YES
SO  LONG
```
(b)
```
SO  LONG
```

QUESTION   Fill in the blanks so that the following program fragment will determine whether an input age is that of a teenager.

```
10   INPUT  "AGE" ; A
20   IF  13<=A  AND _____  THEN  PRINT   "TEENAGER"
                              ELSE  PRINT   "NOT  TEENAGER"
```

ANSWER   The IF condition is IF 13< = A AND A< = 19 (Note that IF 13< = A< = 19 is incorrect syntax, because the word AND must appear for this compound condition.)

OR.   In an IF (condition) OR (condition) THEN statement, the computer executes the THEN branch if at least one of the conditions is true (i.e., one or the other, or both).

QUESTION   What will the printout be for **(a)** X = 25, Y = 5, **(b)** X = 25, Y = 2, **(c)** X = 15, Y = 2, **(d)** X = 15, Y = 5?

```
10   INPUT  X , Y
20   IF  X>18  OR  Y = 2  THEN  PRINT   "HELLO"
                          ELSE  PRINT   "PHONE  HOME "

30   END
```

ANSWER   The printout for inputs **(a)**, **(b)**, and **(c)** will be HELLO . The printout for **(d)** will be PHONE HOME .

NOT.   In an IF NOT (condition) THEN statement, the computer executes the THEN branch only if the condition is *false*.

QUESTION   What will the printout be for **(a)** AGE = 75, YRS = 10, **(b)** AGE = 63, YRS = 15, **(c)** AGE = 67, YRS = 12, **(d)** AGE = 64, YRS = 8?

```
10   INPUT AGE, YRS
20   IF NOT (AGE>65 OR YRS>=10) THEN PRINT "EMPLOYED"
                                ELSE PRINT "RETIRED"
30   END
```

ANSWER   The printout for inputs **(a)**, **(b)**, and **(c)** will be RETIRED . The printout for **(d)** will be EMPLOYED .

6.4 Transfer of Control

Execution of program lines in other than numerically ascending sequences can be accomplished by the transfer of control statements: GOTO and IF-THEN (line #).

GOTO Statements: Unconditional Transfer.   When the computer executes a statement of the form GOTO (line #), the computer will go directly to whatever line number is indicated. For example:

QUESTION   What will the printout be?

```
10   PRINT "EASY AS"
20   PRINT "ONE"
30   GOTO 50
40   PRINT "TWO"
50   PRINT "THREE"
60   END
```

ANSWER   The printout will be

EASY AS
ONE
THREE

The computer does not print the word TWO, because line 30 sends the computer directly to line 50.

IF-THEN (line #) Statements: Conditional Transfer.   When the computer executes the statement IF X=3 THEN 60, if the current value of X equals 3, the computer will go to line 60; if X is not equal to 3, the computer will simply go to the next line (in the usual numerical order).

REMARK: IF X=3 THEN 60 can also be written as IF X=3 THEN GOTO 60.

QUESTION   In the program below **(a)** What will the printout be for an input of X = 1? **(b)** What will it be for an input of X = 3?

```
10   INPUT  X
20   IF  X=3  THEN  60
30   PRINT  "HI"
40   PRINT  "JOE"
50   GOTO  70
60   PRINT  "SO LONG"
70   END
```

ANSWER   **(a)**   **(b)**

                      HI   SO LONG
                      JOE

(a) When X = 1, line 20 does not send the computer to line 60. Moreover, the statement GOTO 70 has the computer skip line 60 entirely.

(b) When X = 3, line 20 sends the computer directly to line 60.

PROBLEM   The only IF-THEN available in the first version of BASIC was IF-THEN (line #). Rewrite the Pass-Fail program of Section 6.2 using an IF-THEN (line #) test to branch to the appropriate PRINT statement.

      HINT: You will need a GOTO statement as well.

ANSWER

```
10   INPUT  "ENTER  GRADE";G
20   IF  G>=65  THEN  50
30   PRINT  "YOU FAIL"
40   GOTO  60
50   PRINT  "YOU PASS"
60   END
```

For an input of 83 the printout would be YOU PASS , because in line 20 the computer is sent to line 50. Note that for an input of 62, the printout would be YOU FAIL , because the IF-THEN condition would not be satisfied. The computer would proceed to the next line, without executing the THEN condition. In short, this program will give the appropriate printout for any input.

QUESTION   **(a)** Explain the purpose of line 40. **(b)** What would be the printout if line 40 were omitted and the input was 61?

ANSWER   **(a)** The purpose of line 40 is to ensure that the computer does not execute both PRINT statements for an input less than 65. **(b)** For an input of 61, the printout would be

```
YOU FAIL
YOU PASS
```

6.5 Multiple Statements

It is permissible to type more than one statement per line. A *colon* separator must be typed between such statements. For example,

```
10   A=5  :  B=7
20   PRINT A  :  PRINT B
30   PRINT A+B
40   END
```

The printout is

```
5
7
12
```

For our purposes, the main application of this feature will be when the THEN or ELSE branches of an IF test contain multiple statements, as illustrated in the next problem. (Many experts consider it poor style to use the colon separator in other situations.)

PROBLEM   Let us write a program in which a person's age is input. The printout will depend on whether that age is at least 21. Here are two sample printouts:

The printout for input 25 is

```
YOUR AGE IS 25
CAN VOTE
```

The printout for input 14 is

```
YOU ARE ONLY 14
CANNOT VOTE
```

SOLUTION 1.   Using a colon.

```
5    REM VOTING AGE
6    REM ****
10   INPUT "ENTER YOUR AGE";AGE
20   IF AGE>=18 THEN PRINT "YOUR AGE IS";AGE :
               PRINT "CAN VOTE"
               ELSE PRINT "YOU ARE ONLY";AGE :
               PRINT "CANNOT VOTE"
30   END
```

As you can see, the THEN and ELSE branches are long, since they contain multiple statements. There is a method of writing this program that is better suited to long THEN or ELSE branches. Here are two similar versions of this branching method:

SOLUTION 2(a).   Using IF-THEN (line #).

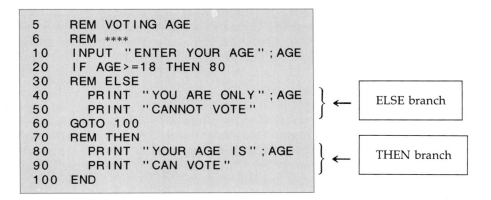

```
5     REM VOTING AGE
6     REM ****
10    INPUT "ENTER YOUR AGE" ; AGE
20    IF AGE>=18 THEN 80
30    REM ELSE
40       PRINT "YOU ARE ONLY" ; AGE     ⎫  ← ELSE branch
50       PRINT "CANNOT VOTE"            ⎭
60    GOTO 100
70    REM THEN
80       PRINT "YOUR AGE IS" ; AGE      ⎫  ← THEN branch
90       PRINT "CAN VOTE"               ⎭
100   END
```

SOLUTION 2(b).   Using IF-THEN (line #) ELSE (line #).

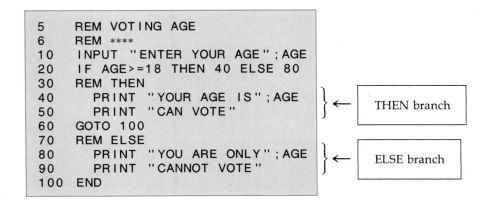

```
5     REM VOTING AGE
6     REM ****
10    INPUT "ENTER YOUR AGE" ; AGE
20    IF AGE>=18 THEN 40 ELSE 80
30    REM THEN
40       PRINT "YOUR AGE IS" ; AGE      ⎫  ← THEN branch
50       PRINT "CAN VOTE"               ⎭
60    GOTO 100
70    REM ELSE
80       PRINT "YOU ARE ONLY" ; AGE     ⎫  ← ELSE branch
90       PRINT "CANNOT VOTE"            ⎭
100   END
```

REMARKS
1. The THEN and ELSE branches have been indented to increase readability.
2. In solution 2(a) the ELSE branch comes first. In solution 2(b) the THEN branch comes first; this was accomplished using an IF-THEN-ELSE test in line 20.
3. Note that the GOTO statement separating the THEN and ELSE branches has not been indented.

▬▬▬ 6.6 Program Testing

The programmer's job is to write a general program that will produce an appropriate printout for any acceptable input of data. However, often it is not possible to test the program for all possible data. Therefore, the programmer must choose the values that would most effectively test the program. How does one choose these test values?

It is most important to have enough tests so that each of the possible THEN or ELSE branches is reached and executed. In this way, there should be an example of every type of possible printout that can be produced.

It is also important to test around the significant boundary values of each IF condition. For example, the retirement program of section 6.3 should probably be tested for ages 64 through 66 in various combinations with years of 9 through 11.

Several other meaningful values may be used for testing. For example, if the program allows for input from 1 to 100, you may wish to try values 1 and 100. Similarly, if the program allows any integer as input, you can try a negative number, zero, and a positive number. The appropriate test values are specific to each program.

▬▬▬ Exercises

CAUTION: *For any printouts on paper remember that input prompts and values will not appear on paper. (See Section 4.6 for ways to avoid this difficulty.)*

1. What printout will be produced by the following fragment if at the start of line 50,
   (a) A = 7 and D = 4
   (b) A = 4 and D = 7
   (c) A = 5 and D = 2
   (d) A = 0 and D = 3

   ```
   50  IF A<=5 THEN D=D+A
   60  PRINT D
   ```

2. Write an IF-THEN-ELSE program to produce a printout that will state whether an input number is at least nine. Here are two typical printouts:

   ```
   14 IS AT LEAST NINE
   ```
   or
   ```
   5 IS LESS THAN NINE
   ```

3. Write an IF-THEN-ELSE program so that for two distinct input numbers the printout will be the difference of the larger number minus the smaller. Be sure that your program will give printout of ⌐6⌐ both for input 9, 15 and for input 15, 9.

4. Basketballs are priced at $12 each if fewer than 5 are purchased and $10 each if at least 5 are purchased. Write a program to print out the total cost for an input number of basketballs. (Have your program contain a single PRINT statement.)

5. Write a program in which two DATA numbers are added together only if both numbers are positive. The printout should be the sum, or NOT BOTH POSITIVE if either of the two numbers is negative.

6. Write a program in which a pair of input numbers represents the ages of two sisters so that the printout will be either AT LEAST ONE OF THE SISTERS IS OVER TWENTY or NEITHER IS OVER TWENTY. Run it for input 12, 19; then 22, 18; then 23, 26; then 14, 22; then 20, 20.

7. (a) Write a program in which two input numbers represent someone's height (in inches) and weight (in pounds). The printout will be DEFINITELY OVERWEIGHT for people who are less than 72 inches tall and heavier than 200 pounds. Otherwise the printout will be MAYBE OKAY. Use an IF (condition) AND (condition) THEN-ELSE statement.

   (b) Rewrite the program using OR instead of AND.

8. (a) For the program below, what will the printout be
   (*i*) for input of 79   (*ii*) for input of 88?

```
10  INPUT "TYPE YOUR IQ"; IQ
20  IF IQ>84 THEN PRINT "HIRED" : GOTO 40
30  PRINT "GOOD LUCK"
40  END
```

   (b) Rewrite this program replacing lines 20 and 30 with an equivalent IF-THEN-ELSE statement.

9. An employee receives $5 per hour for working 30 hours or less. An employee who works over 30 hours receives $5 per hour for the first 30 hours and $7 per hour for each hour over 30 hours.

★ 10. An employee receives the regular pay rate for the first 40 hours and is paid at 1½ times the normal rate for each hour over 40 hours. Have both the pay rate R, and the number of hours worked be entered by a statement INPUT R, H. When you run your program with an input of 6,42 the printout should be RATE $6 HOURS 42 WAGE $258. Rerun your program with input of 8,41. *Do not change any of the program lines.*

★ **11.** Your quiz show score is entered by an input statement. If your score was at least 25 you receive a cash prize of double your score. If your score was under 25 you receive no prize. In either case the printout should consist of three lines. Here are two typical printouts:

The printout for input 32 is   The printout for input 14 is

```
CONGRATULATIONS, SCORE 32
YOUR SCORE WAS AT LEAST 25
YOU WIN $ 64
```

```
SORRY, SCORE ONLY 14
YOUR SCORE WAS UNDER 25
YOU DO NOT WIN A PRIZE
```

12. Also see Appendix B, Exercise 4.

7

More on Punctuation and PRINT Statements

It is desirable to format your printout so that it has a neat, orderly appearance. A main topic of this chapter is the use of commas within PRINT statements to produce a printout in table form. We also discuss trailing punctuation and blank PRINT statements.

7.1 Semicolon versus Comma

PRINT X;Y causes the computer to print the values of X and Y close together with two blank spaces between them if Y is not negative. By contrast, PRINT X,Y causes the computer to print the values of X and Y much farther apart, because they will be printed in different zones (see Section 7.2). Suppose X = 328 and Y = 5. Compare the effects of these two PRINT statements:

```
60  PRINT X;Y          60  PRINT X,Y
```

The printouts are

```
328   5          328          5
```

7.2 Print Zones and Commas

For many implementations of BASIC, each output line contains 5 print zones, each zone being 14 print positions wide.

Zone 1	Zone 2	Zone 3	Zone 4	Zone 5

When a PRINT statement contains several items separated by commas, the first item is printed in Zone 1, the second item is printed in Zone 2 and so on.

EXAMPLE

```
10   A=5  :  B=6  :  C=7
20   PRINT A,B,C
30   PRINT A;B;C
40   END
```

The printout is

Zone 1	Zone 2	Zone 3	Zone 4	Zone 5
5	6	7		
5 6 7				

Number and Width of Zeros Are System Dependent.   The number of zones and their width varies from system to system. Furthermore, for some systems the hard copy may differ from the screen output.

Investigate Your System.   (Find out the details for your system and then fill in the blanks.) Each output line contains _____ print positions and is subdivided into _____ zones of width _____.

NOTE: On some systems the last zone may be of shorter width than its other zones.

Using Commas to Produce a Table.

EXAMPLE

```
10   PRINT  "NAME" , "SCORE"
20   PRINT  "SMITH" ,82
30   PRINT  "HALL" ,91
40   PRINT  "JOHNSON" ,85
50   END
```

Printout

```
NAME                    SCORE
SMITH                    82
HALL                     91
JOHNSON                  85
```

QUESTION What will the printout be?

```
10  PRINT  "NUMBER" , "SQUARE" , "CUBE"
20  PRINT  4 ,  4∧2 ,  4∧3
30  PRINT  5 ,  5∧2 ,  5∧3
40  PRINT  6 ,  6∧2 ,  6∧3
50  END
```

ANSWER

```
NUMBER          SQUARE        CUBE
   4              16           64
   5              25          125
   6              36          216
```

Skipping over Print Zones. Each comma in a PRINT statement causes the computer to move to the next print zone. Thus, a statement such as PRINT ,6 will cause the computer to print 6 in Zone 2.

QUESTION What will the printout be?

```
10  PRINT  "COL A" , "COL B" , "COL C"
20  PRINT  3 , 4 , 5
30  PRINT  , 6
40  PRINT  , , 7
50  PRINT  , 8 , 9
60  END
```

ANSWER

COL A	COL B	COL C
3	4	5
	6	
		7
	8	9

◼ 7.3 Trailing Punctuation and Blank PRINT

Trailing Punctuation. A statement with no trailing punctuation—such as PRINT X—will cause the computer to print the value of X and then drop the carriage to the first position in the next line. Trailing punctuation, however, prevents the carriage from dropping to the next line (unless the carriage is already at the end of the line). For example, PRINT X; will cause the computer to print the value of X and then leave the carriage on the same line.

QUESTION Suppose for these program fragments X=1, Y=2, and Z=3. What are the printouts?

(a)
```
50  PRINT X;
60  PRINT Y
70  PRINT Z;
```

(b)
```
50  PRINT X;
60  PRINT Y;
70  PRINT Z
```

(c)
```
50  PRINT X;Y
60  PRINT Z
```

ANSWER The printouts are

(a)
```
1 2
3
```

(b)
```
1 2 3
```

(c)
```
1 2
3
```

Note that in program (a), the carriage does not drop to the next line until after line 60 is executed. In program (b), the carriage does not drop to the next line until after line 70 is executed. In program (c), the carriage drops to the next line after line 50 is executed.

Blank PRINT Statements. When a line consisting of only PRINT (and nothing else) is executed, the carriage moves to the beginning of the next line. This will produce a "skipped line" in the printout (unless the previous PRINT statement contains trailing punctuation).

QUESTION What will the printouts be if A=5 and B=6?

(a)
```
50  PRINT A
60  PRINT
70  PRINT B
```

(b)
```
50  PRINT A;
60  PRINT
70  PRINT B
```

(c)
```
50  PRINT A;
60  PRINT B
```

ANSWER

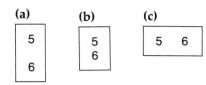

(a)
```
5

6
```

(b)
```
5
6
```

(c)
```
5   6
```

EXAMPLE   For X = 7 and Y = 8 the printout is

```
50  PRINT  X;
60  PRINT  Y;
70  PRINT  "GOODBYE"
```

Printout

```
7   8  GOODBYE
```

QUESTION   Modify the above program segment so that the printout is

```
7   8
GOODBYE
```

ANSWER   Include line 65 PRINT. This will drop the carriage, so that GOODBYE will be printed on its own line.

7.4 TAB and PRINT USING

For a discussion of more advanced techniques for controlling the format of a printout see Chapter 13 on TAB and PRINT USING.

Exercises

1. Give the printouts.

(a)
```
10  A=4 : B=6 : C=8
20  PRINT A,B,C
30  PRINT A;B
40  PRINT C
50  END
```

(b)
```
10  PRINT "COL A" , "COL B"
20  PRINT 4,4*4
30  PRINT 5,5*5
40  PRINT 6,6∧2
50  END
```
square

2. Assuming a system has 5 print zones, what will the printouts be?

(a)

```
10  PRINT 1,2,3,4,5,6,7,8
20  END
```

(b)

```
10  PRINT 1,2
20  PRINT 3,4,5,6,7,8
30  END
```

3. Give the printouts.

(a)

```
10  A=4 : B=5 : C=6
20  PRINT A;
30  PRINT B;
40  PRINT C;
50  PRINT "BING"
60  END
```

(b)

```
10  A=4 : B=5 : C=6
20  PRINT A;
30  PRINT B;
40  PRINT C;
50  PRINT
60  PRINT "BING"
70  END
```

4. Give the printout.

```
10  PRINT "COL A","COL B","COL C"
20  PRINT 5,6,7
30  PRINT ,8
40  PRINT ,9,10
50  END
```

5. What will the printout be for the following on a system that has 5 print zones with 14 spaces to a zone?

```
10  PRINT "ZONE ONE","ZONE TWO","ZONE THREE"
20  PRINT "ZONE ONE","IS THIS IN ZONE TWO?","ZONE THREE?"
30  END
```

★ **6. (a)** How many spaces does SECOND HALF SALES use? Will it fit in one zone if the computer system has 14 spaces to a zone?
(b) Write a two-line program fragment using two PRINT statements with commas that gives the output

```
YEAR    FIRST HALF    SECOND HALF    TOTAL
        SALES         SALES          SALES
```

★ **7.** Write a program that will allow you to determine the width for each of the zones and the number of zones on your system. (*Hint:* You may have to examine the printout closely.)

CHAPTER 8

FOR-NEXT Loops

In the programs considered so far, the computer has *not* executed any line more than once. A powerful feature of the computer is its ability to execute the same block of lines a number of times—an action called **looping**—and the block of lines to be executed repeatedly is called the **loop body**. Looping enables a computer program to handle a problem involving a number of repetitions of essentially the same task—for example, calculating and printing paychecks for 1000 different employees.

The three looping constructs available in IBM and Microsoft BASIC are (1) FOR-NEXT loops, (2) WHILE loops, and (3) hand-made loops.

When the programmer *knows in advance* how many times the loop body needs to be executed, FOR-NEXT loops provide the simplest means of looping.

8.1 Some Elementary Illustrations

Loop Body. The block of lines sandwiched between the FOR and NEXT statements is the loop body. This block will be executed for each of the values indicated in the FOR statement.

EXAMPLE

```
10   FOR J=1 TO 4
20      PRINT "HELLO"
30   NEXT J
40   PRINT "SO LONG"
50   END
```

Printout

```
HELLO
HELLO
HELLO
HELLO
SO LONG
```

69

REMARKS

1. In the above example the loop body, consisting of the single statement PRINT "HELLO", was executed four times. First when J = 1, next when J = 2, then when J = 3, and *finally* when J = 4.
2. Note that we *indented* the loop body. This is done to make the program easier for humans to read—the computer would have given the same printout even if the loop body had not been indented.

Control Variable.   The variable immediately following the word FOR is called the **control variable**, or **index**. Any valid numeric variable may be used as the control variable.

QUESTION   What will the printouts be?

(a)
```
10  FOR TIME=1 TO 3
20      PRINT "HI"
30      PRINT "BYE"
40  NEXT TIME
50  END
```

(b)
```
10  FOR TIME=1 TO 3
20  PRINT "HI"
30  PRINT "BYE"
40  NEXT TIME
50  END
```

ANSWER   These two programs will give the same printout—indentation of the loop body is good style but is not necessary for the computer's sake. The printout will be

```
HI
BYE
HI
BYE
HI
BYE
```

You will note that the loop body was executed three times.

QUESTION   Write a program using a FOR-NEXT loop to produce the following printout:

```
JOHN DOE
52 APPLE ST.
N.Y., N.Y. 10021
JOHN DOE
52 APPLE ST.
N.Y., N.Y. 10021
```

ANSWER   Obviously, we should use the FOR statement FOR J = 1 TO 2, since we want *two* copies of the address. The loop body will consist of three PRINT statements.

```
10  FOR J=1 TO 2
20    PRINT "JOHN DOE"
30    PRINT "52 APPLE ST"
40    PRINT "N.Y., N.Y. 10021"
50  NEXT J
60  END
```

Of course, if we wanted to print 25 copies of this address, we would change line 10 to FOR J = 1 TO 25.

Control Variable Can Appear in Loop Body.

EXAMPLE

```
10  PRINT "GREETINGS"
20  FOR J=1 TO 4
30    PRINT J
40  NEXT J
50  END
```

Printout

```
GREETINGS
 1
 2
 3
 4
```

Control Variable Need Not Start at One.   FOR statements such as FOR J = 5 to 7 are permissible—in this case, the loop body would be executed first with J = 5, then with J = 6, and finally with J = 7.

QUESTION   What will the printout be?

```
10  FOR J=5 TO 7
20    PRINT "THIS TIME J EQUALS";J
30    PRINT J;"SQUARED IS";J*J
40  NEXT J
50  END
```

ANSWER

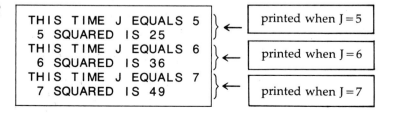

QUESTION   Write a program to produce the following printout:

HINT: What should the loop body be?

```
SOME  SQUARES  AND  CUBES
 3  SQUARED  IS  9
 3  CUBED  IS  27
 4  SQUARED  IS  16
 4  CUBED  IS  64
 5  SQUARED  IS  25
 5  CUBED  IS  125
```

ANSWER

```
10   PRINT  "SOME  SQUARES  AND  CUBES"
20   FOR  J=3  TO  5
30      PRINT  J; "SQUARED  IS"; J∧2
40      PRINT  J; "CUBED  IS"; J∧3
50   NEXT  J
60   END
```

8.2 Processing DATA Line One Element at a Time

Reusing Same Variable.   If a dessert recipe called for six tablespoons of chocolate powder, would you use *six different* spoons or a single spoon six times? Obviously, you would use a single spoon.

By the same token, it is often efficient to keep reusing the same variable in processing a list of DATA numbers. Not only does this method use less memory space, but even more importantly, makes it possible to use a loop.

EXAMPLE

```
10   FOR  J=1  TO  4
20      READ  X
30      PRINT  X
40   NEXT  J
50   DATA  31,18,25,42
60   END
```

Printout

```
31
18
25
42
```

Note that each time the computer executes READ X, it assigns to X the next *unused* DATA value.

QUESTION   What value was assigned to X during the execution of the loop body with J = 3?

ANSWER   X was assigned the third DATA value, namely 25.

Using Counters.

QUESTION   What will the printout be?

```
10   COUNT=0
20   COUNT=COUNT+1
30   COUNT=COUNT+1
40   COUNT=COUNT+1
50   PRINT COUNT
60   END
```

ANSWER   The printout is $\boxed{3}$. Here is why: COUNT starts out at 0. Each time COUNT = COUNT + 1 is executed the value of COUNT is increased by 1.

COUNT will be 3 by line 50, since COUNT = COUNT + 1 will have been executed three times.

QUESTION   The DATA line gives a student's scores on seven exams. What will the printout be?

```
10   COUNT=0
20   FOR EXAM=1 TO 7
30      READ SCORE
40       IF SCORE > 85 THEN COUNT=COUNT+1
50   NEXT EXAM
60   PRINT COUNT
70   DATA 84,88,90,92,70,94,81
80   END
```

ANSWER   COUNT is being used as a counter. COUNT is increased by 1 each time that a score is over 85. *Thus,* COUNT *counts the number of scores over 85.* The printout will be $\boxed{4}$.

Initialization.   Note that in the previous program, the statement COUNT = 0 is positioned before the loop. The variable COUNT is said to be *initialized* at 0.

Automatic Initialization Should Not Be Used.   Recall from Chapter 5 that a numeric variable that has no value assigned to it prior to its use, on the right side of a LET statement, will automatically be given the value 0 for that computation. Thus, the previous program would have produced the correct printout even if line 10 initializing COUNT at 0 had been omitted. *However, relying on automatic initialization is considered very poor style and should never be used.* In more complicated programs, relying on automatic initialization can lead to actual errors; for this reason, most other computer languages do not have automatic initialization.

8.3 Processing DATA Groups

EXAMPLE   Suppose we know that the DATA lines will contain the names and political parties for *six* people. The following program will print the names of just the Democrats and also the final count for the number of Democrats. We can use FOR J = 1 TO 6 because we know that there will be *six* data groups. Note the use of READ NAM\$,PARTY\$ to read in *pairs* of DATA items.

```
5    REM COUNT AND PRINT THE DEMOCRATS
6    REM ********
10   PRINT "DEMOCRATS"
20   DEM.COUNT=0
30   FOR J=1 TO 6
40     READ NAM$,PARTY$
50     IF PARTY$="D" THEN PRINT NAM$ : DEM.COUNT=DEM.COUNT+1
60   NEXT J
70   PRINT DEM.COUNT; "WERE DEMOCRATS"
80   DATA "FOY","R","BOND","D","MANN","D"
90   DATA "CHAN","D","HALL","R","HART","R"
100  END
```

The printout will be

```
DEMOCRATS
BOND
MANN
CHAN
  3 WERE DEMOCRATS
```

QUESTION In the previous example, what values will NAM$ and PARTY$ have when J = 3?

ANSWER When J = 3, the third DATA group will be read in and processed. Thus, NAM$ will be "MANN" and PARTY$ will be "D". For this DATA group, DEM.COUNT will be increased by 1.

8.4 Using Summing Variables

QUESTION What will the printout be?

```
10   SUM=0
20   SUM=SUM+8
30   SUM=SUM+9
40   SUM=SUM+11
50   PRINT SUM
60   END
```

ANSWER SUM is being used as a summing variable. SUM starts out at 0. First 8 is added to it. Then 9 is added to it. Finally 11 is added to it. By line 50, the value of SUM will be 8+9+11. The printout will be [28].

REMARK: There is no magic in the variable name SUM. If in the previous program, the variable S had been used instead of SUM, the computer would still have computed and printed the sum.

EXAMPLE **Sum of DATA Numbers** If you know in advance how many numbers there will be in the DATA line(s), you can use a FOR-NEXT loop for finding their sum. Consider this program that will print the sum for any five DATA numbers:

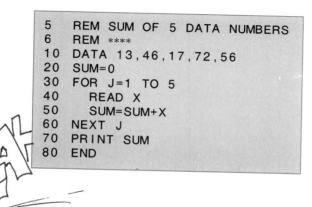

```
5    REM SUM OF 5 DATA NUMBERS
6    REM ****
10   DATA 13,46,17,72,56
20   SUM=0
30   FOR J=1 TO 5
40     READ X
50     SUM=SUM+X
60   NEXT J
70   PRINT SUM
80   END
```

Printout

204

Pay particular attention to what happens *BEFORE, DURING,* and *AFTER* the loop. *Before* the loop SUM is initialized at 0. *After* the loop, the final value of SUM is printed.

During the loop, the values are read in and added on to SUM. When J = 1, the first data number is read in and added to SUM. When J = 2, the second data number is read in and added on, and so on.

REMARK: If you wished to reuse this program to find the sum of the following five numbers:

23,14,8,25,19

you would replace line 70 by 70 DATA 23,14,8,25,19.

Initialization.   Note that in the previous program the statement SUM = 0, which gives SUM a first value, is positioned before the loop. Recall that the variable SUM is said to be initialized at 0.

QUESTION   In the following incorrect program, the summing variable is set equal to 0 inside the loop. What will the printout be?

```
5    REM INCORRECT SUM
6    REM ****
10   FOR J=1 TO 4
20      SUM=0
30      READ X
40      SUM=SUM+X
50   NEXT J
60   PRINT SUM
70   DATA 9,11,13,15
80   END
```

ANSWER   It will be $\boxed{15}$, because the fourth time the loop body is executed, SUM is reset at 0. Then X becomes 15, and 15 is added to 0. Thus, the final value of SUM will be 15.

8.5 Applications with Control Variable Appearing in Loop Body

PROBLEM   Write a program to find the sum of the first one hundred integers—that is, 1 + 2 + 3 + . . . + 100.

PROGRAM IDEAS

Obviously, we would prefer to avoid typing DATA lines with the integers 1 through 100; we can avoid this since each number to be added to the sum follows a pattern that can be expressed in terms of the control variable. Here is the program:

```
5    REM  SUM  OF  1  THROUGH  100
6    REM  ****
10   SUM=0
20   FOR  K=1  TO  100
30       SUM=SUM+K
40   NEXT  K
50   PRINT  "SUM  OF  FIRST  100"
60   PRINT  "INTEGERS" ; SUM
70   END
```

Printout

```
SUM  OF  FIRST  100
INTEGERS  5050
```

When K = 1, line 30 is the same as SUM = SUM + 1; thus, 1 is added to SUM. When K = 2, line 30 is the same as SUM = SUM + 2; thus, 2 is added to SUM. Similarly, when K = 3, 3 is added to SUM; when K = 4, 4 is added to SUM, and so on. Thus, by the end of the FOR-NEXT loop, SUM will be 1 + 2 + 3 + . . . + 100.

QUESTION   Modify the previous program so that it prints the sum 1 + 2 + 3 + . . . + 50, along with an appropriate message.

ANSWER   Change line 20 to FOR K = 1 TO 50 and line 50 to PRINT "SUM OF FIRST 50"

QUESTION   Contrast the printouts for these two programs.

HINT: Pay attention to what is printed *during* a loop and what is printed *after*.

(a)
```
10   SUM=0
20   FOR  J=1  TO  4
30       SUM=SUM+J
40   NEXT  J
50   PRINT  SUM
60   END
```

(b)
```
10   SUM=0
20   FOR  J=1  TO  4
30       SUM=SUM+J
40       PRINT  SUM
50   NEXT  J
60   PRINT  SUM
70   END
```

ANSWER In program (a), the sum $1+2+3+4$ will be computed, and then, after the FOR-NEXT loop is completed, this sum will be printed. In the program (b), PRINT SUM is executed during the loop as well as after.

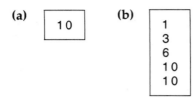

(a)

```
10
```

(b)

```
1
3
6
10
10
```

PROBLEM Write a FOR-NEXT program to print the following table:

NUMBER	ITS SQUARE
5	25
6	36
7	49
8	64
9	81

ANSWER The statement PRINT "NUMBER","ITS SQUARE" comes before the loop. It provides the heading for the table.

```
10  PRINT "NUMBER","ITS SQUARE"
20  FOR K=5 TO 9
30    PRINT K,K*K
40  NEXT K
50  END
```

EXAMPLE **Price-Profit Table** The Shirts-to-Go retail store has just received a new supply of shirts. Preliminary market research for that shirt indicates that the profit obtainable from a given sales price X is given by the formula PROFIT $= X(100-2X)$. Write a program that will produce the following PROFIT $= X(100-2X)$ tabular printout for integer sales prices ranging from $15 to $30.

PRICE	PROFIT
15	1050
16	1088
.	.
.	.
.	.
30	1200

PROGRAM IDEAS

The heading for the table will be produced by the program line PRINT "PRICE","PROFIT". (This will appear before the FOR-NEXT loop.) In the FOR-NEXT loop, the control variable will take on the various prices from 15 to 30. (We will use FOR PRICE=15 TO 30.) For each value of PRICE, we must print both PRICE and the PROFIT calculated from that value of PRICE.

QUESTION   Complete lines 30 and 40 for the PRICE-PROFIT table program.

```
5    REM PRICE-PROFIT
6    REM ****
10   PRINT "PRICE","PROFIT"
20   FOR PRICE=15 TO 30
30      PROFIT=_____
40      PRINT _____
50   NEXT PRICE
60   END
```

ANSWER   Line 30 should be PROFIT = PRICE*(100−2*PRICE). Line 40 should be PRINT PRICE,PROFIT.

8.6 Miscellaneous Applications

Pay attention to whether the FOR statement is used only to specify how many times the loop body is to be executed, or whether the control variable actually appears in the loop body.

PROBLEM   For the following wage calculation program, each DATA triple gives an employee's name, hours worked, and rate per hour. Fill in lines 50 and 70 so that the printout is

```
NAME            WAGE
SMITH            200
CHAN             150
KATZ             210
TOTAL PAID $ 560
```

Here is the program:

```
5     REM WAGE CALCULATION PROGRAM
6     REM ****
10    PRINT "NAME","WAGE"
20    TOTAL=0
30    FOR J=1 TO 3
40      READ NAM$,HRS,RATE
50      _____
60      PRINT NAM$,WAGE
70      _____
80    NEXT J
90    PRINT "TOTAL PAID $";TOTAL
100   DATA "SMITH",40,5,"CHAN",30,5,"KATZ",30,7
110   END
```

ANSWER Line 50 should be WAGE=HRS*RATE, which calculates the employee's wage. Line 70 should be TOTAL=TOTAL+WAGE, which adds the computed wage to the summing variable.

PROBLEM Penny Pincher buys a car on a twenty-year installment plan. She pays $2 the first year, $4 the second year, $8 the third, $16 the fourth and so on. Her payment for the Nth year is 2^N. Writing a program to produce the following printout is Exercise 13.

```
PENNY PINCHER PAYMENT SCHEDULE
YEAR            PAYMENT
 1               2
 2               4
 3               8
 4               16
 .               .
 .               .
 .
 20
TOTAL AMOUNT PAID $_____
```

8.7 Steps Other Than 1

So far in FOR-NEXT Loops, the control variable has been increased by one each time. If you want the control variable to be changed by an amount other than one, you must specify this in the FOR statement using the keyword STEP.

EXAMPLE

```
10  FOR K=1 TO 9 STEP 2
20      PRINT K
30  NEXT K
40  END
```

The printout will be

```
1
3
5
7
9
```

If you wish the control variable to decrease in size, you must use a negative step and put the larger limit first. (If you were to put the larger limit first but *without a negative step, the computer would skip the loop.*)

QUESTION   What will the printouts be?

(a)

```
10  FOR K=4 TO 1 STEP -1
20      PRINT K
30  NEXT K
40  PRINT "SO LONG"
50  END
```

(b)

```
10  FOR K=4 TO 1
20      PRINT K
30  NEXT K
40  PRINT "SO LONG"
50  END
```

ANSWER   **(a)**

```
4
3
2
1
SO LONG
```

(b)

```
SO LONG
```

8.8 OUT OF DATA Error Message

In a program, each time a READ statement is executed, the computer uses the next DATA value(s) from those DATA value(s) not yet used. In the event that there are not enough unused DATA values to assign a value to every variable in the READ statement, the computer will terminate execution with the following error message:

```
OUT OF DATA IN (line #)
```

For example

```
10   DATA 1,2,3
20   READ X,Y
30   PRINT X;Y
40   READ A,B
50   PRINT A,B
60   END
```

Since there will not be enough data to assign values to A and B in line 40, the program will terminate with an error message. The printout will be

```
1   2
OUT OF DATA IN 40
```

NOTE: The line number in the OUT OF DATA message is that of the READ statement that caused the error.

QUESTION   What will the printouts be (including any error message)?

(a)
```
10   READ A,B
20   PRINT A;B
30   READ A,B
40   PRINT A;B
50   DATA 5,7,9,8
60   END
```

(b)
```
10   READ A,B
20   PRINT A;B
30   READ A,B
40   PRINT A;B
50   DATA 5,7,9
60   END
```

ANSWER   (a)
```
5   7
9   8
```

(b)
```
5   7
OUT OF DATA IN 30
```

NOTE: In program (b) the computer never reaches line 40.

QUESTION   What will the printouts in these poorly designed programs be?

(a)

```
10   FOR  J=1  TO  3
20      READ  X,Y
30      PRINT  X;Y
40   NEXT  J
50   PRINT  "SO  LONG"
60   DATA  1,2,3,4,5
70   END
```

(b)

```
10   FOR  J=1  TO  3
20      READ  X,Y
30      PRINT  X;Y
40   NEXT  J
50   PRINT  "SO  LONG"
60   DATA  1,2,3,4,5,6,7,8
70   END
```

ANSWER   Note that program (a) has too little DATA and program (b) has too much.

Printouts

(a)

```
1    2
3    4
OUT  OF  DATA  IN  20
```

(b)

```
1    2
3    4
5    6
SO  LONG
```

RESTORE and DATA Pointer.   After you type RUN, the computer collects all the DATA from your program and sets the DATA pointer to the first DATA value. Each time a READ statement assigns value(s) to variable(s), the DATA pointer is moved further along. If you wish to send the DATA pointer back to the first value, you may do so by including a RESTORE statement in your program. For example, you could use a RESTORE statement if you wanted your program to go through the DATA twice.

```
10    FOR  J=1  TO  3
20       READ  X
30       PRINT  X
40    NEXT  J
50    RESTORE
60    FOR  J=1  TO  3
70       READ  X
80       PRINT  X*X
90    NEXT  5
100   DATA  5,8,9
110   END
```

Printout

```
5
8
9
25
64
81
```

QUESTION What would the printout be if line 50 were omitted?

ANSWER

```
5
8
9
OUT  OF  DATA  IN  70
```

8.9 Trailing Punctuation and FOR-NEXT

Recall from Chapter 7 that a trailing semicolon in a PRINT statement prevents the carriage from dropping to the next line after the item is printed. Thus, trailing semicolons can be used to keep printouts across a line.

QUESTION What will the printouts be?

(a)
```
10   FOR  J=1  TO  4
20      PRINT  J;
30   NEXT  J
40   PRINT  "OKAY"
50   END
```

(b)
```
10   FOR  J=1  TO  4
20      PRINT  J;
30   NEXT  J
40   PRINT
50   PRINT  "OKAY"
60   END
```

ANSWER **(a)**
```
1   2   3   4   OKAY
```

(b)
```
1   2   3   4
OKAY
```

8.10 Using Variable Limit to Increase Program Flexibility

Consider the statement FOR J = 1 TO N. When the computer reaches such a FOR-NEXT loop, how many times will it execute the loop body? The answer is that the computer will use the current value of N. Thus, if N is 8 when the computer first reaches this FOR-NEXT loop, the loop body will be executed 8 times.

EXAMPLE   This program allows the user to specify the value for the upper limit.

```
10   INPUT  "HOW  MANY  TIMES" ; N
20   FOR  J=1  TO  N
30      PRINT  J ;
40   NEXT  J
50   END
```

Typical printout

```
HOW  MANY  TIMES?   5
1   2   3   4   5
```

EXAMPLE   Completing lines 20,40, and 70 is Exercise 9.

```
5    REM  SUM  OF  1  THROUGH  N
6    REM ****
10   PRINT  "SUM  OF  FIRST  N  INTEGERS"
20   INPUT  _____
30   SUM=0
40   FOR  J=1  TO  _____
50      SUM=SUM+J
60   NEXT  J
70   PRINT  "SUM  OF  FIRST" ; _____
80   END
```

Here is a typical printout:

```
SUM  OF  FIRST  N  INTEGERS
TYPE  VALUE  FOR  N?  10
SUM  OF  FIRST  10  INTEGERS  IS  55
```

NOTE: In order to rerun this program with a different value of N, the user simply types in that value in response to the question mark. *The user does not need to retype anything within the program.*

8.11   Using First DATA Number to Specify Number of Sets of Data

In the DATA line of the program below, the first DATA number, 4, specifies that there will be four sets of data. (This value is called the header.)

```
5    REM WAGES
6    REM ****
10   READ HEADER
20   FOR J=1 TO HEADER
30      READ NAM$,HRS,RATE
40      PRINT NAM$;" WAGE $";HRS*RATE
50   NEXT J
60   DATA 4
70   DATA "FOY",35,6,"MIN",41,5,"HALL",40,7,"COHN",50,6
80   END
```

REMARK: The header value of line 60 could have been included as the first value of a single DATA line along with the four DATA groups, but it is generally considered good style to place the header value on its own DATA line.

To rerun this program for 7 employees, the DATA lines would start with a header value of 7 followed by seven data sets giving the seven employees' work information.

Exercises for 8.1–8.4

1. Write a program that will print out ten copies of your name.
2. What will the printouts be?

(a)

```
10   FOR N=1 TO 3
20      PRINT N
30      PRINT "GOOD DAY"
40   NEXT N
50   PRINT "JOE"
60   END
```

(b)

```
10   S=0
20   FOR K=1 TO 5
30      S=S+K
40      PRINT S
50   NEXT K
60   END
```

(c)

```
10   PRINT "COL A","COL B"
20   FOR J=1 TO 4
30      PRINT J^2, 2*J
40   NEXT J
50   END
```

(d)

```
10   FOR  K=1  TO  5
20        IF  K=4  THEN  40
30        PRINT  "HOWDY" ; K
40   NEXT  K
50   END
```

3. **(a)** Write a FOR-NEXT program that will give the printout

```
11  SQUARED  EQUALS  121
12  SQUARED  EQUALS  144
13  SQUARED  EQUALS  169
14  SQUARED  EQUALS  196
15  SQUARED  EQUALS  225
```

(b) SQR( ) is the square root function. For example, SQR(9) equals 3. SQR(2) equals 1.414214. Write a program that prints the square roots of 2 through 10.

4. **(a)** Write a program that will print the name of each student who scored a total of at least 15 points on two quizzes. Use the following DATA lines:

    10   DATA"JOHN",8,6,"MARY",10,8

    20   DATA"SAM",7,5,"LOU",8,7

    Each DATA group represents the student's name and two quiz scores. Your program can assume there will be *four* DATA groups.

    (b) Rewrite your program so that it will also print the number of students who scored at least 15.

5. Write a program that produces the following list of Centigrade and Fahrenheit equivalents, in steps of ten degrees.
    Hint: FAHR = (CELS*9/5) + 32

CENTIGRADE	FAHRENHEIT
0	32
10	50
20	68
.	.
.	.
.	.
100	212

6. Write a program that computes and prints the sum of $1^2 + 2^2 + 3^2 + \cdots + 10^2$.

7. Write a program that will find the average of *five* numbers. Run it with DATA 23, 14, 48, 17, 22.

Exercises for 8.5–8.11

8. Write a program that computes $1 + 1/2 + 1/3 + \cdots + 1/100$.

9. Complete the program of Section 8.10 to find the sum of the first N integers, when the user inputs the value for N.

10. Write a program so that if the DATA line consists of five numbers (representing a student's grades on five tests), the printout will be

A AVERAGE	or	NOT AN A AVERAGE

depending on whether or not the average for the 5 tests is greater than or equal to 90. Run it for DATA 88, 92, 87, 86, 94. Rerun it for DATA 91, 93, 80, 98, 95.

11. 4! is read "4 factorial" and is equal to the product of 4·3·3·1, which is 24. Similarly, 6! is equal to 6·5·4·3·2·1, which equals 720. Write a program that will compute the factorial of an input positive integer. When 4 is input, the printout should be | 4 FACTORIAL EQUALS 24 |. Run it for input of 4; then rerun it for 6, then for 10.

12. Write a FOR-NEXT program to produce the following table for multiplication by 7:

```
7  TIMES  10  EQUALS  70
7  TIMES  11  EQUALS  77
7  TIMES  12  EQUALS  84
7  TIMES  13  EQUALS  91
7  TIMES  14  EQUALS  98
```

13. Penny Pincher buys a car on a 20-year installment plan and pays $2 the first year, $4 the second year, $8 the third year, etc. Note that for year J the payment is 2 to the power J. Write a program that will print out the amount to be paid each year and also the total amount that will have been paid after twenty years.

14. **(a)** Write a program that will either print each of the five DATA numbers greater than 90 or print NONE OVER 90. Thus, for DATA 88,92,92,90,91 the printout should be 92 92 91 . Rerun it with DATA 60,83,80,85,40. The printout should be NONE OVER 90 .
    (b) Modify your program so that a header value gives how many DATA numbers there are.

15. Write FOR-NEXT programs with the printouts

(a)

```
5    4    3    2    1    BLAST  OFF
```

(b)

```
5    4    3    2    1
BLAST  OFF
```

16. Write a program to print 5 copies of your name and address so that there is a *blank line* separating the copies.

17. The Peoria-by-Night Guided Tours estimates that if it prices its tickets at x dollars per ticket, the number sold will be 84 − 6x. Write a program to produce the following table for integer ticket prices ranging from $1 to $14:

TICKET PRICE	NUMBER SOLD	REVENUE $
1	78	78
2	72	144
.	.	.
.	.	.
.	.	.
14	0	0

18. The data gives the sales for the twelve months of the year. DATA 35,50,20,12,18,9,28,36,15,40,31,37. Write a program with a printout of the form

MONTH NUMBER	MONTH'S SALES	TOTAL TO DATE
1	35	35
2	50	85
3	20	105
.	.	.
.	.	.
.	.	.
12	.	.

19. The following DATA line contains the names and ages of four students.

DATA "SMITH",52,"CHAN",17,"DIAZ",15,"HOPE",29

Write a program that will produce the following printout:

```
SMITH AT LEAST 25
CHAN UNDER 25
DIAZ UNDER 25
HOPE AT LEAST 25
```

(*Hint:* You may wish to use a separate PRINT statement for the students' names.)

20. Write a program to compute the sum of $\frac{1}{2} + \frac{2}{3} + \frac{3}{4} + \frac{4}{5} + \ldots + \frac{99}{100}$.

21. Also see Appendix B, Exercises 1–3.

CHAPTER 9

WHILE Loops

A serious limitation of FOR-NEXT loops is that they are count-controlled. Generally, with FOR-NEXT loops the number of times the loop body is to be executed must either be *known in advance* by the programmer or *supplied* by the person entering the data.

WHILE loops, by contrast, offer greater flexibility. There are many situations in which it cannot be known in advance how many times the loop body should be executed. For example, the programmer might want the computer to continue executing the loop body until a certain task is completed but may not know how many repetitions will be needed. A WHILE loop is designed with that situation in mind. In a WHILE loop the programmer includes a "test condition" in the WHILE statement. This enables the loop to be designed so that the computer will continue executing the loop body until the intended task is completed.

NOTE: In WHILE/WEND loops, the order of certain statements in the loop body is usually somewhat different from that of FOR-NEXT loops. Particular attention should be paid to this point.

9.1 First Illustrations

General Form of the WHILE Loop.

    WHILE condition
        loop body
    WEND

In a properly designed WHILE loop, the value of the variable(s) in the condition will be changed by execution of the loop body. This makes it possible to exit eventually. Here is how the WHILE loop works: The computer starts by testing the WHILE condition. If the condition tests out as True, the entire loop body is executed and then control is returned to the top to retest the WHILE condition. This process is repeated as long as the condition tests out as True. The first time that the condition tests out as False, the computer exits from the loop.

NOTE: If the condition becomes False within the body of the loop, the remaining body of the loop is still completed. The loop can be exited from only when the computer is at the top of the loop, testing the condition.

EXAMPLE

```
10   J=1
20   WHILE  J<=3
30      PRINT  J
40      J=J+1
50   WEND
60   PRINT  "SO  LONG"
70   END
```

Printout

```
1
2
3
SO  LONG
```

Here is a step-by-step trace of the program:

J is initialized at 1 and then the computer reaches the WHILE loop.

Since $J<=3$, the loop body will be executed. During this execution of the loop body, 1 is printed and then J becomes 2. The computer is then sent to the top to test the WHILE condition.

Since $J<=3$, the loop body will be executed again. During this execution 2 is printed and then J becomes 3. The computer is then sent to test the WHILE condition.

Since $J<=3$, the loop body is executed again. During this execution 3 is printed and J becomes 4. The computer is then sent to test the WHILE condition.

Now $J<=3$ is false. Thus, the computer exits and moves on to line 60.

REMARK: Of course, this same printout could be produced more simply by using a FOR-NEXT loop. The next example, however, cannot be done more readily by using FOR-NEXT. Try to understand why not.

EXAMPLE   **First Power of 2 to Exceed 200**   The powers of 2 are 1,2,4,8,16,32,64, ... One way to obtain this list is to keep multiplying the previous number on the list by 2.

Let us give a program that will print the first power of 2 that exceeds 200. A FOR-NEXT loop is *not* appropriate because we do not know how many times the loop body (doubling the previous result) should be executed.

```
10   RESULT=1
20   WHILE RESULT<=200
30      RESULT=RESULT*2
40   WEND
50   PRINT RESULT;"IS FIRST POWER OF 2 OVER 200"
60   END
```

The printout will be

```
256 IS FIRST POWER OF 2 OVER 200
```

9.2 DATA Flag as Exit Condition

A DATA **flag**, or **sentinel value**, is used to signal to the computer that the end of the DATA has been reached. Generally, a DATA flag should not be processed the same way other DATA items are processed.

PROBLEM Write a program with a WHILE loop so that for any DATA line ending with the flag 999, the printout will be the sum of the non-flag numbers. For example, use as line 10

        10   DATA 6,14,8,5,999

The printout should be $\overline{33}$.

ANSWER We give the WHILE loop program and a similar FOR-NEXT version side by side. Note that in the FOR-NEXT version, the DATA line does not end with a flag. *Instead the programmer must count by hand that there are four numbers to be summed.*

(a)
```
10   DATA 6,14,8,5,999
20   SUM=0
30   READ X
40   WHILE X<>999
50      SUM=SUM+X
60      READ X
70   WEND
80   PRINT SUM
90   END
```

(b)
```
10   DATA 6,14,8,5
20   SUM=0
30   FOR J=1 TO 4
40      READ X
50      SUM=SUM+X
60   NEXT J
70   PRINT SUM
80   END
```

REMARKS

1. Note that in program (a) (the WHILE/WEND version), there are *two* READ X statements—one within the loop body and another positioned *before* the loop. The READ X that occurs before the loop (in line 30) is called **priming the pump**.

2. Another important difference between the two programs is that in the WHILE/WEND loop body, the READ X statement is located in the last line of the loop body instead of in the first line. This is because you have already read the first data number before entering the loop (**primed the pump**), and must first add that number to the sum before reading the next number.

Rerunning to Find a Different Sum.   Consider rerunning each of these programs to find the sum $41 + 18 + 36 + 52 + 11 + 6 + 45 + 34$. The WHILE version could be rerun by replacing line 10 with this new DATA line:

10   DATA   41,18,36,52,11,6,45,34,999

QUESTION   What must be done to rerun the FOR-NEXT version (program (b)) to find the sum $41 + 38 + 36 + 52 + 11 + 6 + 45 + 34$?

ANSWER   Not only would the user have to type a new DATA line, but the user would also have to count by hand the number of DATA numbers and then change line 30 to FOR J = 1 to 8.

Clearly, if the user needs to run a summing program for a number of sums of different *lengths*, the WHILE version is much more convenient.

Incorrect WHILE/WEND Version of Previous Program.   This program will *not* print the sum of the nonflag data numbers. What will it print?

```
5    REM  BAD  CODE
6    REM  ****
10   DATA  6,14,8,5,999
20   SUM=0
30   WHILE  X<>999
40      READ  X
50      SUM=SUM+X
60   WEND
70   PRINT  SUM
80   END
```

ANSWER   The printout will be 1032 , not 33 as expected. The computer does not exit from the WHILE loop the instant the WHILE condition becomes false. It still must finish the remainder of the loop body. The computer can only exit when it comes back to the WHILE condition. Because of this, the flag value 999 was added to SUM in line 50.

Another Common Numerical Flag Value.   A numerical flag value should be some number that is clearly different from the nonflag numbers. Another common DATA flag is the number −1.

QUESTION   Fill in lines 20, 30, and 50 in the WHILE/WEND version of the program to print each of the DATA numbers greater than 21, where the DATA line ends with the flag −1. The printout should be 25 28 23.

```
10   DATA 25,19,28,23,14,-1
20   _____
30   WHILE X_____
40      IF X>21 THEN PRINT X;
50   _____
60   WEND
70   END
```

ANSWER   The WHILE/WEND program contains two READ X statements, a pump-priming READ X in line 20, and a READ X in line 50. Line 30 should be WHILE X<>−1.

PROBLEM   **Finding the Average**   Write a program to find the average for a list of DATA numbers ending with the flag −1. For DATA 5,12,4,−1 the printout would be 7.

PROGRAM IDEAS

We will need a summing variable, SUM, and also a variable, COUNT, to keep track of how many nonflag DATA numbers there are. Both of these variables will be initialized at 0 before the start of the WHILE loop. Complete lines 30, 60, and 70.

```
5    REM FINDING THE AVERAGE
6    REM ********
10   SUM=0
20   COUNT=0
30   _____
40   WHILE X<>-1
50      SUM=SUM+X
60   _____
70   _____
80   WEND
90   PRINT "AVERAGE IS";SUM/COUNT
100  DATA 5,12,4,-1
110  END
```

ANSWER Line 30 is the pump-priming READ X. Line 60 is COUNT=COUNT+1. Line 70 is READ X.

9.3 OUT OF DATA Error Message

Remember that when the computer reaches a READ statement and there are not enough unused DATA values to provide a value for each variable in the READ statement, the computer terminates execution with an error message.

QUESTION In each of these programs, the flag −1 was incorrectly omitted from the DATA line. Give the printouts.

(a)
```
10   READ X
20   WHILE X<>-1
30      PRINT X
40      READ X
50   WEND
60   PRINT "SO LONG"
70   DATA 5,6,7
80   END
```

(b)
```
10   SUM=0
20   READ X
30   WHILE X<>-1
40      SUM=SUM+X
50      READ X
60   WEND
70   PRINT SUM
80   DATA 5,6,7
```

ANSWER (a)
```
5
6
7
OUT OF DATA IN 40
```

(b)
```
OUT OF DATA IN 50
```

9.4 Using a Flag Group

In the following program the DATA triple "SMITH",40,5 represents the information that SMITH worked 40 hours at $5 per hour. Note the use of the **flag group**, "XYZ",−1,−1.

QUESTION Complete lines 40 and 80 of the program below so that it will print not only each employee's wage, but also the total paid in wages. Here is the printout:

```
5     REM  WAGES
6     REM  ****
10    PRINT  "NAME" ,   "WAGE "
20    TOTAL = 0
30    READ  NAM$ , HRS , RATE
40    WHILE  NAM$ < > _____
50      WAGE = HRS * RATE
60      PRINT  NAM$ , WAGE
70      TOTAL = TOTAL + WAGE
80      _____
90    WEND
100   PRINT  "TOTAL  PAID  $ " ; TOTAL
110   DATA  "SMITH" , 40 , 5 , "CHAN" , 30 , 5
120   DATA  "KATZ" , 30 , 7 , "XYZ" , − 1 , − 1
130   END
```

NAME	WAGE
SMITH	200
CHAN	150
KATZ	210
TOTAL PAID $	560

ANSWER   Line 40 is WHILE NAM$<>"XYZ". Line 80 reads in the next DATA group; line 80 is READ NAM$,HRS,RATE.

QUESTION   What would the printout have been if the DATA line 120 had not ended with the flag triple, but instead had ended with just "XYZ"? This is Exercise 6.

9.5 Infinite WHILE Loops

EXAMPLE   The following program will keep printing HI indefinitely. This is an example of an infinite loop. To stop an infinite loop, press the CTRL key and hit the letter C.

```
10  X=1
20  WHILE  X=1
30    PRINT  "HI"
40  WEND
50  END
```

Printout

```
HI
HI
HI
.
.
.
```

QUESTION   What will happen in the following program?

```
10   X=1
20   WHILE X<>10
30      PRINT X
40      X=X+2
50   WEND
60   END
```

ANSWER   X will never become 10 because it will start at 1 and continue being increased by 2. The computer will continue printing odd numbers until X becomes so large that the program halts with an error.

9.6 Using INPUT Flag Values

```
10   PRINT  "PRODUCTS OF TWO NUMBERS "
20   INPUT  "TYPE TWO NUMBERS OR -1,-1 TO STOP " ; NUM1 , NUM2
30   WHILE NUM1 <> -1
40      PRINT NUM1 ; "TIMES" ; NUM2 ; "IS" ; NUM1*NUM2
50      INPUT "TYPE TWO NUMBERS OR -1,-1 TO STOP " ; NUM1 , NUM2
60   WEND
70   END
```

Here is a sample run:

```
PRODUCTS OF TWO NUMBERS
TYPE TWO NUMBERS OR -1,-1 TO STOP? 9,7
   9 TIMES 7 IS 63
TYPE TWO NUMBERS OR -1,-1 TO STOP? 8,6
   8 TIMES 6 IS 48
TYPE TWO NUMBERS OR -1,-1 TO STOP? 9,12
   9 TIMES 12 IS 108
TYPE TWO NUMBERS OR -1,-1 TO STOP? -1,-1
```

REMARK: Note how similar this INPUT statement is to READ—this program contains both a pump-priming INPUT statement and also an INPUT statement as the last line of the loop body.

9.7 Compound WHILE Conditions

In the following program, the computer is using 5 and 13 as two mystery integers. The human is to continue inputting guesses, until one is correct. Note the use of the *compound* WHILE condition.

50   WHILE GUESS<>5 AND GUESS<>13

```
5     REM MYSTERY NUMBERS
6     REM ****
10    PRINT "I AM THINKING OF TWO MYSTERY INTEGERS"
20    PRINT "FROM 1 TO 20. KEEP GUESSING UNTIL YOU GET ONE"
30    COUNT=1
40    INPUT "TYPE A GUESS";GUESS
50    WHILE GUESS<>5 AND GUESS<>13
60       COUNT=COUNT+1
70       INPUT "TYPE A GUESS";GUESS
80    WEND
90    PRINT "*** YOU FOUND ONE IN";COUNT;"GUESSES ***"
100   END
```

Here is a sample run:

```
I AM THINKING OF TWO MYSTERY INTEGERS
FROM 1 TO 20. KEEP GUESSING UNTIL YOU GET ONE
TYPE A GUESS? 8
TYPE A GUESS? 11
TYPE A GUESS? 7
TYPE A GUESS? 13
*** YOU FOUND ONE IN 4 GUESSES ***
```

QUESTION In line 30, why do we initialize COUNT to 1 rather than to 0?

ANSWER One way to realize that initializing COUNT to 0 would be incorrect is to consider what would happen if the human were to input a mystery number on the very first guess. The computer would not enter the WHILE loop body at all, and therefore COUNT would still be 0 by line 90, producing the incorrect output

*** YOU FOUND ONE IN 0 GUESSES ***

Here is a more general explanation: Although 5 and 13 are sentinel values, we want *some processing* to be done if one of them is input—namely, we still want COUNT to be increased by 1. Since the loop body will not be entered for a correct guess, we must increase the counter *before* each input guess. Accordingly, we start COUNT at 1.

9.8 Computer Finishes Remainder of Loop Body

QUESTION What will the printout be? Make sure you wrote *everything* that will be printed.

```
10    N=1
20    SUM=0
30    WHILE SUM <=5
40       SUM=SUM+N
50       PRINT SUM
60       N=N+1
70       PRINT "JOE"
80    WEND
90    PRINT "OUT OF LOOP"
100   END
```

ANSWER The printout will be

```
  1
JOE
  3
JOE
  6
JOE
OUT OF LOOP
```

NOTE: The computer does not exit from the loop the *instant* that SUM exceeds 5. It can only exit at the top of the loop.

Statements Affecting Variables in WHILE Condition. Recall that in programs with a DATA flag, the last line of the loop body has been a READ statement. In this way we have avoided having the DATA flag processed like other DATA items—the computer did not enter the loop body to process the flag since the test condition was of the form WHILE X<>flag. In many situations, statements that affect variables in the WHILE condition are placed at the end of the loop body.

READ X Need Not Be Last Line of Loop Body.   Consider the following program, which will print the data number that first put the sum of the data numbers over 100. (The program assumes that the sum will eventually exceed 100.)

```
10    DATA 52,38,36,41,43
20    SUM=0
30    WHILE SUM<=100
40       READ X
50        SUM=SUM+X
60    WEND
70    PRINT "SUM GOES OVER 100 WHEN ADD";X
80    END
```

The printout will be

```
SUM GOES OVER 100 WHEN ADD 36
```

REMARK: The last line of this loop body is the statement that affects the value of the variable SUM—note that SUM is the variable in the WHILE condition.

QUESTION   What will be the printout for the following incorrect program to find the term that first puts the sum over 100?

```
5     REM INCORRECT PROGRAM
6     REM *****
10    DATA 52,38,36,41,43
20    SUM=0
30    READ X
40    WHILE SUM<=100
50       SUM=SUM+X
60       READ X
70    WEND
80    PRINT "SUM GOES OVER 100 WHEN ADD";X
90    END
```

ANSWER   The printout will be SUM GOES OVER 100 WHEN ADD 41 . SUM first exceeds 100 when 36 is added to it. However, in line 60 the computer assigns the next DATA value to X, and that is the value that is printed.

Another Correct Program for Finding the Term That Puts Sum Over 100. Here is another correct program. Insert in the incorrect program the line

    55   IF SUM>100 THEN OVER.ON = X

and change line 80 to

    80   PRINT "SUM GOES OVER 100 WHEN ADD";OVER.ON

Exercises

1. What will the printout be?

```
10   PROD=1
20   WHILE PROD<=20
30      PROD=PROD*3
40   WEND
50   PRINT PROD
60   END
```

2. (a) Write a program using a WHILE loop that will print the name of each student who scored a total of at least 180 on two exams. Use the following DATA lines, but your program should work for any similarly flagged DATA lines.

       DATA "SMITH",75,93,"BOND",82,87
       DATA "JONES",92,94,"PARK",85,96
       DATA "XYZ",-1,-1

   (b) Modify your program so that it will also print how many students scored at least 180.

3. Write a WHILE/WEND program that reads a list of DATA numbers with the flag value -1. The program should print all numbers greater than 21 and also keep count of how many there are. For DATA 25,19,28,23,14-1 the printout should be

```
25   28   23 COUNT=3
```

4. For DATA lines formatted as follows:

> 10   DATA "CHANG","D",36,"LANG","R",20
> 20   DATA "LOM","D",32,"MACK","R",80
> 30   DATA "XYZ","XYZ",−1

   (a) Write a program that will print the sum of the ages of all the *Democrats*.
   (b) Modify the program so it will print the average age for the Democrats.

5. Write a program in which the DATA line will contain a student's exam scores and will terminate with the flag −1. The printout should give the student's average and also whether or not the student receives an A. (The criterion for an A is an average of at least 90.)

6. In the wage program of section 9.4, what would the printout have been if the DATA line 120 had not ended with a flag triple but instead with just "XYZ"?

7. What will the printout be for the following incorrect wage-calculating program?

```
5    REM  INCORRECT WAGE
6    REM ****
10   PRINT  "SOC SEC #","WAGE $"
20   WHILE SOC.SEC<>−1
30     READ SOC.SEC,HRS,RATE
40     PRINT SOC.SEC,HRS*RATE
50   WEND
60   DATA 111111111,40,5,222222222,30,6
70   DATA 333333333,40,6,−1,−1,−1
80   END
```

8. Write an interactive program that will find the sum of positive numbers input one at a time by a user. Let the flag value be −1.

9. What will the printout be?

```
10   S=0 : N=0
20   WHILE S<=40
30     N=N+1
40     S=S+(N*N)
50     PRINT S;
60   WEND
70   END
```

10. For the sum $1+2+3+4+5+6+$ . . . on which integer does the sum first go over 50? Which of the two programs below will correctly determine what that integer is? What will be the printout for each of the programs?

(a)
```
10  N=0
20  SUM=0
30  WHILE SUM<=100
40     N=N+1
50     SUM=SUM+N
60  WEND
70  PRINT "GOES OVER 100 ON";N
80  END
```

(b)
```
10  N=0
20  SUM=0
30  WHILE SUM<=100
40     SUM=SUM+N
50     N=N+1
60  WEND
70  PRINT "GOES OVER 100 ON";N
80  END
```

11. What will the printout be? (Be careful.)

```
10  SUM=0
20  READ X
30  WHILE X<>-1
40     SUM=SUM+X
50     READ X
60  WEND
70  PRINT SUM
80  DATA 9,8,6,4,2,999
90  END
```

12. What will the printouts be?

(a)
```
10  X=1
20  WHILE X<5 AND X>8
30     PRINT X
40     X=X+1
50  WEND
60  PRINT "X EQUALS";X
70  END
```

(b)
```
10  X=1
20  WHILE X>5 OR X<8
30     PRINT X
40     X=X+1
50  WEND
60  PRINT "X EQUALS";X
70  END
```

13. Write a program in which the computer takes 5 and 13 as mystery integers and has the human continue inputting an integer from 1 to 20. When the human finally inputs one of the mystery integers, the computer congratulates the human and lets the human know what the other mystery integer was.

14. Write a program that has as its printout the number of data numbers required for the sum first to exceed 100. For DATA 52,38,36,41,43 the printout should be

> IT TOOK 3 NUMBERS TO GO OVER 100

15. Write a single program so that for a DATA line with a flag like DATA 50,40,30,70,999 the printout is

> SUM FIRST GOES OVER 100 WHEN ADD 30

but for data like DATA 25,5,2,7,6,999 the printout is

> THE SUM DOES NOT GO OVER 100

16. Using a WHILE loop, write a program to find the sum $\frac{1}{2} + \frac{2}{3} + \frac{3}{4} + \ldots \frac{99}{100}$.

★ 17. (a) Write a program in which the user is asked to input a positive integer. The printout will state whether that integer is odd or even. Use test

> IF NUM MOD 2 = 0 . . .

(b) *Ulam's conjecture* is the following: Start with any positive integer. If it is even, divide it by two; if it is odd, multiply it by three and add one. Obtain successive integers by repeating this process. The mathematician S. Ulam has conjectured that no matter what the starting integer is, eventually the number 1 will be obtained. For example, when 22 is the starting integer, the procedure outputs

> 22 11 34 17 52 26 13 40 20 10 5 16 8 4 2 1

Write a program in which the user is asked to input a positive integer and that then prints out its Ulam sequence.

18. Also, see Appendix C, Exercises 3 and 4.

CHAPTER

10

Handmade Loops

So far, we have considered two methods of looping—FOR-NEXT loops and WHILE loops. There is also a third method that uses IF-THEN (line #) tests to exit. We call this third method **handmade** loops.

Since WHILE loops were not available in the early versions of BASIC, handmade loops were once an essential part of a BASIC programmer's repertoire. Now, however, handmade loops are not often used. In this chapter, after providing illustrations of handmade loops, we discuss some of their drawbacks and limitations.

10.1 Illustrations

EXAMPLE Consider the following program, which uses a WHILE loop and is similar to those we have already seen in Chapter 9:

```
5    REM WHILE LOOP TO PRINT LIST OF NAMES
6    REM *****
10   DATA "JOHN", "MARY", "KEN", "SUE", "FLAG"
20   READ NAM$
30   WHILE NAM$ < > "FLAG"
40     PRINT NAM$
50     READ NAM$
60   WEND
70   PRINT "ARE PRESENT"
80   END
```

It will produce the printout

```
JOHN
MARY
KEN
SUE
ARE  PRESENT
```

We could rewrite this program using a handmade loop as follows:

```
5    REM HANDMADE  LOOP  TO PRINT  LIST  OF  NAMES
6    REM *****
10   DATA  "JOHN" , "MARY" , "KEN" , "SUE" , "FLAG"
20   READ NAM$
30   IF NAM$="FLAG"  THEN 60
40   PRINT NAM$
50   GOTO 20
60   PRINT "ARE PRESENT"
70   END
```

Notice that the loop body in the second example consists of lines 20–50, as these are the lines that are repeated several times. In contrast, the loop body in the first example consists of only two lines, 40 and 50.

REMARK: The WHILE loop is the preferred method for this program, since it does not contain IF-THEN-(line #) and GOTO statements and is easier to follow.

However, the WHILE loop was not part of the original BASIC, and programmers therefore had to resort to handmade loops instead, as the only method then available. It is advantageous to become familiar with handmade loops, since early programs often use them.

Clarifying Handmade Loops.   The loop body in a handmade loop can be made clearer by using a REM LOOP heading and indentation. For example, the above program could be rewritten as follows:

```
5    REM HANDMADE  LOOP
6    REM ****
10   DATA  "JOHN" ,  "MARY" ,  "KEN" ,  "SUE" ,  "FLAG"
20   REM LOOP
30      READ NAM$
40      IF NAM$="FLAG"  THEN 70
50      PRINT NAM$
60      GOTO 30
70   PRINT  "ARE PRESENT"
80   END
```

You may have noticed another disadvantage of handmade loops. By changing the line numbers of the program, as we did when inserting the REM statement as line 20, we were also required to make two additional changes. Namely, we had to change the line numbers to which we wished to branch, at the ends of lines 40 and 60 in the loop body, from 60 to 70 and from 20 to 30, respectively. Whenever we use IF-THEN-(line #) or GOTO statements in our programs, we would have to be aware of this difficulty.

10.2 Converting to and from Handmade Loops

Any of the loops we have seen in previous chapters can be rewritten using handmade loops.

QUESTION   What will the printouts be for the following two programs?

(a)

```
5    REM FOR-NEXT LOOP
6    REM ****
10   FOR X=1 TO 5
20      PRINT X
30   NEXT X
40   PRINT "SO LONG"
50   END
```

(b)

```
5    REM HANDMADE LOOP
6    REM ****
10   X=1
20   REM LOOP
30      PRINT X
40      X=X+1
50      IF X<=5 THEN 30
60   PRINT "SO LONG"
70   END
```

ANSWER   Both programs will produce the same printout:

```
1
2
3
4
5
SO LONG
```

In fact, program (b) simulates exactly what is done internally by the computer when it executes program (a). Program (b) is evidently more cumbersome—another reason why handmade loops are the least preferred method.

Here is a WHILE loop version of the same program:

```
5    REM WHILE LOOP
6    REM ****
10   X=1
20   WHILE X<=5
30      PRINT X
40      X=X+1
50   WEND
60   PRINT "SO LONG"
70   END
```

Notice that there is no need to escape from inside the loop body using an IF-THEN-(line #) test, as we must do with the handmade version.

10.3 Structured Programming

The disadvantages of handmade loops make them more difficult to follow and therefore harder to debug than FOR-NEXT and WHILE loops. Structured programs in BASIC that only include FOR-NEXT and WHILE loops are easier to follow and more advantageous to use.

Imagine a long, unstructured program consisting only of handmade loops. Because of its many branching statements, it would be very difficult to trace. A program of this sort is often referred to as having "spaghetti GOTOs," because of the way the lines are interwoven by branching.

A structured program, on the other hand, is much easier to follow. All of the loops are entered from the top and "fall through" at the end. What this means is that after the loop has completed its task, the computer continues by "falling through" the end of the loop to the line that follows it. Handmade loops, by contrast, often escape from the middle of their loop bodies when they are done and theoretically can be entered at any point.

One of the benefits of structured programs is that they can easily be divided into loops and other program segments, each of which has an assigned task.

Exercises

1. Using a handmade loop, write a program that will print 5 copies of your address.

2. This exercise provides a good illustration of the difficulties involved in using handmade loops.

```
10    DATA 42,58,74,81,36,41,999
20    SUM=0
30    COUNT=0
40    REM LOOP
50      READ X
60       IF X=999 THEN 90
70      SUM=SUM+X
75      COUNT=COUNT+1
80      GOTO 50
90    PRINT "AVERAGE: ";AVG
100   END
```

Suppose that after typing this program, the programmer realizes that a line to compute the average has been omitted. Suppose that a line 85 is then inserted

85   AVG=SUM/COUNT

The program will still have a bug in it. Explain what the bug is and why this difficulty would not arise in the WHILE loop version.

11

More on Writing Programs: Stepwise Refinement

Up to this point, the programs have been simple enough so that their organization did not require much forethought. In writing more complicated programs, it is important to take a more systematic and disciplined approach.

In this chapter, we introduce the method of **stepwise refinement**, which involves first breaking up a problem into smaller subproblems and then fleshing out the details for solving these subproblems.

11.1 Programming in Industry

Actual programs in business and industry are enormously more complicated than any programs we have discussed so far. Not surprisingly, new programs very rarely work properly on the first run; instead, they require a certain amount of debugging to remove errors. The principal cost to a company for the development of a new program is not in the original writing of the program, but rather in its testing, debugging, and maintenance—that is, correcting errors and modifying the program from time to time to fit new needs. Typically, a company might spend 25 percent of the total cost for the creation of the program and 75 percent for testing, debugging, and general maintenance. Quite often the maintenance is done by someone other than the creator of the program. Thus, programmers should give top priority to producing programs that are

1. Clear and readable (especially to others)
2. Easy to debug
3. Easy to modify

One step that a programmer can take towards attaining these goals is to provide ample documentation—that is, lots of REM statements in the program itself.

Beyond the simple but important matter of ample documentation, there is an entire approach to writing programs called **structured programming**. The primary concern in structured programming is to produce clear, reliable programs by using specific techniques to keep a program's organization straightforward. Obviously, tricky shortcuts that save several lines but that are hard to comprehend should be avoided. GOTO statements should also be avoided when better means for looping, namely FOR-NEXT and WHILE loops, can be used. Two other techniques used in structured programming are **stepwise refinement** and **modularization** (discussed in Chapter 16).

11.2 Stepwise Refinement

The principle behind stepwise refinement is that some things that are difficult to do in one or two giant steps can be done easily by taking a number of small steps. Thus, we approach a problem by dividing it into smaller subproblems, and by making a list of steps. After we have performed each of these steps, the original problem will be solved.

Stepwise Refinement

1. Select meaningful variable names.
2. Make a step-by-step list of what you need to do to produce the desired printout.
3. Replace some of the steps from part 2 by a more detailed description when necessary (this is called refinement). For a difficult program it may be useful to do several refinements.
4. Write the actual program.

Since the human mind is not always immediately able to foresee a complete list of steps for solving a given programming problem, the following are further suggestions for getting started:

1. Make sure you understand the problem. Can you imitate and adapt programs you have already seen?

2. Work out by hand the calculation for a specific example (with actual numbers). Can you solve at least part of the problem?

3. Will the program contain a loop? If so what happens *before, during,* and *after*?

4. How is the data set up? Is there a flag? Are counters or summing variables needed?

11.3 Illustrations

PROBLEM **Compound Interest** Suppose you deposit $200 in a bank at 5% interest compounded annually. After how many years will the balance first exceed $400?

PROGRAM IDEAS

Suppose you are having trouble getting started. You might solve part of the problem by computing the balance after two years. You will receive $10 interest (200*.05) at the end of the first year. Thus, you will have $210 at the end of the first year. At the end of the second year you will receive $10.50 in interest ($210*.05) and thus you will have $220.50. Use a loop to keep repeating this procedure of computing and adding the interest until the balance exceeds $400.

Variable names: BALANCE, INTEREST, YRS

Type of loop: Use a WHILE loop, since we do not know in advance how many executions of the loop body will be needed—each execution will compute new balance and increase the year counter by 1.

List of Steps

> *Before loop*   Initialize variables.
> *During loop* Compute new balance and update year counter.
> *After loop*   Print results.

List of Steps—Refinement (i.e., more details)

> *Before*   BALANCE = 200 : YRS = 0
> *During* WHILE BALANCE < = 400
> >   increase YRS counter.
> >   compute current year's INTEREST.
> >   add current INTEREST to BALANCE.
> >   WEND
> *After*   Print result—current value of YRS.

Pseudocode: In the preceding refinement, note the informal mixture of actual program code and ordinary English—such a mixture is called **pseudocode**.

Here is the actual program:

```
5     REM COMPOUND INTEREST
6     REM ****
10    BALANCE=200
20    YRS=0
30    WHILE BALANCE<=400
40       YRS=YRS+1
50       INTEREST=BALANCE*.05
60       BALANCE=BALANCE+INTEREST
70    WEND
80    PRINT "OVER $400 IN YEAR";YRS
90    PRINT "BALANCE OF $";BALANCE
100   END
```

PROBLEM **Two Salespeople's Sales Totals**   DATA 1,17,2,35,2,24,1,43,1,52,1,25,2,23,999,999. In this DATA line each pair of numbers gives information on a sale. The first number tells whether it was salesperson 1 or 2; the second number tells how many items were sold. Write a program that will compute separately the total number of items sold for each salesperson.

PROGRAM IDEAS

Variable names: We will use ID and QUANTITY for a pair of DATA numbers. Also, we need two separate variables to keep track of the totals for the two salespeople; let us use SUM1 and SUM2 for that purpose.

Type of loop: Use a WHILE loop, since the DATA is set up with a *flag* group.

List of Steps

Before	Initialize SUM1 and SUM2.
	Prime the pump.
During	Use a WHILE loop to process all the DATA pairs; each execution processes one DATA group.
After	Print results.

Refinement

Before	SUM1=0 : SUM2=0
	READ first data group.

During   WHILE ID <> flag
    IF ID = 1 THEN add QUANTITY to SUM1
    IF ID = 2 THEN . . .
    READ next data group
   WEND

After Use two separate PRINT statements.

Writing the program based on this outline is Exercise 2.

PROBLEM **Interactive Junk Food Order** Ye Olde Fast Food Shoppe has a simple menu. Code #1 represents a burger—cost $.75; code #2 a hot dog—cost $1.00; code #3 a sundae—cost $1.25. To enter an order, the attendant types the code numbers, terminating the order by typing − 1; so that if the attendant inputs 3,2,6,3, − 1 the printout slip would be

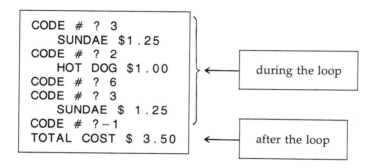

NOTE: *Hardcopy versus screen printout.* Recall that on most systems, input values and prompting messages will not appear in the hardcopy. On such systems, to obtain the desired hardcopy—in addition to changing PRINT statements to LPRINT statements—you would also need to include the echo statement, LPRINT "CODE #";ID.

PROGRAM IDEAS

Variable names: ID for the code number of the item and TOT for the total cost.

Type of loop: WHILE since the exit condition is the flag − 1. (Note also that as an aid we have drawn brackets on the printout, labeling the part produced *during* the loop and the part produced *after* the loop.)

List of Steps

Before Initialize TOT.
    Prime the pump with an INPUT statement.

During WHILE _____
　　　　　IF ID = 1 THEN PRINT " BURGER $.75" : TOT = TOT + .75
　　　　　IF ID = 2 THEN . . .
　　　　　IF ID = 3 THEN
　　　　　more input
　　　　WEND
After　　Print total cost.

Completing this program is Exercise 7.

PROBLEM　**SALES-R-US Bonus Program**　A salesperson for SALES-R-US receives a bonus of 2% of weekly sales, if the sales exceed $1500. The DATA line is to give information on each of *three* salespeople, the printout should give a table with each salesperson's results. It also should give the bonus total and whether the bonus total was within budget—$125 is allocated for bonuses each week. For DATA "JONES",1200,"FOY",2000,"DIAZ",2800, the printout should be

```
SALESPERSON      SALES $          BONUS $
JONES              1200           0
FOY                2000           40
DIAZ               2800           56
BONUS TOTAL $ 96
BONUS TOTAL IS WITHIN BUDGET
```

PROGRAM IDEAS

Use brackets to label parts of the printout as *before, during,* or *after* the loop. Draw brackets on the printout given above. (Of course, if there is anything printed during the loop, the loop body will contain a print statement.)

Variable names:　NAM$ and SALES for the READ statement. BONUS for each individual's bonus, and BONUS.TOT for the total of all the bonuses.

Type of loop:　FOR-NEXT since we know in advance that there will be DATA for *three* salespeople.

List of Steps and Refinement.　Before reading on, try to write a list of steps and a refinement. Writing the program is Exercise 9. You may wish to do so by filling in the blank lines here:

```
 5     REM SALES-R-US-BONUS
 6     REM ****
10     DATA  "JONES",1200,"FOY",2000,"DIAZ",2800
20     _____
30     BONUS.TOT=0
40     FOR SALESMAN=1 TO _____
50       READ NAM$,SALES
60       IF _____ THEN _____
                      ELSE _____
70       BONUS.TOT=BONUS.TOT+BONUS
80     _____
90     NEXT SALESMAN
100    _____
110    IF _____ THEN _____
                   ELSE _____
120    END
```

11.4 More on Debugging

Hand Tracing.   The hand-tracing method described in Chapter 1 is an important debugging tool. However, it is also useful to know debugging techniques in which the computer does some of the work.

Inserting Debugging PRINT Statements within Programs.   Additional PRINT statements can be used to output the values of certain variables at the time key calculations are made. Consider the following incorrect program for calculating the average of a list of DATA numbers with a flag:

Printout

```
 5     REM INCORRECT PROGRAM FOR AVERAGE
 6     REM *****
10     DATA 30,60,40,50,20,-1
20     S=0 : C=0
30     READ X
40     WHILE X<>-1
50        C=C+1
60        S=S+C
70        READ X
80     WEND
90     PRINT "AVERAGE";S/C
100    END
```

AVERAGE 3

Clearly the average of the five numbers 30, 60, 40, 50, and 20 is not 3. What makes it hard to spot the error is that the printout provides only the end result; none of the intermediate steps are shown. To know the values of S and C at the time S/C was calculated, we can insert line 95.

    95   PRINT "AT LINE 95, S IS";S;"C is";C

When this program is run, the printout is

```
AVERAGE 3
AT LINE 95, S IS 15 C IS 5
```

QUESTION We know S cannot be 15. What is wrong? Before reading on, try to find the mistake in the program. It may even be helpful to insert an additional line 45.

    45   PRINT "AT LINE 45, S IS";S;"C IS";C;"X IS";X

inside the loop body, to see the intermediate steps taken by the computer for each pass through the WHILE loop.

HINT: What could have caused S to have a value of only 15 by line 95?

ANSWER   Line 60, the only statement in which S is assigned a value, is incorrect. It should be $S = S + X$. Perhaps the programmer could have avoided this mistake in the first place by using meaningful variable names, such as SUM and COUNT. After you correct the error in the program you should also delete the additional PRINT statements (lines 95 and 45 here), since they are no longer needed.

STOP Statement/Immediate Mode Combination.
NOTE: The STOP statement described here is not available on all systems. This combination functions very much like the insertion of additional (temporary) PRINT statements. In executing a program, when the computer reaches a STOP statement, the computer halts execution with the message BREAK IN (line #) and returns to the immediate mode. You may type PRINT statements (without line numbers) to determine the values that various variables had at the time the computer halted execution. For example, in the previous program line 95 could have been 95 STOP. The printout for the program with that STOP statement would then be

```
AVERAGE 3
BREAK IN 95
```

You could then learn the values of S and C in line 95 by typing PRINT statements and hitting the return key:

```
PRINT S
  15
PRINT C
  5
```

TRON and TROFF.   The TRON command can be used to ascertain the order in which the lines of a program are executed. TRON and TROFF are short for TRace ON and TRace OFF. You may turn on the TRON command by typing TRON before you run a program. When the TRON command is on, the computer will execute a program as it normally does. However, in addition to printing whatever printout the program produces, the computer will also print the line number of each line as it is executed. This sort of line trace is useful in debugging programs with loops. The TRON command stays on until the TROFF command is typed from the immediate mode.

Instead of typing TRON before you run a program, you can also include TRON and TROFF inside a program to produce just a partial trace of a program.

NOTE: On some implementations, TRON and TROFF may work somewhat differently.

Variable Keys.   Errors commonly occur in long programs when the programmer loses track of the variables. The easiest way to solve this problem is to create a variable key on paper while writing the program. Each time a new variable is introduced in the program, it would be added to the key. The variable key consists of all the variable names and descriptions. This key, as well as the use of meaningful variable names, will help the programmer avoid using the wrong variables in calculations, and avoid reusing variable names for new variables. It is also often included with the program listing to help any readers follow the program. (The key is usually alphabetized after the program is completed.)

Here is a sample variable key for the Compound Interest program of Section 11.3:

Variable	Description
BALANCE	The current balance in dollars
INTEREST	The calculated compounded interest
YRS	The number of years since deposit

Exercises

1. Write a program that will separately count the number of 6's and 8's in a DATA line with ten data numbers. For DATA 4,7,6,2,8,6,6,9,1,8 the printout should be

```
3 SIXES
2 EIGHTS
```

2. Write the two-salespeople program from Section 11.3.

3. A simple method of computing compound interest is by the formula BALANCE = PRINCIPAL * (1 + RATE)$\wedge$YRS. Rewrite the compound-interest program of Section 11.3 in which PRINCIPAL equals 200 and RATE equals .05.

4. The following DATA lines contain information on college freshmen. The first number tells whether the student is male or female (1 for male and 2 for female). The second number gives the age of that student. Write a program to find the average age for male freshmen and the average age for female freshmen. (Do not do anything by hand; have the computer do everything.)

    10   DATA 1,17,1,19,2,18,2,17,1,18,1,17
    20   DATA 1,17,2,18,2,17,2,17,999,999

5. Suppose Tyler deposits $100 at 8%, whereas Smith deposits $200 at 3%. In how many years will Tyler have more money than Smith? Run a compound interest program to determine the result.

6. Suppose someone buys something and pays for it in installments: 1¢ during the first year, 2¢ during the second, 4¢ during the third, and every year payments keep doubling. Write a program that will determine the first year for which the payment will be greater than $1,000,000.

7. Write the Interactive Junk Food Order program from Section 11.3.

8. The following DATA lines give the scoring in a basketball game, where H stands for Home team and V for Visiting, and 1 or 2 indicates the number of points for that team:

    DATA "H",2,"H",2,"V",1,"H",2,"V",2,"H",1
    DATA "V",1,"H",2,"V",1,"V",2,"H",2,"XYZ",0

Write a program that will give a running count of the score and also tell which team won the game. Your program may assume the game does not end in a tie.

```
HOME        VIS
  2           0
  4           0
  4           1
  6           1
  6           3
     and so on
```

9. Complete the SALES-R-US Bonus Program from Section 11.3.

10. The SALES-R-US Company from Section 11.3 pays its three salespeople 25% of their weekly sales plus whatever bonus they have earned. Write a program so that for the same data the printout will give each salesperson's name, bonus, and earnings. Also the last line of the printout should give the total earnings, which would be $1596 (this comes from 300 + 540 + 756).

11. Write a program that will calculate the weekly salaries for the salespeople of SALES-R-US, and find the sum of the salaries. Each DATA triplet will contain the salesperson's name, hours, and sales. Each salesperson earns $5 per hour, plus a bonus of 5% of the weekly sales (regardless of how high sales were). The printout should include the salary of each salesperson and the sum of the salaries. The first DATA number is a header value that represents the number of salespeople. Use a FOR-NEXT loop and the following DATA:

```
10   DATA 4
20   DATA "JONES",38,1500,"SMITH",42,1700,"DIAZ",35,2400,"CLARK",47,1000
```

12. What message will be printed when the computer reaches the following line?

```
40   STOP
```

13. Suppose you were given the following DATA line

```
10   DATA 3,10,7,5,2, −1
```

where −1 is a flag and were asked to write a program that used a loop to produce the following printout:

```
THERE ARE 5 NON−FLAG DATA
THEIR PRODUCT IS 2100
THEIR SUM IS 27
```

    (a) What kind of loop would you use? Use pseudocode to describe what would be done before, during, and after the loop. Be specific.

    (b) Write the program.

14. Suppose a program has the DATA lines

    10   DATA "JOHN","SMITH","SUE","JONES","TOM","SMITH"

    20   DATA "GREG","WHITE","LARRY","JONES","GREG","SMITH"

    30   DATA "XYZ","XYZ"

and produces the following printout when run:

```
ENTER  A  LAST  NAME?  SMITH
JOHN
TOM
GREG
3 HAD  LAST  NAME  SMITH
```

(Note that the underlined "SMITH" was entered by the user.)

    (a) Label the parts of the printout that were probably produced before, during, and after the program's loop.

    (b) Write the program.

15. Create a variable key for one of the Sales-R-Us exercises (numbers 9, 10, or 11) from this chapter.

16. Also see Appendix B, Exercises 5 and 6.

17. Also see Appendix C, Exercise 8.

12

Multiway Selection Using IF-THEN

In Chapter 6, we saw how IF-THEN ELSE could be used to choose between two alternatives. However, there may be times when you need the computer to select the appropriate alternative from a list of *more than two* alternatives. This selection is called **multiway selection**.

In this chapter, we first give several IF-THEN methods for achieving multiway selection. We also present an entirely different method using ON K GOTO (list of line numbers).

12.1 Three-Way Selection Using Three IF-THEN Tests

EXAMPLE The following program will give the appropriate output for any pair of input numbers:

```
10  INPUT "PICK TWO NUMBERS";A,B
20  IF A<B THEN PRINT A;"LESS THAN";B
30  IF A>B THEN PRINT A;"GREATER THAN";B
40  IF A=B THEN PRINT A;"EQUALS";B
50  END
```

For example, for input of 5,9 the printout is

```
5 LESS THAN 9
```

EXAMPLE   Team jackets are priced at $33 each if fewer than 5 are purchased, $31 each if at least 5 but fewer than 10 are purchased, and $30 each if at least 10 are purchased.

```
10   INPUT  "ENTER  NUMBER  OF  JACKETS" ; N
20   IF  N<5  THEN  COST=N*33
30   IF  N>=5  AND  N<10  THEN  COST=N*31
40   IF  N>=10  THEN  COST=N*30
50   PRINT  N; "JACKETS  COST  $" ; COST
60   END
```

Note the use of the AND connective for the case at least 5 but fewer than 10.

EXAMPLE   Let's Make a Deal

```
10   INPUT  "DO  YOU  WANT  WHAT  IS  BEHIND  DOOR  1 ,  2 ,  OR  3" ; DOOR
20   IF  DOOR=1  THEN  PRINT  "YOU  WON  A  COLOR  TV"
30   IF  DOOR=2  THEN  PRINT  "YOU  WON  A  NEW  CAR"
40   IF  DOOR=3  THEN  PRINT  "YOU  WON  A  CAN  OF  DOG  FOOD"
50   END
```

12.2 Three-Way Selection Using Two IF-THEN Tests and Default Case

Let us rewrite the program to compare two input numbers, using just two IF-THEN tests and a **default case** (a case to be reached only if the two tests both fail).

```
10   INPUT  "PICK  TWO  NUMBERS" ; A , B
20   IF  A<B  THEN  PRINT  A; "LESS  THAN" ; B  :  GOTO  50
30   IF  A>B  THEN  PRINT  A; "GREATER  THAN" ; B  :  GOTO  50
40   PRINT  A; "EQUALS" ; B
50   END
```

Note that GOTO statements in lines 20 and 30 are used to ensure that line 40, the default case, is reached only if both tests fail. This method is more efficient because for certain input, unnecessary tests are avoided. (See Exercise 6.)

REMARK: The version from Section 12.1 is the better version of the above program, because the logic is clearer. Extra GOTO statements generally make it harder to understand a program.

The main situation in which two IF-THEN tests and a default case are the preferred method for handling three-way selection occurs when the third case is difficult to describe by an IF-THEN test. Here is an illustration:

EXAMPLE   An employee at ACME products can retire if one of the following retirement conditions is fulfilled:

1. The employee is at least 65 years old.
2. The employee is at least 59 and has worked at ACME for at least 20 years.

Otherwise the employee may not retire.

This situation is ideally suited to the default case method because the simplest way to describe the conditions under which the employee MAY NOT RETIRE is as: not case (1) and not case (2).

Writing a program to produce the appropriate printout for an input age and years worked is Exercise 10.

12.3 Nested IF-THEN Tests

Sometimes an IF-THEN test will occur within the THEN or ELSE branches of an IF-THEN test. This structure is called **nested IF-THEN tests**.

EXAMPLE

```
10    INPUT "HOW MUCH IS 2 TIMES 2";YOUR.ANS
20    IF YOUR.ANS=4 THEN 40 ELSE 90
30    REM THEN BRANCH
40       PRINT "YOU WIN A PRIZE"
50       INPUT "TYPE A OR B FOR PRIZE";PRIZE$
60       IF PRIZE$="A" THEN PRINT "YOU WON A CAR"
                       ELSE PRINT "YOU WON A TV"
70    GOTO 100
80    REM ELSE BRANCH
90       PRINT "SORRY, NO PRIZE"
100   END
```

◼◼◼ 12.4 Grade Assignment Program

PROBLEM   Students will receive a grade of GOOD if their exam average is at least 85, a grade of FAIR if their average is at least 75 but less than 85, and a grade of POOR if their average is less than 75. The DATA line should terminate with the flag −1. For a student named Jones

DATA "JONES",82,91,94,86, −1

the printout should be

```
JONES
   81   91   94    86
AVERAGE 88
GRADE:  GOOD
```

PROGRAM IDEAS

Obviously, you need to use a WHILE loop. You will also need to use three-way selection. Pay attention to what is done before, during, and after that loop. Try labeling the printout with brackets.

Writing this program is Exercise 7. As aids to writing the program, first write a list of steps and then a refinement.

◼◼◼ 12.5 Other Topics

Three-Way Selection by Branching.   Let us rewrite the Let's Make a Deal program using this method.

```
10    INPUT "DO YOU WANT WHAT IS BEHIND DOOR 1, 2, OR 3";DOOR
20    IF DOOR=1 THEN 50
30    IF DOOR=2 THEN 70
40    IF DOOR=3 THEN 90
50       PRINT "DOOR 1. YOU WON A COLOR TV"
60    GOTO 100
70       PRINT "DOOR 2. YOU WON A NEW CAR"
80    GOTO 100
90       PRINT "DOOR 3. YOU WON A CAN OF DOG FOOD"
100   END
```

This version assumes that the user will input 1, 2, or 3. In Exercise 14(b), you are asked to modify this program with an **error trap** in line 15. If the user inputs an integer other than 1, 2, or 3, the computer will print INVALID ENTRY and branch to the END line.

Four-Way Selection and Higher.   In Exercises 4 and 8, you are asked to write a program involving four- and five-way selection using IF-THEN tests.

ON K GOTO.   The ON K GOTO command has the ability to branch to any one entry in a list of line numbers. For example, the statement

ON K GOTO   90,160,210

will have the computer branch to one of the three line numbers listed. The computer will branch to the Kth line number from the list.

Thus, in the above example, the computer will branch to line 90 if K has the value 1, to line 160 if K has the value 2, and to line 210 if K has the value 3.

General Form of ON K GOTO.

ON (variable or expression) GOTO (list of line numbers)

If the value of the variable or expression is zero or greater than the number of lines in the list, the computer will simply fall through to the next line in the program. If the value of the variable or expression is a noninteger, the computer will round it off to the nearest integer (for example, 2.7 will be rounded off to 3).

The Let's Make a Deal program can be rewritten as follows:

```
10    INPUT "DO YOU WANT WHAT IS BEHIND DOOR 1, 2, OR 3"; DOOR
20   ON DOOR GOTO 50,70,90
30      PRINT "INVALID ENTRY"
40   GOTO 100
50      PRINT "DOOR 1. YOU WON A COLOR TV"
60   GOTO 100
70      PRINT "DOOR 2. YOU WON A NEW CAR"
80   GOTO 100
90      PRINT "DOOR 3. YOU WON A CAN OF DOG FOOD"
100  END
```

Exercises

1. Write a program in which the student will receive a grade of GOOD if the test score is at least 85, a grade of FAIR if the score is at least 75

but less than 85, and a grade of $\boxed{\text{POOR}}$ for under 75. Have the user input the score.

2. Footballs are priced at $28 each if fewer than 5 are purchased, $27 each if at least 5 but fewer than 10 are purchased, and $26 each if at least 10 are purchased. Write a program to print the cost for an input number of footballs. Run it for input 5, then for 6, then for 11, and finally for 15.

3. An employee receives $4 per hour for working 40 hours or less, $6 per hour for each hour over 40 hours and not exceeding 50 hours, and $8 per hour for each hour over 50 hours. For example, an employee working 42 hours would receive $172, whereas an employee working 51 hours would receive $228. Write a program to print the wage earned for an input number of hours.

4. Write a program that will produce whichever printout is appropriate for an input number: $\boxed{\text{LESS THAN 5}}$, $\boxed{\text{AT LEAST 5 BUT LESS THAN 12}}$, $\boxed{\text{AT LEAST 12 BUT LESS THAN 20}}$, or $\boxed{\text{AT LEAST 20}}$.

5. The quadratic equation $X^2 + BX + C = 0$ has two distinct real roots, provided $B^2 - 4C > 0$. Then the two roots are $X1 = (-B + SQR(B*B - 4*C))/2$ and $X2 = (-B - SQR(B*B - 4*C))/2$. If $B^2 - 4C = 0$, then the roots $X1$ and $X2$ are both equal to $-B/2$. However, if $B^2 - 4C < 0$, then there are no real roots. Write a program that will print $\boxed{\text{THERE ARE NO REAL ROOTS}}$ or the values of the two roots $X1$ and $X2$ and whether the two roots are distinct or equal. Run it for $X^2 - 3X + 2 = 0$; that is, use DATA -3, 2 to give the coefficients B and C.

6. In the two IF-THEN tests and a default case program of Section 12.2, which determines whether A is less than, greater than, or equal to B, what would the printout be for an input of 5,9 if GOTO 50 were dropped from lines 20 and 30?

7. Write the Grade Assignment program from Section 12.4.

8. Write a Grade Assignment program for which an average of at least 90 is an A, at least 80 but less than 90 is B, at least 70 but less than 80 is C, at least 60 but less than 70 is D, and under 60 is F. Use the same sort of DATA line as is used in Exercise 7.

9. The following DATA line gives the name and exam average for a number of students and terminates with the flag group "XYZ", -1.

    DATA "SMITH",84,"FOY",88,"DEAN",63,"XYZ", -1

An average of at least 85 receives a grade of GOOD, at least 75 but less than 85 a grade of FAIR, and under 75 a grade of POOR. Write a program that will print a table giving each student's name and grade.

10. Using INPUT "ENTER AGE, YEARS WORKED";A,W as line 10, write the ACME retirement program of Section 12.2. Run it for input pairs 68,10; 68,25; 63,28; 63,5; and 54,30.

11. **(a)** Try to write the ACME retirement program without using the default case method. Use three IF-THEN tests instead.

    (b) Rewrite the ACME retirement program using nested IF-THEN.

12. Redo the Team Jackets program from Section 12.1 using two IF-THEN tests and a default case.

★ 13. A person's name, class (1, 2, 3, 4, or 5), and grade are entered by the statement INPUT N$,C,G$.

    If the person is in class 1, the printout should give the person's name and whether or not he or she got an A.

    If the person is *not* in class 1, the printout should just give the person's name and the message | NOT IN CLASS 1 |.

    This program can use three IF-THEN tests or nested IF-THEN tests.

14. **(a)** In the first version of the Let's Make a Deal program of Section 12.5, what would happen if the user input the number 4?

    (b) Insert line 15 so that if the user inputs anything other than 1, 2, or 3, the only printout will be | INVALID ENTRY |.

15. Job applicants for the AMCO must take five separate aptitude tests.

    1. If they score at least 9 points on three of the tests, they will be hired.

    2. If they do not satisfy (1) but do score 7 or higher on at least 4 of the tests, they will be put on the waiting list.

    3. Otherwise, they will be rejected outright.

    Write a program to process a single applicant and run it with DATA 9,8,7,9,5. The printout should be | WAITING LIST |. Rerun it with DATA 7,7,9,9,9, then with DATA 9,9,6,5,7.

16. Also see Appendix B, Exercise 7.

13

TAB and PRINT USING

A printout with a neat, orderly appearance is preferable to one that looks haphazard. In Chapter 7, we discussed the use of commas to produce a printout in table form. One shortcoming of that method is that when a column of numbers is printed, the numbers are always *left-aligned*. For example, when printing the numbers 2, 25.8, and 264 in a column, the computer would align the 2s. Another shortcoming is the inflexibility of the 14-space zone width.

In real-world applications, such as printing a business report with a centered heading, it is useful to have more powerful features for individualizing the format of the printout. TAB and PRINT USING can be employed to achieve detailed control over the format of a printout.

13.1 TAB Function

The TAB function within a PRINT statement enables you to specify the column position at which the printing is to begin. For example, PRINT TAB(8)"HELLO" would have the computer start the printing of "HELLO" in column 8.

In the program below, note the use of the PRINT statement in line 10. This heading has been included to help you identify the print columns.

```
10  PRINT  "12345678901234567890"
20  PRINT  TAB(5)"NO"
30  PRINT  TAB(2)"PARKING"
40  PRINT  TAB(15)"HERE"
50  PRINT  TAB(1)"TODAY"
60  END
```

The printout is

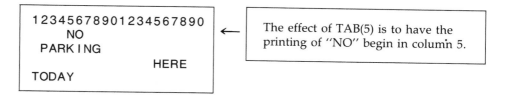

```
12345678901234567890
        NO
    PARKING
                    HERE
TODAY
```

The effect of TAB(5) is to have the printing of "NO" begin in column 5.

Additional Features

1. The parentheses following the word TAB may contain a variable or even a variable expression.
2. A PRINT statement may contain several TAB functions. In such cases, a semicolon should be used to separate the different items.

```
10   PRINT "12345678901234567890"
20   N=5
30   PRINT "JOE SMITH"
40   PRINT TAB(3)"JIM"; TAB(2*N)"BEAM"
50   END
```

```
12345678901234567890
JOE SMITH
   JIM      BEAM
```

Note that the printing of BEAM began at position 10 because 2*N was 10.

EXAMPLE   The following program gives sales figures for each of three employees for three days. Again, note that the same TAB format is used for both the table-heading PRINT statement and the PRINT statement within the loop.

```
10   PRINT "NAME"; TAB(10)"DAY1"; TAB(16)"DAY2"; TAB(22)"DAY3"
20   FOR J=1 TO 3
30     READ N$,D1,D2,D3
40     PRINT N$; TAB(10)D1; TAB(16)D2; TAB(22)D3
50   NEXT J
60   DATA "SMITH",25,14,12,"KOHN",18,15,15
70   DATA "DIAZ",20,15,11
80   END
```

```
NAME       DAY1   DAY2   DAY3
SMITH       25     14     12
KOHN        18     15     15
DIAZ        20     15     11
```

NOTE: If the column indicated in TAB is beyond the current position of the cursor, the material is printed beginning at the appropriate column on the next line. For example

    10   PRINT "FIRST"; TAB(3)"NAME"

produces the printout

```
FIRST
NAME
```

13.2 PRINT USING with Numeric Values

A serious drawback of the formatting of numbers so far is the lack of decimal point alignment and lack of right-margin justification. For example, the following are undesirable formats:

```
1.413          9
25.6          16
```

PRINT USING statements enable you to (1) align a table of numbers according to their decimal points, (2) specify how many decimal places you want, (3) include commas or dollar signs with numbers, and (4) ensure that a number will be printed in a fixed point decimal form (as opposed to floating point form).

The syntax of the PRINT USING statement is as follows:

    PRINT USING format string; value-list

The format string is a string or string variable that contains groups, called **variable fields**, of symbols that represent how the values in the value list will be printed. The value list must contain exactly one value for each variable field in the format string. If there is more than one value or variable in the value list, separate them with commas or semicolons.

Right Margin Alignment of Integers.   Compare the outputs for the following two program fragments:

(a)

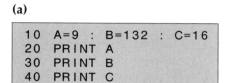

(b)

Printouts

(a)

```
9
132
16
```

(b)

```
  9
132
 16
```

The # symbol in the format string represents a place holder for one numeric digit, or a blank, so that the numbers can be right-justified in each variable field.

Decimal Point Alignment.   Compare the outputs for the following two program fragments:

(a)

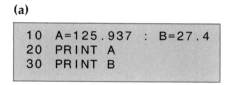

(b)

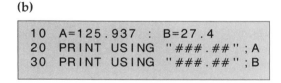

Printouts

(a)

```
125.937
27.4
```

(b)

```
125.94
 27.40
```

The PRINT USING statement can be used to produce alignment of the decimal point. The format string "###.##" specifies that the number printed is to be given to two decimal places (with right-margin alignment). Thus, 125.937 is *rounded off* to 125.94 and a *trailing zero* is supplied for 27.4 so that it is printed as 27.40.

Error Message %.   On some systems, if you try to print a number larger than that specified in the format string, the number will be preceded by a % symbol in the printout. On other systems, there will only be an error message such as **.* instead of an actual number.

Two Dollar Signs \$\$.   If the format string begins with two dollar signs, the printed number will have a dollar sign immediately to its left. (This protects against the possibility of altering the printed copy by inserting an extra digit.)

```
10   DATA 350.6,4.73,56.748
20   FOR J=1 TO 3
30     READ X
40      PRINT USING "$$###.##";X
50   NEXT J
```

Printout

```
$350.60
  $4.73
 $56.75
```

Printing Commas in Large Numbers.   If the format string contains a comma immediately to the left of the decimal point, then the number will be printed with commas inserted in the usual way.

```
10   A=1234567.8
20   PRINT USING "#######,.##";A
```

Printout

```
1,234,567.80
```

If you want to format the printout so that no decimal places appear, omit .## from the format string.

13.3 Format Variables

If a particular format is to be used at several different points in a program, that format can be established by assigning it to a **format variable**. For example

```
10   F$="$$###.##"
20   A=348.712 : B=25.9
30   PRINT USING F$;A
40   PRINT USING F$;B
```

Printout

```
$348.71
 $25.90
```

13.4 Literal Fields

Part of a format string or variable can consist of literal fields, that is, items that will be reproduced verbatim. Moreover, a format string can contain several variable fields.

EXAMPLE

```
10  F$="THE SQUARE ROOT OF ## IS #.##"
20  FOR J=1 TO 3
30    R=SQR(J)
40      PRINT USING F$;J;R
50  NEXT J
```

The printout will be

```
THE SQUARE ROOT OF  1 IS 1.00
THE SQUARE ROOT OF  2 IS 1.41
THE SQUARE ROOT OF  3 IS 1.73
```

A useful technique is to align a format variable with a PRINT statement heading as in the next example.

```
5    REM 10% INFLATION TABLE
6    REM ****
10   PRINT "ITEM NO.     OLD PRICE     NEW PRICE"
20   F$=   "###          $$##.##        $$##.##"
30   FOR I=1 TO 4
40     READ ID,P1
50     P2=1.1*P1
60     PRINT USING F$;ID;P1;P2
70   NEXT I
80   DATA 305,20,317,13.50,325,27.50,311,45
90   END
```

The printout will be

ITEM NO.	OLD PRICE	NEW PRICE
305	$20.00	$22.00
317	$13.50	$14.85
325	$27.50	$30.25
311	$45.00	$49.50

Format variables are especially convenient for printing business reports because a miniature model of the finished report can be produced by putting the format strings together at the beginning of the report. Following a few simple rules helps to keep the format strings readable. For example

```
5     REM BUSINESS REPORT
6     REM ****
10    HEAD1$="        FRED'S STORE"
20    HEAD2$="        MAY 22, 1986"
30    HEAD3$="   SALES          PROFITS"
40    DET$  ="   ####.##         ####.##"
50    TTAL1$="********TOTALS********"
60    TTAL2$="$$####.##        $$####.##"
70    REM PRINT HEADINGS
80    PRINT HEAD1$
90    PRINT HEAD2$
100   PRINT HEAD3$
110   REM READ AND PRINT DETAIL LINES
120   TOTSALES=0
130   TOTPROFITS=0
140   READ SALES,PROFITS
150   WHILE SALES<>-1
160     PRINT USING DET$;SALES,PROFITS
170     TOTSALES=TOTSALES+SALES
180     TOTPROFITS=TOTPROFITS+PROFITS
190     READ SALES,PROFITS
200   WEND
210   REM PRINT TOTALS
220   PRINT TTAL1$
230   PRINT USING TTAL2$;TOTSALES,TOTPROFITS
240   DATA 105.27,52.17,1473.33,622.79,-1,-1
250   END
```

The printout will be

```
        FRED'S STORE
        MAY 22, 1986
   SALES          PROFITS
   105.27           52.17
   1473.33         622.79
   ********TOTALS********
$1578.60        $674.96
```

REMARKS

1. Note how much the material on the right sides of the string assignment statements in lines 10 through 60 looks like the final report. Setting up a "miniature report" in this way will make it easier to print out neat output. It is important to line up the left quotation marks in the miniature report format lines, as we did in lines 10–60, to ensure that the strings in the final report will match up character-for-character in the output.

2. Also note that we did *not* use PRINT USING statements in the program to print out material without variable fields. When a string is made up completely of literal material in quotes, we use a PRINT statement instead. For example, we used PRINT to print out the headings. However, we still assigned these literal strings to variables in the miniature report of lines 10–60 and printed these string variables to ensure that our final report is neat and centered.

13.5   Starting PRINT USING in Zone 2

In the next example we use trailing punctuation in line 60 so that the output of PRINT USING will start at the beginning of zone 2. The value of a string variable is printed in zone 1.

```
10    PRINT  "NAME",
20    PRINT  "WEEK1       WEEK2"
30    F$=      " $$##        $$##"
40    FOR  J=1  TO  3
50      READ  N$,W1,W2
60      PRINT  N$,
70      PRINT  USING  F$;W1,W2
80    NEXT  J
90    DATA  "HALL",24,18,"BOND",15,10,"FOY",18,9
100   END
```

The printout will be

```
NAME      WEEK1    WEEK2
HALL      $24      $18
BOND      $15      $10
FOY       $18       $9
```

13.6 PRINT USING with String Variables

So far we have seen PRINT USING statements being used to print the contents of numeric variables in a neat format, sometimes among characters of literal fields. PRINT USING can be used to print the contents of *string* variables as well.

[Ampersand.] If you want the contents of a string variable to print as is, taking up as many print positions as the length of the string, you can use an ampersand ("&") to specify the position of the string in the format string. For example

```
10   F$= "---&---"
20   FOR J=1 TO 3
30     READ NAM$
40     PRINT USING F$;NAM$
50   NEXT J
60   DATA "BOND", "FOY", "JONES"
70   END
```

Printout

```
---BOND---
---FOY---
---JONES---
```

Note that the printout would be the same if we changed line 40 to

    40   PRINT "---";NAM$;"---"

The benefit of the ampersand, however, is that it can be used among any other symbols in format strings.

Fixed-Length String Fields. *Optional*   We can also use PRINT USING to print the truncated or padded contents of a string variable so that it fits into a format field of a fixed length. For example, in the program of Section 13.5, we may wish to ensure that any names in the DATA line that extend into zone 2 are printed without disturbing the alignment of the rest of the output line. The backslash character ("\") can be used in the format string to mark the first and last positions of the string variable contents when using PRINT USING. For example

    F$ = "---\ \---"

will print three characters between the sets of dashes when it is used by a PRINT USING statement with one string variable, such as

    PRINT USING F$;SUBJECT$

Note that there is only one space between the backslashes because the backslash characters themselves count as place holders.

If the string to be printed is longer than the number of characters reserved for it, only the leftmost characters are printed. For example, if "LONG*STRING" were to be printed in a field of seven characters, only "LONG*ST" would print. This is called **truncation**. On the other hand, if the string to be printed is shorter than the space reserved for it, the string is printed left justified, with spaces filling the string out on the right. This is called **padding**.

QUESTION What will the printout be for the following program?

```
10  F$="\\\\"
20  A$="*" : B$="***"
30  PRINT USING F$;A$,B$
40  END
```

ANSWER The printout will be ▢`* **`. The odd-looking format string consists of two fields of two characters each. Therefore, the single asterisk of A$ will be printed left justified with one space padded to the right, and the three asterisks of B$ will be truncated to a length of two characters in the printout.

Single-Character String Fields. What about one-character strings? Since we have to use two backslashes (one at the start and one at the end) to mark the area to be occupied by the string variable, we can not use this method to mark areas to be occupied by a one-character string value. Instead, we use an exclamation point ("!").

QUESTION What will the printout be? (There are five spaces between the backslashes in line 10.)

```
10  F$="\     \, MR. !. AND MRS. !."
20  FOR J=1 TO 3
30    READ LAST$,HUSBAND$,WIFE$
40    PRINT USING F$;LAST$,HUSBAND$,WIFE$
50  NEXT J
60  DATA "JONES","FRED","ANN"
70  DATA "SIMPSON","GEORGE","MARY"
80  DATA "WASHINGTON","HENRY","SUE"
90  END
```

ANSWER

```
JONES  , MR. F. AND MRS. A.
SIMPSON, MR. G. AND MRS. M.
WASHING, MR. H. AND MRS. S.
```

Exercises

TAB FUNCTION

1. What will the printouts be?

(a)
```
10   FOR  J=1  TO  5
20      PRINT  TAB(J)"*"
30   NEXT  J
40   END
```

(b)
```
10   PRINT  "HELLO"
20   PRINT  TAB(1)"A"
30   PRINT  TAB(8)23
40   END
```

2. Modify the last program of Section 13.1 so that the printout also gives each employee's separate total.

NAME	DAY1	DAY2	DAY3	TOTAL
SMITH	25	14	12	51
KOHN	18	15	15	48
DIAZ	20	15	11	46

PRINT USING

3. **(a)** What will the printout be?

```
10   DATA  3.52,4.916,7
20   F$="#.##"
30   FOR  J=1  TO  3
40      READ  X
50      PRINT  USING  F$;X
60   NEXT  J
70   END
```

(b) Write a program to produce a table of the squares of integers 3 through 10.

3	9
4	16
5	25
6	36
7	49
8	64
9	81
10	100

4. Write a program to produce the following list of Celsius and Fahrenheit equivalents in steps of ten degrees Celsius (F = (C*9/5) + 32):

```
    0  CELSIUS  EQUALS    32  FAHRENHEIT
   10  CELSIUS  EQUALS    50  FAHRENHEIT
   20
    .
    .
    .

  100  CELSIUS  EQUALS  212  FAHRENHEIT
```

5. Write a program to print the following table of square roots given to three decimal places:

```
  NUMBER       SQR.ROOT
    2            1.414
    4            2.000
    6              .
    8              .
   10              .
```

6. Write a program to produce the following printout table for three sales-people using
DATA "JONES",5000,4200,"MUTT",3000,5000,"BOND",1000,2500:

```
  NAME      WEEK 1    WEEK 2    TOTAL
  JONES     $5,000    $4,200    $9,200
  MUTT      $3,000    $5,000    $8,000
  BOND      $1,000    $2,500    $3,500
```

(*Hint:* You will need to insert a comma in the format variable to have the commas appear in the printout.)

7. What will the printouts be?

(a)

```
10  F$=" >&< "
20  FOR J=1 TO 3
30     READ X$
40       PRINT USING F$;X$
50  NEXT J
60  DATA "A","AB","ABC"
70  END
```

(b)

```
10  F$=" >\\< "
20  FOR J=1 TO 3
30     READ X$
40       PRINT USING F$;X$
50  NEXT J
60  DATA "A","AB","ABC"
70  END
```

8. Each of the following DATA lines gives the first name, last name, date of birth (by month, day, and year), and major for one student.

DATA "FRED","JONES",7,30,1965,"GEOLOGY"

DATA "MARY","HALL",12,8,1957,"ENGLISH"

DATA "TOM","ALCOTT",3,6,1961,"BIOLOGY"

Note that only the last two digits of the year of birth are printed (use YR − 1900), and that the major is abbreviated to three letters. Using a single-format string to print out *all* the information for each student, apply the DATA for *three* students to write a program that will produce the following printout:

```
BIRTHDAY   NAME  (MAJOR)
 7-30-65   F.  JONES  (GEO)
12- 8-57   M.  HALL  (ENG)
 3- 6-61   T.  ALCOTT  (BIO)
```

9. Also see Appendix C, Exercises 9 and 10.

14

Finding the Maximum

In this chapter, we provide a simple method for finding the maximum number from a list of DATA numbers. This method is very similar to what a person would actually do when confronted with that problem.

14.1 Developing the Method

The first two programs are drills that will help you understand the final program of this chapter.

QUESTION What will the printout be?

```
10   DATA 8,6,5,10
20   READ L
30   FOR K=2 TO 4
40      READ X
50      PRINT X*X
60   NEXT K
70   PRINT L
80   END
```

HINT: Does the value of L change during the course of the program? Does the value of X change?

ANSWER In line 20 (the first READ statement), L is assigned 8, the first DATA value. There are no statements in the program that will change the value of L. In the FOR-NEXT loop, each time READ X is executed a new DATA value will be assigned to X. The printout will be

```
36
25
100
8
```

QUESTION   In the next program what will the printout be? What would the printout be for DATA 68,42?

```
10  DATA 3,7
20  READ L
30  READ X
40  IF X>L THEN L=X
50  PRINT L
60  END
```

ANSWER   This program will print the larger of the two DATA numbers. Note that by line 50, the current value of L is the larger of the two DATA numbers. For DATA 3,7 the printout will be ⎕7⎕. For DATA 68,42 the printout will be ⎕68⎕.

14.2 Finding the Maximum in a List of DATA

PROBLEM   Maximum in List of Five Numbers

PROGRAM IDEAS

Let a variable called MAX keep track of the current largest number. Start by letting MAX equal the first DATA number. Then compare MAX with the second DATA number. If the second DATA number is larger than MAX, change the value of MAX to that DATA number. Next compare the current MAX with the third DATA number, and change MAX if necessary. Then compare the current MAX with the fourth DATA number, and change MAX if necessary. Finally, compare the current MAX with the fifth DATA number, and change MAX if necessary. By the end of these comparisons, the current value for MAX will be the largest DATA number.

Here is an outline for the program:

Step 1. Read the first DATA number to initialize MAX.

Step 2. Use the FOR-NEXT loop to compare each of the remaining four

DATA numbers against the current value of MAX, and change the value of MAX when necessary.

Step 3. Print the final value of MAX.

```
10  REM FINDING THE MAXIMUM OF 5 DATA NUMBERS
20  DATA 14,6,18,26,22
30  READ MAX
40  FOR K=2 TO 5
50    READ X
60     IF X>MAX THEN MAX=X
70  NEXT K
80  PRINT MAX
90  END
```

REMARKS

1. The reason that FOR K=2 TO 5 was used to find the largest of *five* DATA numbers is that the statement READ MAX (assigning the first DATA value to MAX) comes before the FOR-NEXT loop. The FOR-NEXT loop compares the current MAX against the remaining four challengers, the second through the fifth DATA numbers.

2. Before the loop, MAX starts off with the value 14. When K=2, the value of MAX does not change because 6 does not exceed 14. When K=3, the value of MAX is changed to 18. When K=4, the value of MAX is changed to 26. When K=5, the value of MAX does not change because 22 does not exceed 26. During the execution of this program, MAX took on the values 14, 18, and 26.

3. Look at line 60. The THEN clause is MAX=X because MAX is to be changed to the value of X. What would happen if, instead of MAX=X, we wrote X=MAX? *Answer:* This would change the value of X but it would leave MAX unchanged. Thus, the computer would incorrectly give as printout ⎡14⎤, which is the starting value for MAX.

PROBLEM **Maximum of a DATA List with a Flag**   As in the FOR-NEXT version, MAX is initialized before the start of the WHILE loop with the first DATA value. However, READ MAX alone is no longer an adequate means of doing that.

Completing the following program is Exercise 4:

```
10  DATA 14,28,19,32,29,30,-1
20  READ X
30  MAX=X
40  WHILE _____
     :
     :
```

■■■■ 14.3 Finding Largest and Smallest of DATA List of Ten Numbers

PROGRAM IDEAS

We will use the variables MAX and MIN to keep track of the current largest and smallest numbers.

Step 1. Read the first DATA number and assign its value to both MAX and MIN.

Step 2. Use a FOR-NEXT loop, FOR J = 2 to 10, to compare the remaining DATA numbers against MAX and MIN.

Step 3. Print the results.

Writing this program is Exercise 6.

■■■■ Exercises

1. Write a program that will find the largest of seven DATA numbers. Run it three times, using different data each time.

2. Write a program that will find the smallest of seven DATA numbers.

3. If the FOR-NEXT program from Section 14.2 is RUN with DATA 8,14,12,19,16, what *values* will MAX have taken on during the program?

4. Write a program to find the largest number in any list of DATA numbers with a flag.

5. The following DATA lines provide information on five salespeople:

    ```
    10   DATA "FOY",38,"JONES",49,"KOHN",44
    20   DATA "BOND",89,"RUSSO",65
    ```

    For each pair of DATA values, the first gives the salesperson's name and the second tells how many sales he or she had in a given week. Write a program that will have printout of the form

    ```
    ┌─────────────────────────────────┐
    │ BOND HAD THE MOST SALES 89       │
    └─────────────────────────────────┘
    ```

    Rerun it with the following DATA lines, which give information on a different set of five salespeople:

    ```
    10   DATA "WARD",74,"AMES",25,"MING",48
    20   DATA "HARRIS",68,"BROWN",44
    ```

6. Write a single program to print both the largest and the smallest numbers from a list of ten numbers.

7. Write a single program to print both the largest and the next-to-largest number from a list of ten numbers.

★ 8. A swimmer keeps track of the number of laps she swims each day. The DATA line uses 999 as the flag. Write a program that counts the number of days in which she swam more laps than on the day *before*. For DATA 20,20,30,21,19,25,18,32,999 the program will count only 30,25, and 32. The printout will be ⌐3 DAYS⌐.

★★ 9. Also see Appendix B, Exercise 15 for a program to determine the mode of a data list.

10. Also see Appendix C, Exercise 11 for a problem on optimal production in a ceramics studio.

CHAPTER
15

Some Everyday Life Programs

As you know, computers are being used in many different settings in today's world, from banks to schools to political campaigns. In this chapter, we look at simplified versions of the following types of programs:

1. "Psychotherapy"
2. Campaign letter
3. State capitals tutorial
4. Simple menu
5. Automatic change maker

In later chapters we consider more complex programs that are closer to real world applications.

15.1 "Psychotherapy"

The next program demonstrates very dramatically the interactive capabilities of a computer.

```
5      REM PSYCHOTHERAPY
6      REM ****
10     INPUT "I AM A COMPUTER THERAPIST. WHAT IS YOUR NAME ";NAM$
20     PRINT "HELLO, ";NAM$;
30     PRINT " GLAD TO MAKE YOUR ACQUAINTANCE"
40     INPUT "TELL ME, HAVE YOU EVER HAD THERAPY";THERAPY$
50     PRINT "THAT IS VERY INTERESTING ";NAM$
60     INPUT "HOW OLD ARE YOU NOW";A
70     IF A<30 THEN PRINT "YOUTH HAS ITS SPECIAL PROBLEMS"
80     IF A>=30 AND A<65 THEN PRINT "MIDDLE AGE HAS ITS PROBLEMS"
90     IF A>=65 THEN PRINT "OLD AGE HAS ITS SPECIAL PROBLEMS"
100    INPUT "HOW ARE YOU FEELING TODAY";FEEL$
110    PRINT "I WOULD BE WORRIED IF YOU"
120    PRINT "NEVER FELT ";FEEL$
130    INPUT "TELL ME, DO YOU LIKE YOUR FATHER";FATHER$
140    IF FATHER$="YES" THEN 210
150    IF FATHER$="NO" THEN 240
160    REM OTHERWISE
170      PRINT "I DIDN'T THINK YOU WOULD GIVE A"
180      PRINT "SIMPLE YES OR NO ANSWER"
190    GO TO 260
200    REM YES
210
```

Adding several more lines to the preceeding program is Exercise 2. A typical printout follows. (What the human types has been underlined.)

```
I AM A COMPUTER THERAPIST. WHAT IS YOUR NAME? SCROOGE
HELLO, SCROOGE, GLAD TO MAKE YOUR ACQUAINTANCE
TELL ME, HAVE YOU EVER HAD THERAPY? HUMBUG
THAT IS VERY INTERESTING SCROOGE
HOW OLD ARE YOU NOW? 73
OLD AGE HAS ITS SPECIAL PROBLEMS
HOW ARE YOU FEELING TODAY? LOUSY
I WOULD BE WORRIED IF YOU
NEVER FELT LOUSY
TELL ME, DO YOU LIKE YOUR FATHER? _____
        :
        :
```

Here is another typical printout:

```
I AM A COMPUTER THERAPIST. WHAT IS YOUR NAME? GEORGE
HELLO, GEORGE, GLAD TO MAKE YOUR ACQUAINTANCE
TELL ME, HAVE YOU EVER HAD THERAPY? NO
THAT IS VERY INTERESTING GEORGE
HOW OLD ARE YOU NOW? 19
YOUTH HAS ITS SPECIAL PROBLEMS
HOW ARE YOU FEELING TODAY? DYNAMITE
I WOULD BE WORRIED IF YOU
NEVER FELT DYNAMITE
TELL ME, DO YOU LIKE YOUR FATHER? _____
```

Note the two main devices used in this program to avoid inappropriate responses by the computer:

1. Vague responses that are appropriate for a wide range of inputs.

2. Testing inputs and then branching to an appropriate response for that input.

Of course, this tongue-in-cheek "psychotherapy" program is much too simple to provide psychotherapy and, in fact, to this date no one has devised a program that seriously could be said to provide effective psychotherapy. Nevertheless, the question of whether psychotherapy is something within computer capability is hotly debated by experts. Some claim that in the near future computers will provide this service, while others argue that such a deep human role is inherently beyond the capability of computers. (The most famous psychotherapy program, "ELIZA", was written by Professor J. Weizenbaum of MIT.)

15.2 Campaign Letter

The campaign director for a certain politician has devised a single program for writing "personalized" letters based on three DATA items. For DATA "MR. JONES", "ENGINEERS", 25000 the letter printout would be

```
DEAR (MR. JONES) :
  I BELIEVE THAT NOW, MORE THAN EVER, THE PROBLEMS OF (MIDDLE)
INCOME GROUPS DESERVE SPECIAL ATTENTION. IN ORDER TO CARRY
OUT MY PROGRAMS, I NEED THE SUPPORT OF (ENGINEERS)
LIKE YOURSELF. PLEASE SUPPORT MY CANDIDACY AND TOGETHER
WE CAN MAKE THIS COUNTRY A BETTER PLACE TO LIVE IN.
```

REMARK: The encircling has been provided to help you understand the program; it would not appear in the actual printout.

For DATA "MRS. SMITH","PEOPLE ON WELFARE",5000 the letter would be

```
DEAR (MRS. SMITH):
  I BELIEVE THAT NOW, MORE THAN EVER, THE PROBLEMS OF (LOWER)
INCOME GROUPS DESERVE SPECIAL ATTENTION. IN ORDER TO CARRY
OUT MY PROGRAMS I NEED THE SUPPORT OF (PEOPLE ON WELFARE)
LIKE YOURSELF. PLEASE SUPPORT MY CANDIDACY AND TOGETHER
WE CAN MAKE THIS COUNTRY A BETTER PLACE TO LIVE IN.
```

For DATA "MRS. BURNS","EXECUTIVES",60000 the letter should have
MRS. BURNS, UPPER, and EXECUTIVES in place of the circled words. Writing this program is Exercise 3.

15.3 State Capitals Tutorial

In the following program the user is asked to give the state capital for each of the four states in the DATA line. Here is a typical run:

```
WHAT IS THE CAPITAL OF NEW YORK? ALBANY
    YOU ARE CORRECT
WHAT IS THE CAPITAL OF MAINE? PORTLAND
    SORRY. THE ANSWER IS AUGUSTA
WHAT IS THE CAPITAL OF IOWA? IOWA CITY
    SORRY. THE ANSWER IS DES MOINES
WHAT IS THE CAPITAL OF OHIO? COLUMBUS
    YOU ARE CORRECT
**** YOUR SCORE WAS 2 CORRECT ****
```

PROBLEM   Complete line 60.

```
5    REM STATE CAPITALS TUTORIAL
6    REM ****
10   COUNT=0
20   FOR J=1 TO 4
30     READ STATE$,CAPITAL$
40     PRINT "WHAT IS THE CAPITAL OF ";STATE$;
50     INPUT TRY$
60     IF _____
         THEN PRINT "   YOU ARE CORRECT" : COUNT=COUNT+1
         ELSE PRINT "   SORRY. THE ANSWER IS ";CAPITAL$
70   NEXT J
80   PRINT "**** YOUR SCORE WAS";COUNT;"CORRECT ****"
90   DATA "NEW YORK","ALBANY","MAINE","AUGUSTA"
100  DATA "IOWA","DES MOINES","OHIO","COLUMBUS"
110  END
```

ANSWER   The IF test in line 60 should be IF TRY$ = CAPITAL$.

REMARKS
1. Do you see why we used two lines, 40 and 50, instead of attempting a single INPUT statement? (See Exercise 7 and Section 4.8.)
2. Of course, a second run of this program would ask for the capitals of the *same* four states. There are various ways of providing further practice for the user: (a) another person could change the DATA line; (b) a more interesting method would be a program in which the computer *randomly* selects *four* states from DATA lines containing all fifty states and their capitals. (See Chapter 18.)

15.4 Simple Menu

```
5     REM MENU
6     REM ****
10    READ WEATHER$,HOROSCOPE$,SCORE$
20    PRINT "MENU OF CHOICES"
30    PRINT "        1)    FOR TODAY'S WEATHER FORECAST"
40    PRINT "        2)    FOR YOUR HOROSCOPE"
50    PRINT "        3)    FOR SCORE OF LAST NIGHT'S GAME"
60    INPUT "TYPE YOUR SELECTION";SEL
70    IF SEL=1 THEN PRINT WEATHER$
80    IF SEL=2 THEN PRINT HOROSCOPE$
90    IF SEL=3 THEN PRINT SCORE$
100   DATA "CLOUDY WITH A CHANCE OF RAIN"
110   DATA "YOU SHOULD MAKE A MAJOR LIFE CHANGE SOON"
120   DATA "CELTICS 120 KNICKS 114"
130   END
```

If the user entered 2 for his selection, the printout would be

```
MENU OF CHOICES
        1)    FOR TODAY'S WEATHER FORECAST
        2)    FOR YOUR HOROSCOPE
        3)    FOR SCORE OF LAST NIGHT'S GAME
TYPE YOUR SELECTION?   2
YOU SHOULD MAKE A MAJOR LIFE CHANGE SOON
```

REMARKS
1. The maximum length for a string value of a string variable is 255 characters. Note that each DATA line represents one string value.

2. In this program the task for each menu selection was very simple—just printing the appropriate string. For more complex tasks there is a better method, using the techniques of the next chapter.

15.5 Automatic Change Maker

In this next program the computer will request an amount of change to be made. After the user inputs the amount, the computer will print out how many quarters, dimes, nickels, and pennies will be used.

```
AMOUNT OF CHANGE IN CENTS? 89
    QUARTERS   3
    DIMES   1
    NICKELS   0
    PENNIES   4
*** YOU HAVE RECEIVED 89 CENTS IN CHANGE ***
```

PROGRAM IDEAS

We use the integer functions MOD and \ of Chapter 5. For example, the number of quarters to be used in making 89 cents is equal to 89\25. (Recall that A\B gives the maximum number of times B goes into A, ignoring the remainder.) After three quarters are supplied, 14¢ change is still *owed*. Note that 14 is equal to 89 MOD 25.

Completing this program is Exercise 8.

```
5    REM AUTOMATIC CHANGE
6    REM ****
10   INPUT "AMOUNT OF CHANGE IN CENTS";AMT
20   OWE=AMT
30   PRINT "   QUARTERS ";OWE\25
40   OWE=OWE MOD 25
50   PRINT "   DIMES ";OWE_____
60      :
        :
```

Exercises

1. Give at least two examples for the "psychotherapy" program, showing how the computer might respond inappropriately to a reasonable input.

2. Extend the "Psychotherapy" program by having the computer ask at least two more questions and give appropriate responses.

3. Write the Campaign Letter program from Section 15.2. Use the criteria over 50,000 as upper income, over 8,000 but not over 50,000 as middle, and less than or equal to 8,000 as lower.

4. Write a looping version of the Campaign Letter program so that it will print out five letters for DATA lines giving information on five voters. There should be two blank lines separating each letter.

5. Write a Multiplication Tutorial program for which the DATA line contains six multiplication questions. In addition to telling how the user did on each question (and the correct answer when the user was wrong) the printout should also give the total number of questions answered correctly.

6. Modify the Multiplication Tutorial program so that the user receives 2 points for each correct answer and loses 1 point for each incorrect answer. The final line of the printout should be the user's final score.

7. Explain what is wrong with a statement such as the following:

INPUT "WHAT IS THE CAPITAL OF";STATE$;TRY$.

8. Complete the Automatic Change Maker program of Section 15.5.

9. Write a tutorial program so that the user is asked, for each of four presidents, which president came next. You may use the following DATA pairs: Lincoln, Johnson, Eisenhower, Kennedy, Washington, Adams, Nixon, Ford.

★ **10.** Rewrite the State Capitals Tutorial program so that it allows someone to input either "C" or "S" depending on whether the user wants to be asked to guess either the capitals or the states for the question. For example, if the user inputs an "S", the first question will be

"ALBANY IS THE CAPITAL OF WHICH STATE"

11. Modify the Simple Menu program so that the user is given a fourth choice—THE THOUGHT FOR THE DAY.

12. See Appendix B, Exercise 29 for a program on guessing a number that the computer has selected.

CHAPTER 16

Modularization and Subroutines

As we already have mentioned, there is more to good programming than merely producing programs that "work." Programming style is also extremely important. Good programming style not only makes it easier to write correct programs but even more importantly, good programming style will lead to programs that are (1) clear and readable and (2) easy to modify should the need arise.

A principal tool in achieving these goals is **modularization**, that is, breaking up a larger problem into separate subtasks. Stepwise refinement initiates the modularization process. As this chapter shows, BASIC facilitates the farming out of subtasks to separate modules in the program through the use of GOSUB and ON GOSUB statements.

Note to the instructor: Although modularization is an important part of structured programming, you may wish to cover Chapters 17 and 18 before this one, since their content is more elementary.

16.1 GOSUB and RETURN

Suppose a program needs to be designed to perform several tasks. It may be best to define and perform each task with a block of program lines called a **subroutine**. Subroutines are a common technique in structured programming. A complete program would then consist of these subroutine modules and the **main** section, which transfers control to the appropriate subroutines.

The GOSUB (line number) statement is used in the main program to branch to each subroutine. The last line of each subroutine must be a RETURN statement. When the computer reaches the RETURN statement of a subroutine, it returns to the statement immediately following the GOSUB statement that transferred the computer to the subroutine.

155

The following example uses a subroutine to print the square of N. The two-line subroutine is in brackets.

Printout

```
10    N=7
20    PRINT  "HELLO"
30    GOSUB  100
40    PRINT  "GOODBYE"
50    END
60    '
99    REM PRINT  THE  SQUARE
100   PRINT N*N
110   RETURN
```

```
HELLO
 49
GOODBYE
```

REMARKS

1. Note the use of line 50 to branch around the subroutine. If line 50 were omitted, the subroutine would have been entered involuntarily, and line 110 would cause the computer to halt with an error message.
2. Also note the REM statement of line 99. Just as it is important to document the program at the beginning, it is likewise good style to label each subroutine with its task using a REM statement.

QUESTION One of the powerful features of subroutines is that they can be reused to perform a certain task many times. What will the printout be?

```
10    FOR N = 1 TO 4
20       GOSUB  100
30    NEXT N
40    END
50    '
99    REM PRINT  THE  SQUARE
100   PRINT N*N
110   RETURN
```

ANSWER

```
1
4
9
16
```

REMARK: Consider what would happen if line 110 RETURN were omitted in this program. For N = 1, line 20 would transfer control to line 100, and 1 would be printed. However, without the RETURN statement, the computer would then reach line 200 END and would halt instead of processing N = 2 through 4.

The program examples have so far been drill and have not shown the benefits of the use of subroutines. The previous program, for example, could more easily have been done with line 20 as PRINT N*N. However, the following example illustrates the benefits of using subroutines.

EXAMPLE   **Personalized Campaign Letters**   Suppose we wanted to write a personalized campaign letter to those people whose names and ages are listed in a flagged DATA line. We might wish the letter to be two paragraphs, the first paragraph being the same for everyone (except for the name) and the second paragraph either the youthful voter's paragraph or the mature voter's paragraph. This selection, of course, is based on the voter's age. Here is the program:

```
5    REM CAMPAIGN LETTER
6    REM *****
10   DATA "JONES",24,"SMITH",62,"TWAIN",33,"XYZ",-1
20   READ NAM$,AGE
30   WHILE NAM$<>"XYZ"
40      GOSUB 100
50      IF AGE<40 THEN GOSUB 200
                  ELSE GOSUB 300
60      READ NAM$,AGE
70   WEND
80   END
90   '
99   REM PARAGRAPH 1
100  PRINT "DEAR MR.  ";NAM$;","
110  PRINT "    MORE THAN EVER THIS COUNTRY NEEDS"
120  PRINT "INTELLIGENT AND COURAGEOUS LEADERSHIP."
130  PRINT "WORKING TOGETHER WE CAN KEEP THIS"
140  PRINT "COUNTRY GREAT.''
150  RETURN
160  '
199  REM PARAGRAPH 2 FOR YOUTH
200  PRINT "    I ESPECIALLY NEED THE SUPPORT OF"
210  PRINT "YOUNG VOTERS. THE FUTURE OF THIS"
220  PRINT "COUNTRY WILL BE SHAPED BY YOUTHFUL"
230  PRINT "CITIZENS LIKE YOURSELF."
240  PRINT : PRINT
250  RETURN
260  '
299  REM PARAGRAPH 2 FOR OLDER
300  PRINT "    I ESPECIALLY NEED THE SUPPORT OF"
310  PRINT "MORE MATURE VOTERS.  IT IS THE"
320  PRINT "EXAMPLE AND WISDOM OF MATURE"
330  PRINT "CITIZENS LIKE YOURSELF THAT WILL"
340  PRINT "SHAPE THIS COUNTRY'S FUTURE."
350  PRINT : PRINT
360  RETURN
```

NOTE: The line number of a GOSUB statement does not have to be greater than the line number at which the GOSUB statement appears. Therefore, 170 GOSUB 20 is valid, but would not be used in structured programming if the subroutines follow the main module.

16.2 ON K GOSUB

We have seen earlier how multiway branching may be achieved using ON K GOTO. A similar command for subroutines is the ON K GOSUB statement. This statement has the capacity to branch to any one of a whole list of subroutines. For example, the statement

ON K GOSUB 200,250,300,350

will have the computer branch to any one of the four subroutines whose starting line numbers are listed. The computer will branch to the appropriate subroutine based on the current value of K (which may be any variable or expression, and not only K).

If the value of the variable or expression (K in our example) is 1, the computer will branch to the subroutine that starts at the *first* line number in the ON K GOSUB list (i.e., the subroutine at line 200 in our example, just as if it had reached the statement GOSUB 200 instead). Similarly, if the value of the variable or expression is 2, the computer will branch to the *second* subroutine in the list (at line 250, in our example). Finally, for values of 3 or 4, the computer will branch to the *third* and *fourth* subroutines, respectively.

If the value of the variable or expression is 0, or greater than the number of line numbers in the list, the computer will simply fall through to the next line in the program. If the value is a noninteger, the computer will round it off to the nearest integer; for example, 2.7 will be rounded off to 3.

Upon reaching the RETURN statement in the subroutine, the computer is sent back to the statement immediately following the ON K GOSUB statement that branched to it.

16.3 Menu Examples

QUESTION In the following program, what would the printout be if the user typed JOE DOE, 2, and 15 in response to the INPUT prompts?

```
95    REM TEMPERATURE CONVERSION MENU
96    REM ****
100   INPUT "TYPE YOUR NAME";N$
110   PRINT "MENU OF CHOICES"
120   PRINT "      1)   CONVERT FAHRENHEIT TO CELSIUS"
130   PRINT "      2)   CONVERT CELSIUS TO FAHRENHEIT"
140   INPUT "TYPE CHOICE, 1 OR 2";SEL
150   ON SEL GOSUB 300,400
160   PRINT "IT WAS A PLEASURE SERVING YOU, ";N$
170   END
180   '
190   '
300   REM CONVERT TO CENTIGRADE *******
310   INPUT "TYPE DEGREES FAHRENHEIT";F
320   PRINT F;"FAHRENHEIT ";(F-32)*5/9;"CELSIUS"
330   RETURN
340   '
350   '
400   REM CONVERT TO FAHRENHEIT ******
410   INPUT "TYPE DEGREES CELSIUS";C
420   PRINT C;"CELSIUS   ";C*9/5+32;"FAHRENHEIT"
430   RETURN
```

REMARK: Note that the END statement appears in line 170; and that we use REM statements (the single quote mark form) in lines 180 and 190 to separate (visually) the subroutines from the main body of the program. Also we use single quote marks to separate different subroutines.

ANSWER

```
TYPE YOUR NAME? JOE DOE
MENU OF CHOICES
    1)   CONVERT FAHRENHEIT TO CELSIUS
    2)   CONVERT CELSIUS TO FAHRENHEIT
TYPE CHOICE, 1 OR 2? 2
TYPE DEGREES CELSIUS? 15
15 CELSIUS    59 FAHRENHEIT
IT WAS A PLEASURE SERVING YOU, JOE DOE
```

Automatic Teller—Single Transaction. This program simulates an automatic teller. Let us suppose that you have $800 in your account before this transaction.

```
95    REM AUTOMATIC TELLER
96    REM ****
100   BAL=800
110   PRINT "MENU OF CHOICES"
120   PRINT "        1)   FOR DEPOSIT"
130   PRINT "        2)   FOR WITHDRAWAL"
140   PRINT "        3)   FOR BALANCE INFORMATION"
150   INPUT " TYPE YOUR SELECTION"; SEL
160   ON SEL GOSUB 300,400,500
170   PRINT "---IT WAS A PLEASURE SERVING YOU---"
180   END
190   '
200   '
300   REM***DEPOSIT***
310   INPUT "   AMOUNT YOU WISH TO DEPOSIT";AMT
320   BAL=BAL+AMT
330   PRINT "   YOUR NEW BALANCE IS $";BAL
340   _____
350   '
360   '
400   REM***WITHDRAWAL***
410   INPUT "   AMOUNT YOU WISH TO WITHDRAW";AMT
420   BAL=BAL-AMT
430   PRINT "   YOUR NEW BALANCE IS ";BAL
440   RETURN
450   '
460   '
500   REM***INFORMATION***
510   PRINT "   YOUR CURRENT BALANCE IS $";BAL
520   RETURN
```

PROBLEM   Fill in line 340. Here is a typical transaction:

```
MENU OF CHOICES
        1)   FOR DEPOSIT
        2)   FOR WITHDRAWAL
        3)   FOR BALANCE INFORMATION
 TYPE YOUR SELECTION? 2
 AMOUNT YOU WISH TO WITHDRAW? 120
 YOUR NEW BALANCE IS $ 680
---IT WAS A PLEASURE SERVING YOU---
```

ANSWER   Line 340 should be RETURN.

Looping Version of Automatic Teller—Multiple Transactions

```
95    REM LOOPING TELLER
96    REM ****
100   BAL=800  :  SEL=0
110   WHILE SEL<>4
120      PRINT "MENU OF CHOICES"
130      PRINT "    1)   FOR DEPOSIT"
140      PRINT "    2)   FOR WITHDRAWAL"
150      PRINT "    3)   FOR BALANCE INFORMATION"
160      PRINT "    4)   NO FURTHER TRANSACTIONS"
170      INPUT "  TYPE YOUR SELECTION";SEL
180      ON SEL GOSUB 300,400,500
190   WEND
200   PRINT "---IT WAS A PLEASURE SERVING YOU---"
210   END
220   '
230   '
300   REM *** DEPOSIT ***
310         and so on
```
(The rest of this program is exactly the same as the Single-Transaction Automatic Teller, that is, it consists of the same subroutines.)

REMARK: Note that if the user inputs 4, the computer will "fall through" the line 180 statement, ON SEL GOSUB 300, 400, 500, since 4 exceeds the number of choices following the word GOSUB. Instead of going to a subroutine, the computer will go to the next program line, 190. WEND will then send the computer to the test condition at the top of the loop. The loop will not be entered again; instead the computer will continue to line 200.

EXAMPLE   **Vacation Plan**   The ROOMS-R-US Hotel offes a vacation plan that includes various options as specified within the following program. In Exercise 8 you will be asked to give the printouts for various inputs.

```
95    REM HOTEL BILLING
96    REM ****
100   PRINT "CHOOSE YOUR VACATION PLAN"
110   INPUT "TYPE 1 FOR ECONOMY, 2 FOR DELUXE";PLAN
120   INPUT "HOTEL: HOW MANY NIGHTS";NITES
130   INPUT "CAR RENTAL: HOW MANY DAYS";CDAYS
140   ON PLAN GOSUB 200,300
150   GOSUB 400          'PRINT ITEMIZED BILL
160   END
170   '
180   '
200   REM ECONOMY PLAN
210   VAC$="ECONOMY"
220   HOTEL=40*NITES
230   CAR=15*CDAYS
240   RMSERV=0
250   RETURN
260   '
270   '
300   REM DELUXE PLAN
310   VAC$="DELUXE"
320   HOTEL=80*NITES
330   INPUT "CAR: TYPE M FOR MERCEDES,J FOR JAGUAR";C$
340   IF C$="M" THEN CAR=90*CDAYS
                    ELSE CAR=120*CDAYS
350   INPUT "DO YOU WISH BREAKFAST IN ROOM,Y OR N";R$
360   IF R$="Y" THEN RMSERV=10*NITES
370   RETURN
380   '
390   '
400   REM PRINT ITEMIZED BILL
410   PRINT VAC$;" VACATION"
420   PRINT "HOTEL ROOM $";HOTEL
430   PRINT "CAR RENTAL $";CAR
440   PRINT "ROOM SERVICE $";RMSERV
450   PRINT "TOTAL BILL $";HOTEL+CAR+RMSERV
460   PRINT "IT WAS A PLEASURE SERVING YOU."
470   RETURN
```

Exercises

1. What will the printouts be?

(a)
```
100   FOR K=1 TO 3
110      READ X
120      GOSUB 200
130   NEXT K
140   END
150   '
200   PRINT K;X*X
210   RETURN
300   DATA 5,7,9
```

(b)
```
100   A=2
110   GOSUB 200
120   PRINT A
130   END
140   '
200   PRINT "HELLO"
210   A=A+1
220   RETURN
```

2. Modify the Single-Transaction Automatic Teller program so that if the user selects withdrawal and inputs an amount exceeding the current balance, the computer does not allow the transaction but instead prints the message SORRY, THAT AMOUNT EXCEEDS YOUR BALANCE.

3. (a) What will happen if the user inputs 5 in the Single-Transaction Automatic Teller?
   (b) Modify that program so that if the user inputs a number less than 1 or greater than 3, the computer prints INVALID SELECTION NUMBER and then repeats the MENU OF CHOICES.

4. A program is needed that will provide the user with a menu of two choices: (a) list all the students with a given input major or (b) list all the students with score over 89. Use as DATA lines

   600 DATA "ADAMS","CHEM",92,"FOY","BIOL",85

   610 DATA "RUSSO","BIOL",88,"COHN","HIST",89

   620 DATA "JONES","CHEM",82,"MOSS","ENGL",95

   Here is a typical printout:

```
MENU   :  WHAT INFORMATION DO YOU NEED?
   1)   LIST STUDENTS WITH INPUT MAJOR
   2)   LIST STUDENTS WITH SCORE OVER AN INPUT SCORE
TYPE CHOICE 1 OR 2? 1
TYPE FIRST FOUR LETTERS OF MAJOR? CHEM
ADAMS
JONES
```

   Rerun your program so that option 2 is selected.

★ **5.** Write a looping version of the Fahrenheit or Centigrade Conversion program of Section 16.3.

★ **6.** Write a loop version of the program in Exercise 4.

7. (a) Rewrite your program from Exercise 4 so that it will also contain a third option on the menu

    3)   COMPUTE CLASS AVERAGE

★ **(b)** Rewrite that program so that it will also contain a fourth option

    4)   COMPUTE AVERAGE FOR ALL STUDENTS WITH INPUT MAJOR

(**Note:** Beware of dividing by 0.)

8. (a) What will be the printout in the vacation plan example for inputs of 1 for type of plan, 5 for hotel nights, and 4 for car days?

(b) What will be the printout for inputs of 2 for type of plan, 5 for hotel nights, 3 for car days, "M" for type of car, "Y" for breakfast in room?

★ **9.** The Pick-Your-Plan Hotel offers a choice of deluxe and economy plans. Under the deluxe plan, the base cost per night is $80. Deluxe options include: first-class plane fare from New York at $600; color TV comes with room, VCR for an extra $10 per night; car rental for $50 per day for any number of days. Under the economy plan, the base price per night is $40. Economy options consist of: plane fare from New York with a choice of tourist class ($400) or standby ($200); black and white TV at $5 per night or radio at $2 per night; car rental at $25 per day for any number of days. Write a program to print out an itemized bill.

CHAPTER 17

Linear Search

In a linear search of a list of items, you examine the items one-by-one until either you find what you are looking for (i.e., a match) or you reach the end of the list. By contrast, when processing an entire list, you continue to the end of the list regardless.

17.1 Processing Entire List

PROBLEM   **Printing Names of Democrats**   Fill in the blanks so that the following program will print the names of just the Democrats:

```
10  PRINT  "DEMOCRATS"
20  READ  NAM$ , PARTY$
30  WHILE  NAM$ <> "XYZ"
40        _____
50        _____
60  WEND
70  DATA  "BOND" , "R" , "JONES" , "D" , "FOY" , "R"
80  DATA  "HALL" , "D" , "HAYES" , "D" , "XYZ" , "XYZ"
90  END
```

Printout

| DEMOCRATS |
| JONES |
| HALL |
| HAYES |

ANSWER

```
40      IF PARTY$ = "D" THEN PRINT NAM$
50      READ NAM$,PARTY$
```

17.2 Linear Search of DATA List

PROBLEM Write a program in which the user is asked to input a name. The computer then searches the DATA list and prints whether or not that input name appears on the DATA list.

> DATA "ALCOTT","SMITH","SIMMS"
>
> DATA "EWING","BRETT","XYZ"

For the preceeding DATA line, here are printouts from two typical runs of the program.

```
WHO ARE YOU LOOKING FOR? JOHNSON
JOHNSON NOT ON LIST
```

```
WHO ARE YOU LOOKING FOR? SMITH
SMITH ON LIST
```

PROGRAM IDEAS

Obviously, we need to use a WHILE loop in which there are *two* exit conditions: (1) the input name has been found, or (2) the computer has reached the flag. This indicates that we should use a *compound* WHILE condition. Here it is in pseudocode:

> WHILE (input name not found yet) AND (flag not found yet)

Note that exiting if either (1) *or* (2), translates into

> WHILE (not 1) <u>AND</u> (not 2)

PROBLEM Complete line 60.

```
10  INPUT "WHO ARE YOU LOOKING FOR";WANT$
20  READ NAM$
30  WHILE NAM$<>WANT$ AND NAM$<>"XYZ"
40    READ NAM$
50  WEND
60  IF NAM$=WANT$_____
                        _____
70  DATA "ALCOTT","SMITH","SIMMS"
80  DATA "EWING","BRETT","XYZ"
90  END
```

ANSWER   The purpose of line 60 is to determine which of the two conditions caused the computer to exit from the WHILE loop. Line 60 is

IF NAM$ = WANT$ THEN PRINT WANT$;" ON LIST"

ELSE PRINT WANT$;" NOT ON LIST"

Note that if we had exited because of reaching the flag, NAM$ would equal "XYZ", and hence "NOT ON LIST" would be printed.

17.3   Further Illustrations

PROBLEM   **First and Last Names**   In the following program, the DATA lines contain a list of first and last names. The user inputs a last name. The printout will be either the first name of that person or the message that the person is not on the list. If the last name BOND is input, the printout would be

```
LAST NAME OF PERSON? BOND
FIRST NAME OF BOND IS ED
```

```
10   INPUT "LAST NAME OF PERSON";L.WANT$
20   READ FIRST$,LAST$
30   WHILE _____ AND _____
40        _____
50   WEND
60   IF LAST$=L.WANT$
        THEN _____
        ELSE _____
70   DATA "TOM","HALL","ED","BOND",
     "AL","FOY"
80   DATA "LEE","CHAN","SAL","ALOU",
     "XYZ","XYZ"
90   END
```

ANSWER   The incomplete lines are

WHILE LAST$<>L.WANT$ AND LAST$<>"XYZ"

READ FIRST$,LAST$

THEN PRINT "FIRST NAME OF ";L.WANT$;" IS ";FIRST$

ELSE PRINT L.WANT$;" NOT ON LIST"

PROBLEM   **Position on List**   This program searches for a name on a DATA list and prints which position the name occupies; if the name is not on the list, then the program prints [_____ NOT ON LIST]. Complete line 20.

NOTE: Recall that when using a counter with a WHILE loop, there is a danger of being off by 1.

```
10   INPUT "WHO ARE YOU LOOKING FOR";WANT$
20   POS=_____
30   READ NAM$
40   WHILE NAM$<>WANT$ AND NAM$<>"XYZ"
50      POS=POS+1
60      READ NAM$
70   WEND
80   IF NAM$=WANT$ THEN PRINT WANT$;" IN POSITION";POS
                    ELSE PRINT WANT$;" NOT ON LIST"
90   DATA "SMITH","CHAN","KATZ"
100  DATA "ORTEGA","BUTKUS","XYZ"
110  END
```

ANSWER   Line 20 should be POS=1. This initializes POS to 1 for the pump-priming READ statement.

17.4 Using Mock Boolean Variable in Linear Search

Mock Boolean Variables. Many computer languages have a type of variable that can take on only the values TRUE or FALSE. Such variables are called **Boolean variables**.

Microsoft BASIC has a somewhat cumbersome, numeric form of Boolean variables. Instead of using these numeric Boolean variables, we will use an ordinary string variable as **mock Boolean variables**. In using a mock Boolean variable, we will allow the program to assign it only two possible values: either "YES" or "NO".

In the linear search program presented in this section, we will use the string variable FOUND$ as a mock Boolean variable. The only values that FOUND$ will ever be assigned are "YES" or "NO".

QUESTION   What will the printout be for inputs of (a) 24 and (b) 16?

```
10  INPUT "AGE";AGE
20  OFAGE$="NO"
30  IF AGE>=18 THEN OFAGE$="YES"
40  PRINT OFAGE$
50  IF OFAGE$="YES" THEN PRINT "EXCELLENT"
60  END
```

ANSWER   **(a)**

YES
EXCELLENT

(b)

NO

PROBLEM   **Linear Search Redone with Mock Boolean Variable**   We will redo the program of Section 17.2 using the variable FOUND$ to keep track of whether the input name has been found. The WHILE condition will be

WHILE FOUND$ = "NO" AND NAM$ <>"XYZ"

Fill in the blank in line 50.

```
10    INPUT "WHO ARE YOU LOOKING FOR"; WANT$
20    FOUND$ = "NO"
30    READ NAM$
40    WHILE FOUND$ = "NO"  AND NAM$ <> "XYZ"
50      IF NAM$ = WANT$ THEN _____
60      READ NAM$
70    WEND
80    IF FOUND$ = "YES"  THEN PRINT WANT$; " ON LIST"
                              ELSE PRINT WANT$; " NOT ON LIST"
90    DATA "ALCOTT", "SMITH", "SIMMS"
100   DATA "EWING", "BRETT", "XYZ"
110   END
```

ANSWER   Line 50 is IF NAM$ = WANT$ THEN FOUND$ = "YES"

REMARK: Note that FOUND$ is initialized to "NO" before the start of the loop, since the name has not been found. This allows the computer to enter the WHILE loop the first time.

Exercises

1. Write a program that will print the names of all the people who received a grade of A. Have the program also print the number of people receiving an A. For

   DATA "SNOW","A","BOND","B","FOSTER","C"
   DATA "HALL","B","JONES","A","XYZ","XYZ"

   the printout would be

SNOW
JONES
2 GOT AN A

2. Write a program tht will list the people who received an A for both semesters. Try it on the DATA list.

DATA "HEINZ","A","B","MORGAN","A","A","BOOLE","C","A"

DATA "TELER","A","A","PASCAL","D","B","LOCKHART","A","B"

DATA "FLAG","FLAG","FLAG"

3. Write a telephone number look-up program that allows the user to input a name. The printout will be either the telephone number of that person or the message that the input name is not on the DATA list.

DATA "BOND","545-1213","JONES","615-2222"

DATA "DERN","666-8152","LING","777-4444"

DATA "XYZ","XYZ"

4. Consider the program in which the user inputs a last name and receives as printout the first name of that person. Suppose that the DATA lines contained *three* SMITHS: JOHN, ED, and PETER. Which first name would be printed or would all three be printed?

5. Write a program so that when a name is input, the computer will give one of the three printouts [_____ RECEIVED AN A], [_____ DID NOT RECEIVE AN A], [_____ IS NOT ON THE DATA LIST]. Use the DATA line DATA "MINELLI","A","POE","B","RAND", "D","FLAG","FLAG". For example, for input of POE, the printout would be [POE DID NOT RECEIVE AN A].

6. In the program of Section 17.2, suppose that we had incorrectly used as line 60

IF NAM$ = WANT$ THEN PRINT NAM$;" ON LIST"

ELSE PRINT NAM$;" NOT ON LIST"

Describe what type of incorrect printout would result.

7. Write a single program so that when a last name is INPUT, the computer will print out either the first names of all the people with that last name or [NONE] if there are none. Use the following DATA lines:

DATA "JONES","TOM","NAMATH","JOE","JONES","ED"

DATA "BEAM","JIM","JONES","MARY","FLAG","FLAG"

Run it first inputting JONES; then run it inputting a name not on the list. Do not tolerate an error message.

★ 8. *Three Guesses to Answer a Multiplication Question—Finding 9×7.* Write such a program using a loop and beginning with lines

10 DATA 9,7

20 READ X,Y

Here are two typical runs:

```
WHAT  IS  9  TIMES  7
?64
     WRONG  TRY  AGAIN
?56
     WRONG  TRY  AGAIN
?54
THE  CORRECT  ANSWER  IS  63
```

```
WHAT  IS  9  TIMES  7
?72
     WRONG  TRY  AGAIN
?63
     VERY  GOOD
     YOU  GOT  IT  ON  GUESS  2
```

★ **9.** Modify the telephone number look-up program described in Exercise 3 so that the program asks whether the user wants to find the telephone number for an input name or the name that has an input phone number.

★ **10.** Using the mock Boolean variable method, rewrite the First and Last Names program of Section 17.3. (*Note:* Beware of being off by 1.)

Also see Appendix B, Exercises 8 and 9 for programs on prime numbers.

CHAPTER 18

Simulation, Coin Flipping, Dice Rolling, and the RND Function

Simulation involves an attempt to give a serviceable imitation of real events. For example, suppose you are asked to roll a pair of ordinary dice 5000 times and count the number of times you rolled 7 followed immediately by an 11. To perform the actual task will take approximately three hours. If, instead, you use a computer program to simulate the dice rolling, it takes approximately five minutes to type in the program and another few seconds to run it.

In business and industry, computer simulation is used for more serious purposes, ranging from various types of forecasting to the testing of specifications for new airplane designs. Obviously, it is much quicker, cheaper, and generally more desirable to find out through computer simulation that a new design for an airplane wing is faulty than to build the planes and have them crash.

The key to computer simulation is the **RND function**, which generates random numbers. By using appropriate expressions involving the RND function, we can cause simulated events to occur with the same frequencies as in the real world.

18.1 RND Function Produces Random* Decimals between 0 and 1

During the running of a program, each time the computer executes a statement containing RND, the computer will use a different random decimal

* Actually, the "random" numbers generated by a computer are "pseudorandom," since they are produced by a function rather than by the results of some random act.

between 0 and 1. Consider

```
10  FOR K=1 TO 3
20     PRINT RND
30  NEXT K
40  END
```

The printout could be the following three decimals:

```
.7151002
.683111
.4821425
```

18.2 Coin Flipping

A random decimal between 0 and 1 has a 50/50 chance of being less than .5. Here is a program that simulates flipping a coin 10 times. T stands for Tails, and H for Heads.

```
10  REM LESS THAN .5 WILL BE A HEAD
20  FOR FLIP=1 TO 10
30     IF RND<.5 THEN PRINT "H";
                 ELSE PRINT "T";
40  NEXT FLIP
50  END
```

The printout might be

```
TTHTTHHTHT
```

Here is why: For each flip, a different random decimal is used. If that decimal is less than .5, then PRINT "H"; is executed. Otherwise PRINT "T"; is executed. When FLIP = 1, the computer simulates the first flip. When FLIP = 2, the computer simulates the second flip, and so on. Note that the computer moves on to the next flip when it gets to line 40 NEXT FLIP. Note also that the effect of the semicolons is to keep the entire printout on the same line. In the above printout there were six tails and four heads.

PROBLEM   In the following program, note the use of the variables TAILS and HEADS as counters. Describe what this program will do.

```
10   TAILS=0 : HEADS=0
20   FOR FLIP=1 TO 20
30     IF RND<.5 THEN PRINT "T"; : TAILS=TAILS+1
                     ELSE PRINT "H"; : HEADS=HEADS+1
40   NEXT FLIP
50   PRINT
60   PRINT HEADS;"HEADS";TAILS;"TAILS"
70   END
```

ANSWER   The program will simulate flipping a coin 20 times. Not only will it print out the Ts and Hs of the individual flips, but it will also print out the final tally for heads and tails. The actual printout will be

```
TTHTTHHTHTHHHTTHHTHH
  11 HEADS 9 TAILS
```

Unfortunately *every* run of this program will produce 11 HEADS and 9 TAILS in *exactly the same order*. To obtain variety in the printouts, it is necessary to use the RANDOMIZE statement of the next section.

18.3 Using RANDOMIZE to Vary Results

The sequence of random decimals used in a program involving RND depends on a beginning value called a **seed**. Unless the computer is instructed otherwise, it will always start with the "standard seed."

```
10   FOR J=1 TO 3
20     PRINT RND
30   NEXT J
40   END
```

Every run produces the same printout. For some systems it will always be as shown in the printout below.

```
.7151002
.683111
.4821425
```

RANDOMIZE Allows User to Supply Seed

```
10   RANDOMIZE
20   FOR J=1 TO 3
30     PRINT RND
40   NEXT J
50   END
```

When this program is run, the computer will halt execution at line 10 with the prompt

```
RUN
RANDOM NUMBER SEED (-32768 TO 32767)?
```

To have the computer resume execution, type any number in the indicated range, such as 754, and hit the return key. The computer will use the number you supply as the seed for generating the three random decimals. In running this program again, if you type a different seed, the printout will be an entirely new list of three decimals.

Here are two sample runs:

```
RANDOM NUMBER SEED (-32768 TO 32767)? 754
.4116724
.2847395
.6032214
```

```
RANDOM NUMBER SEED (-32768 TO 32767)? 41
.5793818
.7698927
.1594805
```

QUESTION   What will the printout be for a run in which you input the seed 754?

ANSWER   The printout will be the same as it was for a previous input of the seed 754:

```
.4116724
.2847395
.6032214
```

More on Coin Flipping Program.   In order to vary the printouts on different runs of the program, include a RANDOMIZE statement at the beginning of the program. Then for each run of the program, select a different seed when the computer halts with the prompt

```
RANDOM NUMBER SEED (-32768 TO 32767)?
```

Using Internal Clock to Provide Seed.   If you use the computer's internal clock to provide the seed, you would use the following two lines in place of RANDOMIZE:

        10   S = VAL(RIGHT$(TIME$,2))
        20   RANDOMIZE S

This will cause the computer to use a seed based on the current time on the computer's internal clock. (The computer will not request a seed from you.)

▄▄▄▄ 18.4 INT Function

Recall that INT(X) truncates the fractional part of X for positive numbers.

> What is INT(.401341)? *Answer:* 0.
>
> What is INT(4*.401341)? *Answer:* 1, because 4*.401341 is approximately equal to 1.6, and when you truncate the fractional part you get 1.
>
> What is INT(9*.401341)? *Answer:* 3, because 9*.401341 is approximately 3.6.

A very important fine point about RND is that it is a number between but *not including* 0 and 1. Thus, RND is always a random number *less* than 1. Thus, 6*RND will be a random number less than 6 and greater than 0, because six times a number between 0 and 1 will be between 0 and 6. INT(6*RND) will be a random number from what list of numbers? *Answer:* It will be from the list 0, 1, 2, 3, 4, 5. (Note that since 6*RND is less than 6, the largest that INT(6*RND) can be is 5.)

▄▄▄▄ 18.5 Dice Rolling

Suppose you want to simulate rolling a six-sided die. You need to generate an integer from the set 1,2,3,4,5,6. As seen earlier, the expression INT(6*RND) produces one of six possible integers, but the smallest is 0 and the largest is 5. To obtain a set with 1 as the smallest and 6 as the largest, we add 1 to this expression. Thus, INT(6*RND) + 1 produces the set we need.

EXAMPLE   To simulate rolling a pair of dice, add two numbers of the form INT(6*RND) + 1. The following program will simulate rolling a pair of dice 100 times, counting separately the number of 7s and 8s rolled.

```
5    REM SEVENS AND EIGHTS
6    REM ****
10   RANDOMIZE
20   SEVENS=0
30   EIGHTS=0
40   FOR ROLL=1 TO 100
50      DIE1=INT(6*RND)+1
60      DIE2=INT(6*RND)+1
70      SUM=DIE1+DIE2
80      IF SUM=7 THEN SEVENS=SEVENS+1
90      IF SUM=8 THEN EIGHTS=EIGHTS+1
100  NEXT ROLL
110  PRINT "THERE WERE ";SEVENS; "SEVENS"
120  PRINT "THERE WERE ";EIGHTS; "EIGHTS"
130  END
```

A typical printout might be

```
RANDOM SEED (-32768 TO 32767)? 524
THERE WERE 16 SEVENS
THERE WERE 13 EIGHTS
```

REMARK: SUM = INT(11*RND)+2 will generate an integer from the list 2,3,4,5,6,7,8,9,10,11,12. However, it should *not* be used to simulate rolling a pair of dice. Exercise 8 explains this issue.

EXAMPLE   Write a program that will keep track of (a) the roll on which the first 11 occurs and (b) how many 7s had been rolled by that time. A typical printout might be

```
6  5  7  4  10  7  9  7  11
11 ON ROLL 9
WERE 3 SEVENS
```

PROGRAM IDEAS

We do not use a FOR-NEXT loop, since we do not know the number of rolls that will be needed.

```
5     REM  SEVENS  AND  ELEVEN
6     REM ****
10    RANDOMIZE
20    ROLLS=0  :  SEVENS=0
30    SUM=0
40    WHILE  SUM<>11
50       DIE1=INT(6*RND)+1
60       DIE2=INT(6*RND)+1
70       SUM=DIE1+DIE2
80       PRINT  SUM;
90 ·     ROLLS=ROLLS+1
100      IF  SUM=7  THEN  SEVENS=SEVENS+1
110   WEND
120   PRINT
130   PRINT  "11  ON  ROLL";ROLLS
140   PRINT  "WERE";SEVENS;"SEVENS"
150   END
```

REMARK: The exit value for SUM is a value that needs to be processed. We must print that value for SUM and increase ROLLS by 1. This is why the last line of the loop body is *not* SUM = DIE1 + DIE2.

▰▰▰ 18.6 Simulating Event with Decimal Probability

Suppose Larry Bird has an 83 percent probability of making a foul shot in basketball. The way to simulate his taking one foul shot is

> IF RND<.83 THEN PRINT "MADE IT"
>
>   ELSE PRINT "MISSED"

The reason that the test IF RND<.83 simulates an event with 83 percent probability is that a random decimal has a .83 probability of being between 0 and .83. Consider the diagram

QUESTION   Suppose that when Moe plays Ping-Pong with Curly, Moe has a 55 percent chance of winning any single point. How would you simulate one point being played?

ANSWER

> IF RND<.55 THEN "MOE WON"
>
>   ELSE "CURLY WON"

QUESTION   What is wrong with this program to simulate Moe and Curly playing *one* point? (See Exercise 18.)

```
10   RANDOMIZE
20   IF RND<.55 THEN PRINT "MOE WON THIS POINT"
30   IF RND>=.55 THEN PRINT "CURLY WON THIS POINT"
40   END
```

ANSWER   *Two* different random decimals will be used in lines 20 and 30. Thus, if the first random decimal is .813652 and the second is .416382, neither player wins the point. Similarly, both players might win the point.

PROBLEM   **Straight-11 Ping-Pong**   In straight-11 Ping-Pong the first player to reach 11 points wins; the player need not be ahead by 2. Write a program to simulate Moe and Curly playing one game of straight-11 Ping-Pong, in which Moe's probability of winning any given point is .55.

A typical printout after inputting a seed might be

```
MOE WON 11  8
```

PROGRAM IDEAS

Step 1. Initialize counters.

Step 2. Use a loop to keep playing points. Each execution of the loop body will play 1 point. Exit when one of the players reaches 11 points.

Step 3. Print the outcome.

Before reading on, try to write a refinement for these three steps; the program is given on the next page.

REFINEMENT

Step 1. MOE=0 : CURLY=0

Step 2. WHILE MOE<11 AND CURLY<11
        Play a point, increasing the counter for the winner of the point.
   WEND

Step 3. Print the outcome, using IF THEN-ELSE.

Try to write the program before reading on.

```
5    REM STRAIGHT 11 PING PONG
6    REM *****
10   RANDOMIZE
20   MOE=0  :  CURLY=0
30   WHILE MOE<11 AND CURLY<11
40      IF RND<.55 THEN MOE=MOE+1
                    ELSE CURLY=CURLY+1
50   WEND
60   IF MOE=11 THEN PRINT "MOE WON";MOE;CURLY
                    ELSE PRINT "CURLY WON";CURLY;MOE
70   END
```

In Exercise 18 you are asked to modify the above program so that it gives a running tally of the score during the game. A typical printout might be

```
MOE                CURLY
 1                  0
 2                  0
 2                  1
 3                  1
 .                  .
 .                  .
 .                  .
11                  8
MOE WON 11    8
```

Exercises

1. **(a)** Type the following program and run it three times.

```
20   FOR K=1 TO 2
30      S = INT(10*RND)
40      PRINT S;
50   NEXT K
60   END
```

(b) Add the line 10 RANDOMIZE and run the program five more times. The first *two* times, enter 542 as a seed. The next three times, enter three *different* seeds.

2. Write a program that will simulate rolling a pair of dice 100 times and will have a printout in the form SEVEN WAS ROLLED _____ TIMES

3. Write a program that will simulate flipping a coin 100 times and will produce one of these printouts, depending on which was the case. MORE HEADS THAN TAILS, MORE TAILS THAN HEADS, or SAME NUMBER OF HEADS AND TAILS

4. Write a program to simulate rolling a pair of dice 100 times. The printout should be of the form

```
5  WAS  ROLLED  _____  TIMES
8  WAS  ROLLED  _____  TIMES
SUM  WAS  AT  LEAST  6  _____  TIMES
```

5. Write a program that will simulate rolling a set of three dice 100 times and will have printout in the form

```
THIRTEEN  WAS  ROLLED  _____  TIMES
```

6. **(a)** If RND has the value .301042, what value will INT(8*RND) have?
   (b) Same question for INT(8*RND)+3.

7. INT(5*RND)+3 will generate a random integer from the list {3, 4, 5, 6, 7}. A way to see this is first to determine the smallest possible value of that expression and then to determine the largest. The smallest INT(5*RND)+3 can be is $0+3=3$. The largest INT(5*RND)+3 can be is $4+3=7$, since 5*RND is less than 5 and hence INT(5*RND) is at most 4.
   (a) INT(8*RND)+2 will generate a random integer from which list?
   (b) What expression should be used to generate a random integer from the list {4, 5, 6, 7, 8}?

8. Is INT(11*RND)+2 a random integer from the list 2, 3, 4, . . . , 12? Explain why it would not be suitable for simulating the rolling of a pair of dice.

9. For the following program, on the average, approximately how many times would you expect the number 3 to be printed?

```
10  FOR  K=1  TO  100
20     A=INT(5*RND)+1
30        PRINT  A
40  NEXT  K
50  END
```

★ **10.** Here are the rules for craps
   (a) If your first roll is 7 or 11, you win outright.
   (b) If your first roll is 2, 3, or 12, you lose outright.
   (c) If your first roll is any other number, then that number becomes your *point number*. You then keep rolling until you either roll a 7 or you

roll your point number. If you roll your point number first you win; if you roll 7 first you lose.

Write a program to play one game. Here are three illustrative printouts:

| 11   YOU WIN | or | 4 5 8 11 4   YOU WIN | or

| 6 4 9 5 12 5 8 4 3 7   YOU LOSE |

11. Write a program that will keep rolling a pair of dice until the third 7 is rolled. In addition to printing each individual roll, the printout should also give the roll on which the third 7 occurred, and how many 8s were rolled by then. (Don't use a FOR-NEXT loop, since you do not have an upper limit for the number of rolls.)

★ 12. (a) Write a program that simulates rolling a pair of dice until 7 is rolled twice in a row and that will print on which roll this occurred.

★★ (b) Write a program that will simulate rolling until 7 is rolled *three* times in a row and that will print out on which roll this occurred.

★★ 13. Write a program that will roll the dice 100 times and will print out the length of the longest run of consecutive 7s. For example, if the maximum number of 7s in a row is three, the printout will be | 3 |.

★ 14. Suppose you start with $200 and play the following game 100 times: You roll a pair of dice and if the roll is 7 or 11, you win $10; but if the roll is anything else, you lose $2. Write a program that will simulate playing this game (100 times) and will print out how much cash you have left at the end.

15. Smith has a .312 batting average. Write a program that simulates a World Series in which Smith has 26 official at-bats and that prints the number of hits he makes.

16. Morgan, Jones, and Hill have batting averages of .327, .301, and .210, respectively. Write a program that prints how many hits each makes in 28 official at-bats.

17. Modify the Straight-11 Ping-Pong program so that it gives a running tally of the score during the game.

18. What is wrong with the following method for trying to simulate Moe and Curly playing 1 point?

```
10  RANDOMIZE
20  IF RND<.55 THEN PRINT "MOE WON"
30  IF RND>=.55 THEN PRINT "CURLY WON"
40  END
```

Run this program 10 times with 10 different seeds. Explain what goes wrong.

★ **19.** Write a program to simulate Moe and Curly playing one *regular* 11-point game (player must win by at least 2 points), where Moe has .55 probability of winning any single point.

20. Write a program to simulate the Cardinals playing the Yankees in the World Series if the Cardinals have a .58 probability of winning any single game. (The first team to win four games wins.)

★★ **21.** Lord Lupner and Earl Edwards have a pistol duel at 20 paces. Lupner (who has a .32 chance of hitting Edwards each time he fires a shot) shoots first. If Lupner misses, Edwards (who has a .41 chance of hitting Lupner) will shoot. The two duelists will keep alternating shots until one of them hits his opponent. Write a program to simulate such a duel, and to print the winner.

★ **22.** A ski lodge operator has estimated that because of weather fluctuations, each year he has a 50% chance of losing $5000, a 25% chance of earning $1000, and a 25% chance of earning $7000. Simulate operation of the lodge for 20 years.

23. Also see Appendix B, Exercise 16 for a way to find an approximation for π.

24. Also see Appendix B, Exercise 29.

CHAPTER 19

Nested Loops

When one loop is completely contained within another, the loops are said to be **nested**. Nested loops are used to repeat a task a number of times when the task itself requires a loop. In this chapter we consider applications, such as finding each individual student's exam average in a class, and programs that involve repeating a simulation a large number of times. In later chapters we will use nested loops in connection with both sorting and the processing of two-dimensional tables.

19.1 Nested FOR-NEXT Loops

In the following example we have put a bracket around the **outer loop body**. The outer loop body will be executed for each value of I in its FOR statement; that is, the entire outer loop body will be executed with I fixed at 2, then with I fixed at 3, then with I fixed at 4. Note that for each fixed value of I, K takes on the value 6, then 7, then 8.

```
10  PRINT " I K PROD"
20  FOR I=2 TO 4
30    FOR K=6 TO 8
40      PRINT I;K;I*K
50    NEXT K
60    PRINT "HELLO"
70  NEXT I
80  END
```

The **inner loop body** consists entirely of line 40 in this program. It is indented further than the rest of the outer loop body for clarity. All nested loops will be similarly *indented*.

The printout will be

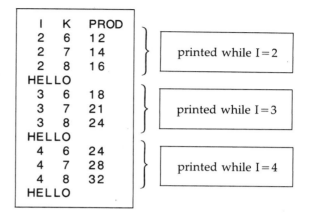

QUESTION What will the printouts be for the following three programs? [You might find it helpful to put a bracket around the outer loop body. We have done so for program (a).]

(a)

```
10   FOR N=7 TO 8
20      PRINT "HELLO"
30      FOR K=3 TO 5
40         PRINT N;K
50      NEXT K
60   NEXT N
70   PRINT "JOE"
80   END
```

(b)

```
10   COUNT=0
20   FOR N=1 TO 3
30      FOR J=7 TO 8
40         PRINT N;J
50         COUNT=COUNT+1
60      NEXT J
70   NEXT N
80   PRINT COUNT
90   END
```

(c)

```
10   FOR N=1 TO 3
20      COUNT=0
30      FOR J=7 TO 8
40         PRINT N;J
50         COUNT=COUNT+1
60      NEXT J
70      PRINT COUNT
80   NEXT N
90   END
```

ANSWER   The printouts are

(a)
```
HELLO
   7   3
   7   4
   7   5
HELLO
   8   3
   8   4
   8   5
JOE
```

(b)
```
1   7
1   8
2   7
2   8
3   7
3   8
6
```

(c)
```
1   7
1   8
2
2   7
2   8
2
3   7
3   8
2
```

Note that in program (b), the counter is initialized before the outer loop. It will have its value increased by 1 six times by the time line 80 is reached. Thus, 6 is printed for COUNT. By contrast, in program (c), COUNT is initialized within the outer loop. Thus, for each new value of N, COUNT is reset at 0 and then increased by 1, twice. Thus, 2 is printed each time in line 70.

19.2   Nested FOR-NEXT Loop Applications

Nested FOR-NEXT loops are useful when you want to *repeat* a certain number of times some process that itself involves a FOR-NEXT loop. The process might be an *experiment*, a *calculation*, or an *analysis*. The outer loop FOR statement should be FOR (variable) = 1 TO (however many times you want to repeat this process). The outer loop body should perform this process once.

PROBLEM   **Grade Averaging**   Each of the following three DATA lines gives the exam scores on five exams for a different student:

DATA 75,85,85,80,75

DATA 90,90,90,85,95

DATA 80,80,80,80,70

Write a program that will compute each student's average. The printout should be in the form

```
STUDENT         AVERAGE
   1              80
   2              90
   3              78
```

PROGRAM IDEAS

Step 1. Print heading

Step 2. FOR STUDENT = 1 TO 3

for a single student, compute the sum of five exams, and print the average.

NEXT STUDENT

This program will involve nested loops, since we will use a loop to compute a sum of five exams. The outer loop FOR statement will be FOR STUDENT = 1 TO 3, since we want to perform a certain calculation three times—once for each student.

Here is the program. Fill in lines 70 and 80.

```
5     REM GRADE AVERAGE FOR EACH OF 3 STUDENTS
6     REM ****
10    PRINT  "STUDENT" , "AVERAGE"
20    FOR STUDENT=1  TO  3
30       SUM=0
40       FOR  EXAM=1  TO  5
50          READ GRADE
60          SUM=SUM+GRADE
70          _____
80       _____
90    NEXT  STUDENT
100   DATA 75,85,85,80,75
110   DATA 90,90,90,85,95
120   DATA 80,80,80,80,70
130   END
```

ANSWER

70   NEXT EXAM

80   PRINT STUDENT,SUM/5

REMARK: The previous program provides an example in which reliance on automatic initialization would result in an incorrect program. Recall that if line 30 were omitted from the program, the computer would automatically use the value 0 for SUM, the *first* time SUM is used to evaluate the expression on the right side in line 60. Nevertheless, the program with line 30 omitted would give an incorrect printout. Can you detect the trouble? See Exercise 6.

19.3 Nested Loops Need Not Be FOR-NEXT Loops

In this next example, the outer loop is FOR-NEXT and the loop within is WHILE/WEND.

QUESTION   What will the printout be?

```
100   FOR LINE=1 TO 3
110      COUNT=0
120      READ NUM
130      WHILE NUM<>-1
140         COUNT=COUNT+1
150         READ NUM
160      WEND
170      PRINT COUNT
180   NEXT LINE
190   DATA 2,8,12,15,9,14,18,-1
200   DATA 4,9,28,12,18,-1
210   DATA 2,5,29,13,-1
220   END
```

ANSWER   The FOR-NEXT loop body, lines 110–170, will be executed three times. Each time COUNT starts out at 0. The WHILE loop counts the number of nonflag data numbers on a DATA line (it terminates when it reaches the -1 flag). The printout will be

```
7
5
4
```

19.4 Nested Loops to Repeat Simulations

PROBLEM   **Repeating a Coin-Flipping Experiment**   If you flip a coin 10 times, how likely is it that there will be exactly 5 heads? Write a program that will perform 100 repetitions of this experiment, and then print the number of times in the 100 tries that there were exactly 5 heads.

PROGRAM IDEAS

The outer loop FOR statement should be FOR REP = 1 TO 100, since we want to repeat the experiment 100 times. Here is a rough outline:

Step 1. EXACTLY5 = 0

Step 2. FOR REP = 1 TO 100

        flip a coin 10 times; if there were exactly 5 heads, then increase EXACTLY5 by 1.

        NEXT REP

Step 3. Print number of times 5 heads were achieved.

Fill in lines 50 and 90 to complete the program.

```
5     REM REPEATING COIN FLIPPING EXPERIMENT
6     REM ****
10    RANDOMIZE
20    REM EXACTLY5 COUNTS # OF SUCCESSES
30    EXACTLY5=0
40    FOR REP=1 TO 100
50    _____
60      FOR FLIP=1 TO 10
70        IF RND<.5 THEN HEADS=HEADS+1
80      NEXT FLIP
90    _____
100   NEXT REP
110   PRINT "EXACTLY 5 HEADS";EXACTLY5;"TIMES"
120   END
```

ANSWER Line 50 should be HEADS = 0, since at the start of each experiment of flipping a coin 10 times, the counter for heads should be set at 0. Line 90 should be IF HEADS = 5 THEN EXACTLY5 = EXACTLY5 + 1, because each time 10 flips are concluded, the program tests whether there were exactly 5 heads.

PROBLEM Write a program to simulate Moe and Curly playing 4 games of straight-11 Ping-Pong; in straight-11, the first player to reach 11 points wins. Assume Moe has a .55 probability of winning any given point. A typical printout might be

```
MOE WON 11   8
MOE WON 11   6
CURLY WON 11   9
MOE WON 11   10
```

HINT: The outer loop should be controlled by FOR GAME = 1 TO 4. The body of the center loop should simulate the playing of one game. Fill in line 70.

```
5    REM  FOUR  GAMES  OF  STRAIGHT-11
6    REM  ****
10   RANDOMIZE
20   FOR  GAME=1  TO  4
30     MOE=0  :  CURLY=0
40     WHILE  MOE<11  AND  CURLY<11
50       IF  RND<.55  THEN  MOE=MOE+1
                      ELSE  CURLY=CURLY+1
60     WEND
70     IF  MOE=11  THEN  _____
                   ELSE  _____
80   NEXT  GAME
90   END
```

ANSWER

THEN PRINT "MOE WON";MOE;CURLY

ELSE PRINT "CURLY WON";CURLY;MOE

19.5 Variable Limits

Variable Upper Limit. What will the printout be for the following program? Note that the inner loop FOR statement has a variable limit.

```
10   FOR  N=2  TO  4
20     FOR  K=1  TO  N
30       PRINT  N;K
40     NEXT  K
50   NEXT  N
60   END
```

ANSWER The printout will be

```
2  1
2  2
3  1
3  2
3  3
4  1
4  2
4  3
4  4
```

When N = 2, line 20 will have the same effect as FOR K = 1 TO 2. When N = 3, line 20 will have the same effect as FOR K = 1 TO 3. When N = 4, what effect will line 20 have? *Answer:* FOR K = 1 TO 4.

Variable Lower Limit.

PROBLEM Write a program to list all pairs (N,K) with N and K integers ≤6 and N≤K. The printout should be of the form

1	1	1	2	1	3	1	4	1	5
1	6	2	2	2	3	2	4	2	5
2	6	3	3	3	4	3	5	3	6
4	4	4	5	4	6	5	5	5	6
6	6								

ANSWER (Note that we are assuming there are five print zones to a line.)

```
10   FOR N=1 TO 6
20      FOR K=N TO 6
30         PRINT N;K,
40      NEXT K
50   NEXT N
60   END
```

Exercises

1. What will the printouts be?

(a)
```
10   FOR N=2 TO 4
20      FOR K=1 TO 3
30         PRINT N;N*K
40      NEXT K
50      PRINT "HI"
60   NEXT N
70   END
```

(b)
```
10   COUNT=0
20   FOR N=3 TO 5
30      FOR J=2 TO 4
40         IF N*J>8 THEN COUNT=COUNT+1
50      NEXT J
60   NEXT N
70   PRINT COUNT
80   END
```

(c) What would be the printout in program (b) if it contained line 25 COUNT = 0?

2. Write a single program that will print out four copies of the following table:

```
16  SQUARED  EQUALS  256
17  SQUARED  EQUALS  289
 .                    .
 .                    .
 .                    .
20  SQUARED  EQUALS  400
```

3. Using the same DATA as in the Grades program of Section 19.2, modify the program so that it will also print the average for all three students.

★ 4. Using the same data as in the Grades program of Section 19.2, produce the printout

```
STUDENT          NO.  OF  GRADES
                 OVER  80
   1                2
   2                5
   3                0
```

★ 5. Write a program for three DATA lines, with each DATA line terminating with the flag −1, so that the printout will be the separate line sums. Run your program with

      DATA 5,8,24,17,19,14,-1

      DATA 3,22,15,-1

      DATA 10,18,14,5,18,-1

The printout will be

```
LINE  1    SUM=  87
LINE  2    SUM=  40
LINE  3    SUM=  65
```

6. In the Grade Averaging program for several students (Section 19.2), what would the printout be if line 30 were omitted from the program?

7. Write a program that will perform 15 times, the experiment of flipping a coin 10 times (the coin will be flipped 150 times), and will have a printout of 15 lines in the form

```
┌─────────────────────────────────────────────┐
│  THERE  WERE  _____  HEADS  THIS  TIME       │
│  THERE  WERE  _____  HEADS  THIS  TIME       │
│  THERE  WERE  _____  HEADS  THIS  TIME       │
│        .                      .               │
│        .                      .               │
│        .                      .               │
│  THERE  WERE  _____  HEADS  THIS  TIME       │
└─────────────────────────────────────────────┘
```

★ **8.** Write a program that will perform 100 times the experiment of flipping a coin 10 times. The printout should have one line and be in the form

```
┌────────────────────────────────────────────────┐
│  THERE  WERE  EXACTLY  FOUR  HEADS  _____  TIMES │
└────────────────────────────────────────────────┘
```

★ **9.** Jones has a .327 batting average. Write a program that will simulate Jones playing in 50 games, with 4 official at-bats in each game. Have the printout be of the form

```
┌──────────────────────────────────────────────────┐
│  JONES  GOT  AT  LEAST  2  HITS  IN  _____  GAMES │
└──────────────────────────────────────────────────┘
```

★ **10.** Jones has a .327 batting average. Simulate Jones playing in 50 games, with 4 official at-bats in each game. Format the printout as follows:

```
┌──────────────────────────────┐
│  # OF HITS        # OF GAMES  │
│     0                 9       │
│     1                21       │
│     2                14       │
│     3                 5       │
│     4                 1       │
└──────────────────────────────┘
```

★ **11. (a)** Write a program to simulate Moe and Curly playing 100 games of straight-11 Ping-Pong, where Moe has a .55 probability of winning any given point. A typical printout might be

```
┌──────────────────────────────────┐
│  MOE WON  71    CURLY WON  29      │
└──────────────────────────────────┘
```

(b) To whose advantage would it be if they played straight-21 Ping-Pong?

★ **12.** Suppose the Knicks and the Lakers are playing a championship series; the first team to win four games will win the series. If the Knicks have a .42 probability of winning any single game, what is the probability of the Knicks winning the series? Rather than using probability theory to give an exact answer, estimate the answer by running a program to play 100 such series.

★ **13.** Write a program to simulate starting with $5 and playing craps for $1 per game so that you keep playing until you either have $10 or you have $0. Here is a typical printout:

```
$5  $4  $5  $4  $3  $2  $3  $4  $3  $2  $1  $0
```

14. What will the printout be?

```
10  FOR  M=1  TO  5
20      FOR  K=1  TO  M
30          PRINT  "*";
40      NEXT  K
50      PRINT
60  NEXT  M
70  END
```

★ **15.** Write a program so that on a system with five print zones it will produce the following printout:

```
1 2     1 3     1 4     1 5     1 6
2 3     2 4     2 5     2 6     3 4
3 5     3 6     4 5     4 6     5 6
```

Note that for each pair (N,K), N is less than K.

★★ **16. (a)** Write a program to find the sum $1! + 2! + 3! + \ldots + 7!$
   (b) Modify it to find $1! + 2! + 3! + \ldots + 9!$

17. Also see Appendix B, Exercises 10–14 and 18–28.

18. Also see Appendix B, Exercise 17, for Ulam's hypothesis.

CHAPTER
20
Arrays: Subscripted Variables

Arrays are often used in processing a long list of data. In this chapter we consider two different types of situations in which arrays are useful: when a large number of related summing or counting variables is needed and when a data list must be processed more than once.

▰▰ 20.1 Problem Using Arrays

PROBLEM **January Sales Program** Suppose that a sloppy store owner kept all his sales receipts for the month of January stuffed in a cigar box and wanted to know the total sales for each day in January. He might type in DATA lines as follows:

```
180   DATA 5,214,3,312,28,250,7,208,3,115
190   DATA . . .
  ⋮      ⋮
290   DATA −1,−1
```

where lines 190 through 280 are DATA lines similar to line 180 and the last DATA pair is a flag. Each of the nonflag DATA pairs represents one receipt that consists of the date in January and a sales figure reported by one of his salespersons. For example, the first DATA pair represents a sales figure from January 5 of $214, the second pair a sales figure from January 3 of $312, and so on. Note that the DATA pairs are *not* in chronological order. Also note that for any given date there might be several DATA pairs with a sales figure for that date, since several salespersons are employed. For example, two figures for January 3 ($312 and $115) are listed in line 180.

The desired printout is as follows:

```
JANUARY              TOTAL  SALES
   1                 $  1146
   2                 $  1284
   3                 $  1592
   .                    .
   .                    .
   .                    .
  31                 $  1486
```

PROGRAM IDEAS

We would like to use a WHILE loop to read through the entire list of DATA. This is what we would need to do before, during, and after the loop.

Before   Initialize one summing variable for each date of the month to 0.
Prime the pump.

During   WHILE DATE <> −1
Add the sales figure to the appropriate summing variable for each date.
READ the next DATA pair.
WEND

After   Print the heading.
Print out each date and its corresponding summing variable.

A Cumbersome Method.   Without the use of arrays, looping in this manner would require a very cumbersome program because you would need 31 different summing variables, such as JAN1,JAN2,JAN3,...,JAN31. This means

1. You would need 31 assignment statements just to initialize the variables.

2. Your loop body would require 31 different IF-THEN tests, as follows:

```
390   READ DATE,SALES
400   WHILE DATE <>−1
410      IF DATE=1 THEN  JAN1=JAN1+SALES
420      IF DATE=2 THEN  JAN2=JAN2+SALES
 .            .
 .            .
 .            .
710      IF DATE=31 THEN  JAN31=JAN31+SALES
720      READ DATE,SALES
730   WEND
```

3. You would need 31 different PRINT statements to print out each of the 31 sums; for example, 790 PRINT 5,"$";JAN5.

As you will see, the use of arrays makes it much easier to solve this problem.

20.2 Arrays

An array can be envisioned as an apartment building. The name of the array would represent the name of the building. Each of the building's apartments (called **elements** of the array) would therefore have a corresponding apartment number (called the **subscript**, or **index**, of that element).

Each element of an array can be represented as a **subscripted variable**. For example, apartment 3 in the apartment building named RISER would be written RISER(3). A subscripted variable consists of an array name followed by a positive integer in parentheses. (We discuss only numeric arrays in this chapter, and therefore the array name can be any acceptable numeric variable name. String arrays are discussed in Chapter 21.) S(3), RISER(1), and JAN(18) are valid subscripted variables.

Array elements function in the same way as memory boxes of simple variables. In fact, an array can be envisioned as a group of memory boxes related by a common name. The contents of an array element will be the current value of that element. When an element receives a new value, the old value is erased and replaced by the new one. Therefore, PRINT RISER(3) will print the current value, or contents, of element 3 in the array RISER.

QUESTION   What will the printouts be?

(a)
```
10   X(1)=8
20   X(2)=5
30   X(3)=9
40   X(4)=7
50   PRINT X(3)
60   PRINT X(2)
70   END
```

(b)
```
10   SCORE(1)=94
20   SCORE(2)=76
30   SCORE(1)=52
40   PRINT SCORE(1)
50   PRINT SCORE(2)
60   END
```

ANSWER   (a)
```
9
5
```

(b)
```
52
76
```

REMARKS

1. By the time the PRINT statements of program (a) are reached, lines 10–40 have filled elements 1 through 4 of the array X as follows:

8	X (1)
5	X (2)
9	X (3)
7	X (4)

2. Notice that line 30 of program (b) has replaced the old value of the first element (formerly 94) with a new value of 52. When the PRINT statements are reached, elements 1 and 2 of SCORE are as follows:

| 52 | SCORE (1) |
| 76 | SCORE (2) |

Better Method, Using the Array JAN.   No longer do we need 31 different summing variables to represent the 31 days of January. Instead, we can have one array, called JAN, that uses elements numbered 1 through 31. We would, therefore, refer to each sum as JAN(1), JAN(2), and so on up to JAN(31). We need the DIM statement to do this.

DIM Statement.   DIM statements are used to reserve memory space for arrays. The dimension of an array is the largest possible subscript it can have. Therefore, the dimension of JAN would be 31. The statement 10 DIM JAN(31) informs the computer that the dimension of the array JAN is 31. This line should be located before the first use of a subscripted variable in JAN. It will set aside elements JAN(0),JAN(1),...,JAN(31) for our use.

Automatic DIM.   If the dimension of an array A is not declared in a DIM statement, the computer will automatically assign it dimension 10 and set aside elements A(0),A(1),...A(10). The two drill programs given earlier in this chapter rely on the automatic DIM to set aside space for X and SCORE. If in a program the computer comes to a statement with a subscript larger than the dimension of the array, then the computer will halt with the error message ⌐SUBSCRIPT OUT OF RANGE⌐.

EXAMPLE   This faulty program will produce the following error message as printout:

```
10  X(15)=4
20  PRINT X(15)
30  END
```

Printout

```
SUBSCRIPT  OUT  OF  RANGE  IN  10
```

Using Variable Subscripts and FOR-NEXT Loops. What makes arrays so powerful and our January Sales program easier to write is the fact that the subscript of a subscripted variable can be a variable or even an expression. For example, the current value of I determines which element X(I) represents in X; if I = 3, then X(I) is the same as X(3). Similarly, if I = 3, X(I + 2) is the same as X(5).

This feature of variable subscripts allows us to use FOR-NEXT loops to assign values to and manipulate arrays, because the *control variable can be used* to determine the subscript.

For example, we can use the following loop in our program to initialize each element of the array JAN to 0. Recall that if we still had 31 ordinary variables instead of an array, we would need 31 assignment statements to do this (unless you were lazy and resorted to the poor style of automatic initialization, which you could not have done if you wished to initialize to a non-zero value).

```
30  FOR I=1 TO 31
40     JAN(I)=0
50  NEXT I
```

In our program, we also use a FOR-NEXT loop to print the table of dates and total sales, instead of using the 31 PRINT statements we would need if we were not using arrays.

QUESTION   What will the printouts be for the following three programs?

(a)
```
10  DATA 7,13,24,8,9,4
20  FOR J=1 TO 6
30     READ A(J)
40  NEXT J
50  PRINT A(5)
60  PRINT A(3)
70  END
```

(b)
```
10  DATA 5,7,43
20  FOR K=1 TO 3
30     READ P(K)
40  NEXT K
50  PRINT P(1)
60  PRINT P(2)+1
70  PRINT P(2+1)
80  END
```

(c)

```
10  FOR I=1 TO 5
20     A(I)=I*I
30  NEXT I
40  FOR N=3 TO 5
50     PRINT A(N)
60  NEXT N
70  END
```

ANSWER   In program (a), the printout is

```
9
24
```

The six DATA values are assigned to the elements A(1), A(2), A(3), A(4), A(5), and A(6), respectively.

In program (b), the printout is

```
5
8
43
```

In line 60, $P(2)+1$ equals 8, since $P(2)=7$. Line 70 has the same effect as PRINT P(3).

In program (c), the printout is

```
9
16
25
```

The FOR-NEXT loop with N as control variable causes the computer to print the contents of A(3), A(4), and A(5).

20.3 Accessing Appropriate Element

As we have seen, the use of variables as subscripts enables us to access any individual element, in order either to assign a new value to it (such as initialize it to 0) or to find out its current value (such as with a PRINT statement).

QUESTION   Suppose the elements 1 through 3 of the array C were initialized to 0 before line 50 was reached below. What will be the effect of the following four program lines?

```
50  C(2)=C(2)+1
60  C(3)=C(3)+1
70  C(1)=C(1)+1
80  C(1)=C(1)+1
```

ANSWER   Each of the three elements acts as a counting variable.

Line 50 will add 1 to the value of the second element, making it 1.

Line 60 increments the third element by 1, making it 1 as well.

Line 70 adds 1 to C(1), also making it 1.

Line 80 adds 1 to C(1), changing it from 1 to 2.

By the end of this program segment, the array C will look like this:

2	C(1)
1	C(2)
1	C(3)

QUESTION   Suppose the elements 1 through 3 of C equal 0 when the following program segments are reached. What will the following program segments do?

(a)
```
50    N=2
60    C(N)=C(N)+1
70    N=3
80    C(N)=C(N)+1
90    N=1
100   C(N)=C(N)+1
110   N=1
120   C(N)=C(N)+1
```

(b)
```
50    READ N
60    WHILE N<>999
70       C(N)=C(N)+1
80       READ N
90    WEND
100   DATA 2,3,1,1,999
```

ANSWER   They will both accomplish the same results as the previous program.

Program segment (a) simply uses the variable N as the subscript of C, assigning the appropriate value to N before each use of N as a subscript.

Program segment (b) assigns the appropriate values to N by using a WHILE loop to read them from a DATA line, eliminating the need to type the statement C(N)=C(N)+1 for each new value of N.

Replacing 31 IF-THEN Tests with Single Statement.   Now consider the 31 IF-THEN tests in the WHILE loop body of the cumbersome version of the January Sales program, beginning with the line

IF DATE = 1 THEN JAN1 = JAN1 + SALES

and continuing until the final test

IF DATE = 31 THEN JAN31 = JAN31 + SALES.

These 31 lines serve only to determine the *appropriate* summing variable—based on the value of DATE—and add SALES to that summing variable. All this can be done with just one statement, using the variable DATE as the subscript of JAN.

Here it is

JAN(DATE) = JAN(DATE) + SALES

This will work because, using the value of DATE, we will add the value of SALES to the appropriate element of JAN.

QUESTION   Here is the solution to the January Sales program. Fill in line 150.

```
5     REM JANUARY SALES
6     REM ****
10    DIM JAN(31)
20    REM INITIALIZE ARRAY
30    FOR I=1 TO 31
40       JAN(I)=0
50    NEXT I
60    REM PROCESS DATA
70    READ DATE,SALES
80    WHILE DATE<>-1
90       JAN(DATE)=JAN(DATE)+SALES
100      READ DATE,SALES
110   WEND
120   REM PRINT RESULTS
130   PRINT "JANUARY","TOTAL SALES"
140   FOR I=1 TO 31
150   _____
160   NEXT I
170   REM DATA LIST
180   DATA 5,314,3,312,28,250,7,208,3,115
190   DATA ...
  :      :
  :      :
  :      :
290   DATA -1,-1
300   END
```

ANSWER Line 150 should be PRINT I,"$";JAN(I) because I represents the dates 1 through 31, and therefore is used as the subscript for the appropriate element of JAN as well.

PROBLEM **Vote Counting** Suppose the DATA line in the following program represents votes for candidates 1, 2, or 3. The array CANDIDATE is used to count the total number of votes for each of the three candidates. Fill in line 70 so that the appropriate element will be increased by 1 when a vote for that candidate is read. The printout will be

CANDIDATE	NO. OF VOTES
1	7
2	4
3	4

```
5    REM VOTE COUNTING
6    REM ****
10   DATA 1,1,2,1,2,1,1,1,2,1,2,3,3,3,3,999
20   FOR I=1 TO 3
30      CANDIDATE(I)=0
40   NEXT I
50   READ VOTE
60   WHILE VOTE<>999
70   _____
80      READ VOTE
90   WEND
100  PRINT "CANDIDATE","NO. OF VOTES"
110  FOR I=1 TO 3
120     PRINT I,CANDIDATE(I)
130  NEXT I
140  END
```

ANSWER Line 70 should be

CANDIDATE(VOTE) = CANDIDATE(VOTE) + 1

20.4 Storing Data for Reuse

Often it is necessary to use arrays to store data that will be reused by the program. The following program shows the usefulness of arrays in this regard.

PROBLEM   **Finding Grades above the Class Average**   Suppose that there are five students in a class and their grades on an exam are given in the DATA line. We wish to write a program that will print how many students scored above the class average. We could follow the following steps:

1. Find the sum of the grades.
2. Compute the average.
3. Count how many students scored above the average.
4. Print that result.

Fill in lines 70 and 120 so that the program produces the correct results.

```
5    REM GRADES ABOVE AVERAGE
6    REM ****
10   DATA 85,72,90,75,78
20   CLASS=5
30   DIM GRADE(CLASS)
40   SUM=0
50   FOR STUDENT=1 TO CLASS
60      READ GRADE(STUDENT)
70      _____
80   NEXT STUDENT
90   AVERAGE=SUM/CLASS
100  COUNT=0
110  FOR STUDENT=1 TO CLASS
120     IF _____
130  NEXT STUDENT
140  PRINT COUNT;"STUDENTS WERE ABOVE"
150  PRINT "THE AVERAGE OF ";AVERAGE
160  END
```

Printout

```
2 STUDENTS WERE ABOVE THE AVERAGE OF 80
```

ANSWER   Line 70 should be SUM=SUM+GRADE(STUDENT). Line 120 should be IF GRADE(STUDENT)>AVERAGE THEN COUNT=COUNT+1.

REMARKS
1. Note that each grade is placed *directly* into GRADE by the READ statement of the first loop, and that this value is added to SUM.
2. Also note that the values in GRADE are reused to find the count in the second loop. If we did not have arrays, we would have to RESTORE the

data pointer and reread the data in the second loop. Exercise 13 uses this method. (In programs of future chapters, it will not be possible to use RESTORE at all times, since the order of the values may change.)

3. This program could have relied on automatic DIM, since there are only five elements used. However, the DIM statement in line 30 is included for good style. Since the dimension of GRADE is based on the value of CLASS, the program could be changed to accept grades for a class with more than 10 students simply by changing line 20.

20.5 Linear Search of Array

Suppose a list of numbers is stored in elements A(1) through A(50), where the array A has dimension 50. The following program segment asks the user to input a number. The printout either will state the index for the box in which the requested number is located or will give the message that the number is not in the list.

QUESTION   Fill in the blank in line 120 with the correct symbol—is it $<$ or $<=$?

HINT: The dimension of the array A is 50.

```
100   INPUT "TYPE NUMBER TO BE LOOKED FOR"; L
110   J = 1
120   WHILE A(J)<>L AND J _____ 50
130      J = J + 1
140   WEND
150   IF A(J)=L THEN PRINT L; "IS IN BOX"; J
              ELSE PRINT L; "NOT ON LIST"
```

ANSWER   We do not want to enter the loop if the index J has the value 50, because J will then be increased to 51 in the loop. This would cause a SUBSCRIPT OUT OF RANGE error message the next time line 120 is encountered. Thus the correct line 120 is WHILE A(J)<>L AND J<50.

Using Zero Element.   You may recall that the DIM statement sets aside elements starting at zero. For example, DIM X(10) sets aside X(0) through X(10). However, the programs we have seen have ignored the element 0. Rather than waste this element, we may use it instead to hold a value that is in some way representative of the array. For example, the zero element may hold the value of the sum, or the average, of the elements of the array. More commonly, it will be used as a header to represent how many elements, beginning at 1, are currently being *used* in the array, although a DIM statement may allow for more. Other uses may become apparent in later chapters dealing with string arrays and two-dimensional arrays.

Exercises

1. Write a program so that for a DATA line consisting of the exam grades of the six students in a class, the printout will be the class average and each grade that was above the average.

2. Suppose that in the vote-counting program the variables A, B, and C have been used to keep track of the votes for candidates 1, 2, and 3, respectively. Replace line 70 by three lines that will ensure that the appropriate counter is incremented.

3. Write a program that will count and print out the totals for eight candidates. Run it with the following data:

   DATA 7,3,5,7,4,1,2,2,8,7,1,6,1,7,1,6,1,7
   DATA 7,3,7,7,3,1,2,6,4,7,8,7,5,7,4,2,3,7,999

4. Using the same DATA lines as in the previous exercise, write a program with printout of the form

CANDIDATE	NO. OF VOTES	PERCENT
1	6	16.6666
2	4	11.1111
:	:	:
:	:	:
8		

5. Write an inventory program that computes how many of each item are sold. Each pair of numbers in the following DATA line gives the Item I.D. Number and Quantity Sold, respectively, for a single order.

   DATA 101,8,103,4,102,6,101,7,104,9,103,1
   DATA 104,5,101,7,102,3,104,6,999,999

   For example, the pair 101,8 means that eight of Item #101 were sold. The DATA line ends with a flag. There are four items, numbered 101 to 104. The printout should be as follows:

```
ITEM  I.D.#        QUANTITY  SOLD
 101                    22
 102                     9
 103                     5
 104                    19
```

6. Write a program to roll a pair of dice 100 times and print the number of times each outcome occurred.

```
 2   WAS  ROLLED  1  TIMES
 3   WAS  ROLLED  4  TIMES
 .
 .
12   WAS  ROLLED  2  TIMES
```

★ 7. Complete line 20 of this program so that the printout will be as follows:

```
10   FOR  K=1  TO  4
20      PRINT  "BETWEEN"; (10*K)+1; _____
30   NEXT  K
40   END
```

```
BETWEEN  11  AND  20
BETWEEN  21  AND  30
BETWEEN  31  AND  40
BETWEEN  41  AND  50
```

★ 8. Suppose that on a certain exam all the students received a grade of at least 10, and that their respective scores are given in the DATA line. Write a program that will count how many grades there are in each 10-point interval. Run it with

DATA 29,38,12,51,62,59,18,21,17,95,18,83,37,999

The printout should be of the form

```
4   GRADES  BETWEEN  10  AND  19
2   GRADES  BETWEEN  20  AND  29
.
.
1   GRADES  BETWEEN  90  AND  99
```

(*Hint:* The grade 29 is in the second grade interval. How can you determine which interval a grade X is in?)

★ 9. Write a program using subscripted variables so that if each of two DATA lines contains four numbers, the computer will print the first number from the first line, the first number from the second line, and so on (alternating).

> DATA 2,7,9,6
>
> DATA 41,63,52,8

Thus, for the above two DATA lines the printout will be

2	41	7	63	9	52	6	8

10. Write a program so that for any DATA line consisting of seven numbers the printout will reverse their order in the DATA line. For DATA 8,5,13,2,4,4,9 the printout should be

9	4	4	2	13	5	8

11. Modify the Grades-above-Average program so that a header value at the beginning of the DATA is used to represent how many scores there are in the DATA list.

12. Rewrite the Grades-above-Average program *without* using subscripted variables; use instead the RESTORE statement.

★ 13. Using the following data:

> 10   REM TAX RATES FOR BRACKETS 1 THROUGH 5
> 20   DATA .25,.22,.16,.14,.10
> 30   REM EACH TRIPLE: NAME, TAX BRACKET, INCOME
> 40   DATA "JONES",3,12000,"WEST",2,20000,"CARR",2,21000
> 50   DATA "ADAMS",1,42000,"BOND",5,6000
> 60   DATA "BOOTH",4,8000,"FLAG",999,999

write a program with printout of the form

NAME	INCOME	TAX RATE	TAX
JONES	12000	.16	1920
WEST	20000	.22	4400
.	.	.	.
.	.	.	.

(*Hint:* In the first part of the program, read the tax rates into RATE(1) through RATE(5).)

★ **14.** The first 10 Fibonacci numbers are 1, 1, 2, 3, 5, 8, 13, 21, 34, 55. Each Fibonacci number (greater than one) is the sum of the 2 previous Fibonacci numbers.

   (a) What is the eleventh Fibonacci number?

   (b) Complete this program, which stores the first 25 Fibonacci numbers in an array and then prints them.

```
10  DIM F(25)
20  F(1)=1
30  _____
40  FOR K=3 TO 25
50
60
 .
 .
```

15. (a) Suppose that NUM is an array containing 25 numbers. Write a program fragment that will print the largest number and its location. Your program may assume that there is no tie.

★ **(b)** Rewrite your program fragment so that if there is a tie, your program will also state how many co-winners there are and give their locations.

★ **16.** Write a program that counts and prints out how many of the eight numbers in the first DATA line are also in the second DATA line.

   DATA 13,72,16,45,19,26,22,87

   DATA 41,13,54,72,25,22,88,47

   For this particular data the printout should be $\boxed{3}$, because 13, 72, 22 are also in the second DATA line.

   (*Hint:* First read the first DATA line numbers into boxes A(1) through A(8). Then read the second DATA line numbers into boxes B(1) through B(8) by using separate FOR-NEXT loops.)

17. Also see Appendix B, Exercises 31–33.

18. Also see Appendix B, Exercises 34–37 for the Sieve of Eratosthenes.

CHAPTER 21

Subscripted String Variables

We have seen that subscripted variables such as A(1), X(J), and GRADE(J) may stand for numeric variables. Likewise, we may have subscripted *string* variables. To distinguish them we use names that end with a dollar sign, such as A$(1),Y$(J) and NAM$(J).

EXAMPLE

```
10   DATA  "JULIUS" , "NERO" , "AUGUSTUS"
20   DATA  "ARNOLD" , "HADRIAN"
30   FOR  J=1  TO  5
40     READ  NAM$(J)
50   NEXT  J
60   PRINT  NAM$(2)
70   PRINT  NAM$(4)
80   END
```

The printout will be

```
NERO
ARNOLD
```

QUESTION   Let us suppose we have a short deck of cards consisting of 13 spades. Here is a program that will pick one of these cards at random. Suppose that when this program is run and a random seed is input, DENOM is assigned the value 11 in line 60. What will the printout be?

```
5     REM DEALING ONE SPADE
6     REM *****
10    RANDOMIZE
20    DIM SPADE$(13)
30    FOR K=1 TO 13
40       READ SPADE$(K)
50    NEXT K
60    DENOM=INT(13*RND)+1
70    PRINT SPADE$(DENOM)
80    DATA "ACE","TWO","THREE","FOUR"
90    DATA "FIVE","SIX","SEVEN"
100   DATA "EIGHT","NINE","TEN"
110   DATA "JACK","QUEEN","KING"
120   END
```

ANSWER   In the FOR-NEXT loop, SPADE$(1) becomes "ACE",SPADE$(2) becomes "TWO", and so on. Since we are assuming that the random integer assigned to DENOM is 11, the printout will be JACK .

21.1 Parallel Arrays

PROBLEM   **Printing Student with Grade above Class Average**   In this program note that the arrays NAM$( ) and GRADE( ) are parallel. The first array NAM$( ) contains the names of the five students. The second array GRADE( ) contains their grades. For any given subscript STUDENT, the box GRADE(STUDENT) contains the grade for student NAM$(STUDENT). For example, say STUDENT=2, the grade of NAM$(2) is given by GRADE(2).

Complete line 180, so that the printout will be the names of those students who have grades above the class average.

```
95    REM STUDENTS ABOVE AVERAGE
96    REM *****
100   SUM=0
110   FOR STUDENT=1 TO 5
120     READ NAM$(STUDENT),GRADE(STUDENT)
130     SUM=SUM+GRADE(STUDENT)
140   NEXT STUDENT
150   AVG=SUM/5
160   PRINT "AVERAGE";AVG
170   FOR STUDENT=1 TO 5
180     IF _____ AVG THEN PRINT _____
190   NEXT STUDENT
200   DATA "FOY",85,"HALL",88,"LOM",91
210   DATA "BOND",70,"BOCH",86
220   END
```

Printout

```
AVERAGE 84
FOY 85
HALL 88
LOM 92
BACH 86
```

By the end of the first FOR-NEXT loop

NAM$(1)	FOY	GRADE(1)	85
NAM$(2)	HALL	GRADE(2)	88
NAM$(3)	LOM	GRADE(3)	92
NAM$(4)	BOND	GRADE(4)	70
NAM$(5)	BOCH	GRADE(5)	86

ANSWER The entire line 180 should be IF GRADE(STUDENT)>AVG THEN PRINT NAM$(STUDENT);GRADE(STUDENT)

21.2 Dealing One Card

Let us try to write a program that will pick a card at random from a full deck of 52 cards. An inefficient program would have 52 strings in the DATA lines. The DATA lines would look like this:

DATA "ACE OF CLUBS","TWO OF CLUBS","THREE OF CLUBS"
DATA "FOUR OF CLUBS","FIVE OF CLUBS"

It would take a long time to type in these data. Here is a more efficient program for selecting a card at random from a full deck of 52 cards. Note that two random numbers are used to generate a card. Also note that DENOM gives the denomination and SUIT gives the suit.

```
5      REM DEALING ONE CARD
6      REM *****
10     RANDOMIZE
20     DIM D$(13),S$(4)
30     FOR J=1 TO 13
40       READ D$(J)
50     NEXT J
60     FOR J=1 TO 4
70       READ S$(J)
80     NEXT J
90     DENOM=INT(13*RND)+1
100    SUIT=INT(4*RND)+1
110    PRINT D$(DENOM);" OF ";S$(SUIT)
120    DATA "ACE","TWO","THREE","FOUR"
130    DATA "FIVE","SIX","SEVEN"
140    DATA "EIGHT","NINE","TEN"
150    DATA "JACK","QUEEN","KING"
160    DATA "CLUBS","DIAMONDS"
170    DATA "HEARTS","SPADES"
180    END
```

QUESTION   What will the printout be if, when the program is run, DENOM becomes 12 and SUIT becomes 2?

HINT: Note that the first 13 DATA words are assigned to D$(1), D$(2), . . . , D$(13). The next 4 DATA words are assigned to S$(1), S$(2), S$(3), S$(4).

ANSWER   QUEEN OF DIAMONDS

QUESTION   What will the printout be if, when the program is run, DENOM becomes 7 and SUIT becomes 1?

ANSWER   SEVEN OF CLUBS

21.3 Dealing Five Cards

Using Single RND to Generate Card.   In the previous program, two random integers were used in generating the DENOMination and SUIT of a card. In the next program we give a method that uses a *single* random integer to generate a card. We will let CARD = INT(52*RND) + 1. Thus, CARD will be an integer from 1 to 52. Then we will generate DENOM and SUIT from CARD as follows:

DENOM = (CARD − 1) MOD 13 + 1

SUIT = (CARD − 1)\13 + 1

As before SUIT = 1,2,3,4 will represent CLUBS, DIAMONDS, HEARTS, and SPADES respectively; DENOM = 1,2 . . . 13 will represent ACE, TWO . . . KING.

QUESTION   What card is generated by:

(a) CARD = 30

(b) CARD = 2

(c) CARD = 42

(d) CARD = 13

(e) CARD = 39

ANSWER

(a) FOUR OF HEARTS because DENOM = 4 and SUIT = 3

(b) TWO OF CLUBS because DENOM = 2, SUIT = 1

(c) THREE OF SPADES

(d) KING OF CLUBS

(e) KING OF HEARTS

Tracking Cards Already Dealt.   In having the computer deal a hand of five cards, you want to ensure that the computer does not deal the same card twice. This will be accomplished by numbering the cards 1, 2 . . . 52. The boxes A(1), A(2) . . . A(52) will be used to keep track of whether a card has been dealt. If a memory box has a 0 in it, then that card has not been dealt yet. If a memory box has a − 1 in it, then that card has already been dealt. Note that at the start of the program (lines 130–150), the boxes A(1) through A(52) are set at 0. Note in line 240 after a card has been dealt, A(CARD) becomes − 1. For example, if the first card dealt is card 17, then A(17) becomes − 1.

For each card dealt, the computer first generates a random integer CARD from 1 to 52; then it checks whether that card has already been dealt by testing whether A(CARD) = − 1. If A(CARD) = − 1, then the computer does not deal that card, but instead goes back to generate another CARD.

PROBLEM   Complete line 240.

```
95    REM DEALING A HAND
96    REM *****
100   RANDOMIZE
110   DIM A(52)
120   DIM D$(13),S$(4)
130   FOR J=1 TO 52
140     A(J)=0
150   NEXT J
160   FOR J=1 TO 13
170     READ D$(J)
180   NEXT J
190   FOR J=1 TO 4
200     READ S$(J)
210   NEXT J
220   FOR J=1 TO 5
230     CARD=INT(52*RND)+1
240     IF A(CARD)=-1 THEN _____
250     DENOM=(CARD-1) MOD 13+1
260     SUIT=(CARD-1)\13+1
270     PRINT D$(DENOM);" OF ";S$(SUIT)
280     A(CARD)=-1
290   NEXT J
300   DATA "ACE","TWO","THREE","FOUR"
310   DATA "FIVE","SIX","SEVEN"
320   DATA "EIGHT","NINE","TEN"
330   DATA "JACK","QUEEN","KING"
340   DATA "CLUBS","DIAMONDS"
350   DATA "HEARTS","SPADES"
360   END
```

ANSWER   Line 240 should be

IF A(CARD) = −1 THEN 230

Exercises

1. **(a)** Using subscripted string variables, write a program to pick someone at random from the following list: TOM, DICK, HARRY, JACK, JILL.
   (b) Rewrite the program without using subscripted string variables.

2. Write a program that will assign a person to guard duty, picking at random both the time of day (whether MORNING, AFTERNOON, or NIGHT) and day of the week. A typical printout might be

GUARD DUTY WEDNESDAY MORNING

3. Use the computer to create five sentences at random of the form subject-verb-object from the lists: subjects (John, Mary, Bowser), verbs (likes, craves, abhors), objects (fire hydrants, caviar, bones).

4. The following DATA lines give the temperatures for the week:

DATA "SUNDAY",85,"MONDAY",78,"TUESDAY",87,"WEDNESDAY",90
DATA "THURSDAY",72,"FRIDAY",65,"SATURDAY",74

Write a program that will print out the average for the week and those days on which the temperature exceeded the average.

★ 5. For the previous DATA lines, write a program that will print the day of the week for which the temperature was closest to the weekly average. You may ignore the possibility of a tie. (Use the absolute value function ABS.)

6. Using the method of Section 21.3 for generating a card from a *single* call of RND, find the suit and denomination that correspond to
(a) CARD = 24
(b) CARD = 8
(c) CARD = 42.

7. In the card-dealing program, how does the computer "cross out a card" after it has been dealt?

8. Write a program to simulate the following situation: The numbers 1, 2 . . . 10 are written on separate slips of paper. There are four blindfolded people. Each one in turn picks a slip of paper. The printout should be in the form

THE NUMBERS PICKED ARE __ __ __ __

Be sure that the four numbers will necessarily be different. (*Hint:* You do not need subscripted *string* variables, but you should use a concept from the last program in this chapter.)

★ 9. Write a program to pick at random first-, second-, and third-place winners from the list TOM, DICK, HARRY, MOE, CURLY, SUE, NAN, TED, FRED, AL, BOB, MARY, PETE. Make sure that the winners are distinct.

★ 10. Write a program that will hold the lottery from Exercise 9, ten times, printing out the results of each lottery and also printing how many times each person won first place.

★ **11.** Write a program that will deal two distinct cards at random. The program should print out what the cards are and also either

(a)

```
A PAIR
```

or   **(b)**

```
NOT A PAIR
```

depending on whether or not the two cards are the same denomination.

★ **12.** Write a program that keeps dealing and printing distinct cards until two cards of the same denomination have been dealt.

★ **13.** In a special election, there are the following eight candidates: Cane, Cocker, Doberman, Hund, Labrador, Pincher, Spaniel, Wolff. A 1 is a vote for Cane, 2 is a vote for Cocker, etc. Write a program that first reads the names of the candidates into N$(1) through N$(8) and then tabulates the vote in the form

```
CANDIDATE     VOTES
CANE            9
COCKER          4
    .
    .
    .
```

DATA 1,1,3,3,1,5,8,1,3,5,7,8,1,2,2,1,2,1,8

DATA 3,5,1,7,1,2,4,3,999

14. Write a program using the following price information: hammers $5, wrenches $4, pliers $3, crowbars $12, files $2, so that if the user inputs a pair of numbers giving the identification number (1 for hammer, 2 for wrench, etc.) and the number purchased, the printout will describe the purchase. For example, for input of 2,20 the printout should be

```
20 WRENCHES 80 DOLLARS
```

★ **15. (a)** Write a program that will create *distinct* guard duty assignments at random (as in Exercise 2) for eight people.

★★ **(b)** Write a program that will create 15 *distinct* sentences at random of the form: subject-verb-object, using the same list as in Exercise 3.

16. Also see Appendix B, Exercises 39 and 40.

22
More Advanced String Manipulations

So far, in all our string manipulations we have processed a string as a whole. We have not examined part of a string, separately. For example, we have not discussed commands for enabling the computer to determine whether a name begins with the letter "J". This chapter deals with various string functions and statements that permit processing parts of a string.

22.1 LEN(A$) Gives Length of String A$

EXAMPLE

```
10  A$="SO LONG"
20  B=LEN(A$)
30  PRINT B
40  END
```

The printout will be $\boxed{7}$. Note that blanks are counted as characters.

REMARK: The value of LEN is an integer and thus is assigned to the numeric variable B.

▬▬ 22.2 Selecting Part of String (LEFT$, RIGHT$, and MID$)

For the three string functions discussed here as well as the LEN function, the string can be either a string variable or an actual string in quotation marks.

LEFT$. LEFT$ (string,n) returns the *first* n characters of the string. Thus (a) LEFT$(Q$,3) returns the first three characters of Q$. (b) LEFT$("HARRY",3) returns HAR.

EXAMPLE

```
10   A$="PAULINE"
20   B$=LEFT$(A$,2)
30   PRINT B$
```

Printout

```
PA
```

RIGHT$. RIGHT$ (string, n) returns the last n characters of the string. Thus, RIGHT$("LOUISE",2) would return SE.

MID$. MID$ is the most important of these three string functions. MID$(string,p,n) returns the substring starting at position p and having length n. Thus, MID$("HARVEY",2,3) returns ARV. By the same token, MID$("HARVEY",4,1) returns V.

It is also permissible to omit the third argument, n. In that case MID$ returns the entire *remaining* string starting from position p. For example, MID$("MARVIN",3) returns RVIN.

QUESTION Using the first form of MID$, write a LET statement that will assign to A$ the third character of B$.

ANSWER A$ = MID$(B$,3,1)

PROBLEM Give the printouts for these two programs.

(a)

```
10   X$="ELVIS"
20   FOR J=1 TO LEN(X$)
30      PRINT MID$(X$,J,1)
40   NEXT J
50   END
```

(b)

```
10   X$="ELVIS"
20   FOR J=1 TO LEN(X$)-1
30      PRINT MID$(X$,J,2)
40   NEXT J
50   END
```

ANSWER (a)   (b)

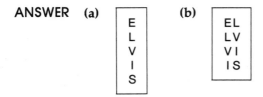

LEN Applications and Substring Functions

EXAMPLE Printing DATA Names Beginning with a Certain Letter

```
10  FOR  K=1  TO  6
20    READ  F$
30    IF  LEFT$(F$,1)="D"  THEN  PRINT  F$
40  NEXT  K
50  DATA  "JOE","DAVE","LOU",
60  DATA  "HAL","DIANE","DOUG"
70  END
```

The printout will be all the names beginning with D.

```
DAVE
DIANE
DOUG
```

REMARK: Line 30 could also have been IF MID$(F$,1,1)="D" THEN PRINT F$

Examining a String, Character by Character

PROBLEM Counting the Number of E's in a String Fill in the blank in line 40.

```
10  INPUT  "TYPE  A  WORD";A$
20  COUNT=0
30  FOR  J=1  TO  LEN(A$)
40    IF  _____  ="E"  THEN  COUNT=COUNT+1
50  NEXT  J
60  PRINT  COUNT;"  E'S  IN  ";A$
70  END
```

Here is a typical run:

```
TYPE A WORD?   ELEMENTARY
3 E'S IN ELEMENTARY
```

ANSWER   The blank in line 40 should be MID$(A$,J,1).

NOTE: MID$(A$,J,1) always returns a string of one character. When J = 1, it returns the first character; when J = 2 it returns the second character; and so on. When J = LEN(A$), it returns the last character of A$.

EXAMPLE   **Replacing First Name with First Initial**   The next program assumes that the input string consists of a first name followed by one blank space and then a last name. Note the use of a linear search to find the location of the blank.

```
10   INPUT "NAME" ; N$
20   REM LOCATE POSITION OF THE BLANK
30   J=1
40   WHILE MID$(N$,J,1)<>" "
50      J=J+1
60   WEND
70   BLANKPOS=J
80   LAST$=MID$(N$,BLANKPOS+1)
90   INIT$=LEFT$(N$,1)
100  PRINT INIT$;". ";LAST$
110  END
```

Printout

```
NAME? JANE DOE
J. DOE
```

REMARK: In the next section we use the INSTR function to give a simpler version of the previous program.

22.3   Other Functions

INSTR.   The INSTR function determines whether one string appears as a substring of another string. INSTR returns either the starting position of the first appearance of the substring or a zero if the substring does not appear.

```
10   A$="ABCDE"
20   J=INSTR(A$,"CD")
30   K=INSTR(A$,"DEF")
40   PRINT J;K
50   END
```

Printout

```
3   0
```

REMARK: Two common uses of INSTR are (1) locating an important position such as a blank separator, and (2) determining whether a character (or string) is present at all. For example, IF INSTR(N$,"E")>0 THEN . . . could be used to test whether N$ contains the letter "E".

EXAMPLE **Using INSTR to Replace First Name with First Initial** Let us now rewrite the program in the previous example. Note that the single line 20 accomplishes the task (lines 20–70 in the previous program) of locating the position of the blank separator.

```
10   INPUT  "NAME" ; N$
20   BLANKPOS=INSTR(N$, "  ")
30   LAST$=MID$(N$,BLANKPOS+1)
40   INIT$=LEFT$(N$,1)
50   PRINT INIT$;".  ";LAST$
60   END
```

EXAMPLE **Counting Number of Words Containing NT or ST**

```
10    C1=0  :  C2=0
20    READ WORD$
30    WHILE WORD$<>"XYZ"
40      IF INSTR(WORD$,"NT")>0 THEN C1=C1+1
50      IF INSTR(WORD$,"ST")>0 THEN C2=C2+1
60      READ WORD$
70    WEND
80    PRINT "NT OCCURRED IN";C1;"WORDS"
90    PRINT "ST OCCURRED IN";C2;"WORDS"
100   DATA "WANT","WART","STAND","START"
110   DATA "WASTE","STORY","PUNT","XYZ"
120   END
```

The printout will be

```
NT OCCURRED IN 2 WORDS
ST OCCURRED IN 4 WORDS
```

Concatenation. The plus symbol can be used to **concatenate**, that is, join strings together. For example,

(a)
```
10   A$="212-"
20   B$="780-5994"
30   C$=A$+B$
40   PRINT C$
```

(b)

```
10  N$="HARRY"
20  P$="********"
30  D$=LEFT$(N$+P$,8)
40  PRINT D$
```

(c)   Note that X$ is initialized as a one-blank string and Y$ is initialized as a null string:

```
10  A$="ABCDEFGH"
20  X$="  "
30  Y$=""
40  FOR J=2 TO LEN(A$) STEP 2
50    X$=X$+MID$(A$,J,1)
60    Y$=Y$+MID$(A$,J,1)
70  NEXT J
80  PRINT X$
90  PRINT Y$
```

The printouts will be

(a)

```
212-780-5994
```

(b)

```
HARRY***
```

(c)

```
BDFH
BDFH
```

VAL (String).   When the characters of a string represent a number, VAL returns that number. This is useful for performing numerical computations.

```
10  A$="13.5"
20  B=VAL(A$)
30  PRINT B
40  PRINT B+1
```

Printout

```
13.5
14.5
```

REMARK: PRINT A$+1 would result in an error. Do you see why?

STR$ (Number or Numerical Variable).   The STR$ will return a string made up of numerical characters. It is the reverse of VAL.

```
10  A=212
20  B=780
30  C=5994
40  PHONE$="("+STR$(A)+")  "+STR$(B)+"-"+STR$(C)
50  PRINT PHONE$
```

Printout

```
(212) 780-5994
```

QUESTION   What is VAL(STR$(17))?

ANSWER   VAL("17"), or 17.

22.4 ASCII Table

Each printable character in BASIC has an ASCII code number (ASCII stands for American Standard Code for Information Interchange). Here is the table:

Code#	Char.	Code#	Char.	Code#	Char.	Code#	Char.	Code#	Char.
32	blank	52	4	72	H	92	\	112	p
33	!	53	5	73	I	93	]	113	q
34	"	54	6	74	J	94	∧	114	r
35	#	55	7	75	K	95	—	115	s
36	$	56	8	76	L	96	'	116	t
37	%	57	9	77	M	97	a	117	u
38	&	58	:	78	N	98	b	118	v
39	'	59	;	79	O	99	c	119	w
40	(	60	>	80	P	100	d	120	x
41	)	61	=	81	Q	101	e	121	y
42	*	62	<	82	R	102	f	122	z
43	+	63	?	83	S	103	g	123	{
44	,	64	@	84	T	104	h	124	|
45	-	65	A	85	U	105	i	125	}
46	.	66	B	86	V	106	j	126	~
47	/	67	C	87	W	107	k		
48	0	68	D	88	X	108	l		
49	1	69	E	89	Y	109	m		
50	2	70	F	90	Z	110	n		
51	3	71	G	91	[	111	o		

QUESTION   The letter A has ASCII code number 65. What is the ASCII code number of the letter F?

ANSWER   It is 70.

QUESTION   What is the code number for a small "a"?

ANSWER   It is 97.

QUESTION   What is the code number of the character *?

ANSWER   It is 42.

QUESTION   We can also ask the reverse question. What character has code number 78?

ANSWER   The letter N.

ASC( ) and CHR$( ) Functions.   The ASC( ) function applied to a character gives the ASCII code number of that character. For example, X = ASC("A") would assign the value 65 to the variable X. The statement PRINT ASC("D") would print the value 68.

The CHR$( ) function applied to a code number gives the character having the code number. For example, PRINT CHR$(66) would print B.

QUESTION   What will the printout be?

```
10  PRINT ASC("E")
20  PRINT ASC("*")
30  PRINT CHR$(66)
40  N=ASC("A")
50  PRINT CHR$(N+3)
```

ANSWER

```
69
42
B
D
```

QUESTION   What will the printout be?

```
10  DATA 70,82,69,68
20  FOR J=1 TO 4
30    READ N
40     PRINT CHR$(N);
50  NEXT J
60  END
```

ANSWER   The DATA line gives the code numbers for the letters in the name FRED. Thus, the printout will be ⟨ FRED ⟩.

CHR\$ and ASC Are Inverse Functions.   Each reverses what the other does.

QUESTION   What is CHR\$(ASC("E")) equal to?

ANSWER   The letter E. Here is why: ASC("E") gives the code number of the letter E. CHR\$(ASC("E")) returns the character whose code number is equal to the code number of the letter E. Therefore, the answer is the letter E.

Changing Lowercase to Uppercase.   Many implementations of BASIC have lowercase as well as uppercase letters.

EXAMPLE   **Changing Lowercase Letter to Uppercase**   For an input lowercase letter, this fragment prints the letter in uppercase. Note that ASC("A") = 65 and ASC("a") = 97, and that $97 - 65 = 32$. In fact, for any letter the uppercase form has an ASC number that is 32 less than the ASC number of the lowercase form of that letter.

```
100  INPUT "TYPE A LOWER CASE LETTER";L$
110  N=ASC(L$)
120  PRINT CHR$(N-32)
```

EXAMPLE   This next fragment requests that the user input a lower-case letter. The printout will be either the uppercase form of the letter or the message that the input character was not a lowercase letter.

```
100  INPUT "TYPE A LOWER CASE LETTER";L$
110  N=ASC(L$)
120  IF N>=97 AND N<=122
        THEN PRINT CHR$(N-32)
        ELSE PRINT L$;" NOT LOWER CASE LETTER"
```

QUESTION   Suppose that you do not have access to an ASCII table. For the above fragment, rewrite the IF condition of line 120 so that 97 and 122 are replaced by expressions involving the ASC function.

ANSWER

IF N> = ASC("a") AND N< = ASC("z")

Encoding Messages: Shift Code.   Following is a program to encode a message by replacing each letter with the letter three places ahead of it in the alphabet. Thus, A will be replaced by D, B by E, and so on. The last three letters of the alphabet, X, Y, and Z will be replaced by A, B, and C respectively.

Thus, the message, AT THE ZOO, YES OR NO? would be encoded as DW WKH CRR. BHV RU QR?

The program below performs this three-shift encoding. Note that the program processes the message one character at a time. For each character, there are three possibilities: (1) it is a letter between A and W, (2) it is a letter between X and Z, or (3) it is a nonletter. For letters, line 50 or 60 shifts the code number for cases (1) and (2). For nonletters, there is no shift; a period should be encoded as a period, blanks as blanks, and so on.

Completing lines 60 and 70 is Exercise 20.

```
5    REM LETTER SHIFT ENCODING
6    REM ****
10   DATA "AT THE ZOO. YES OR NO?"
20   READ MESSAGE$
30   FOR J=1 TO LEN(MESSAGE$)
40     N=ASC(MID$(MESSAGE$,J,1))
50     IF 65<=N AND N<=87 THEN N=N+3
60     IF 88<=N AND N<=90 THEN N= _____
70     PRINT _____
80   NEXT J
90   END
```

Exercises

STRING MANIPULATIONS

1. Write a program to print all the names on the DATA list with second letter A.

   DATA "HARRY","DAN","LOU","AL","JEAN","BABS"

   DATA "ALF","AARON","FLAG"

2. Write a program so that for an INPUT word, the printout will give the separate counts for the number of occurrences of "E" and "A".

3. Write a program so that for a DATA line giving one first and last name with one blank separating them, the printout will give the last name followed by a comma and the first name. For DATA "HENRY HIGGINS", the printout should be ⌐HIGGINS, HENRY⌐.

4. Write a program so that for a DATA line giving one last name followed by a comma, a space and then the first name, the printout will be the

first name followed by the last name. For DATA "HIGGINS, HENRY", the printout should be ⎸ HENRY HIGGINS ⎸.

★ 5. Write a program so that for DATA lines ending with the flag "XYZ" giving first and last names with one blank separating them, the printout will print the names with the last name first and a comma separator. For DATA "BOB JONES", "LEE FONG", "TED MACK", "XYZ", the printout should be

```
JONES , BOB
FONG , LEE
MACK , TED
```

★ 6. Write a program that codes an input name by changing each occurrence of the letter E to R and each occurrence of the letter R to E. For an input of "ROBERT JONES", the output should be ⎸ EOBRET JONRS ⎸. (*Hint:* It is not necessary to locate the blank separator.)

7. Write a program to print the first names of all the people on the list with last names over five characters long.

DATA "HAROLD","BOND","AL","BLALOCK","LOU",

"MARTINO","FLAG","FLAG"

★ 8. Write a program to print the first names of all the people on the list with *last* names over five characters long. (Note that the first and last names are *not* separate DATA entries.)

DATA "HAROLD BOND","AL BLALOCK","LOU MARTINO","FLAG"

★ 9. Write a program that prints out a DATA word in reverse order. For HENRY, the printout should be YRNEH. Use a FOR-NEXT loop.

★ 10. (a) In the concatenation program (b) of Section 22.3, what would the printout be if line 10 were changed to N$ = "JOE"?
   (b) Redo Exercise 9 using concatenation. Use the string REV$ to form the DATA word in reverse order. Let the statement before END be PRINT REV$.

★ 11. Write a program that alphabetizes any two names according to the last name so that for DATA "LOU JONES", "AL COHN" the printout will be

```
AL  COHN
LOU JONES
```

★ 12. To form a pig Latin word from an ordinary word beginning with a consonant, put the first letter at the end of the ordinary word followed by the letters *ay*. Thus, JUICE becomes UICEJAY in pig Latin. Write a program that takes as input an ordinary word beginning with a consonant and gives as printout its pig Latin form.

★ **13.** Suppose that the input will consist of *either* a first name followed by last name *or* first and middle names followed by a last name. Write a program so that the printout will give the first initial(s) followed by the last name. For input DAVID SMITH, the printout would be ⌐D. SMITH⌐ whereas for input JOHN PAUL JONES the printout would be ⌐J. P. JONES⌐.

★ **14.** *Letter Substitution Encoding*

Write a program that will perform a letter substitution coding based on the following:

ABCDEFGHIJKLMNOPQRSTUVWXYZ

HJAZKQYBFDPWTVSCUXLGINOEMR

Thus, A will be replaced by H, B by J, C by A, D by Z, E by K, and so on.

For an input of "AT THE ZOO!", the printout should be

```
HG GBK RSS!
```

Fill in the blank in line 70.

```
 5   REM LETTER SUBSTITUTION ENCODING
 6   REM ****
10   ALPHABET$="ABCDEFGHIJKLMNOPQRSTUVWXYZ"
20   ENCODE$   ="HJAZKQYBFDPWTVSCUXLGINOEMR"
30   LINE INPUT "ENTER A PHRASE";PHRASE$
40   FOR J=1 TO LEN(PHRASE$)
50     X$=MID$(PHRASE$,J,1)
60     P=INSTR(ALPHABET$,X$)
70     IF P>0 THEN PRINT MID$(_____,_____,_____);
              ELSE PRINT _____;
80   NEXT J
90   END
```

(*Hint:* For each J, X$ becomes the Jth character from the phrase. INSTR is used to determine if X$ is a letter. If X$ is a letter, then P gives its position in the alphabet; if X$ is not a letter, then P = 0. For X$ a letter, we want to print the character from the string ENCODE$ in position P; for X$ a nonletter we want to print X$.)

★★ **15.** *Hangman.* Write a Hangman program using 20 seven-letter words contained in the DATA lines. The human blindly selects a seven-letter word by inputting an integer between 1 and 20. Assume HEAVIER is the 12th word in the DATA line. A typical printout might be

```
A  SEVEN  LETTER  WORD  WILL  BE  SELECTED
PICK  AN  INTEGER  BETWEEN  1  AND  20  ?  12
   PICK  A  LETTER  ?  E
E  IS  IN  POSITION  2
E  IS  IN  POSITION  6
   PICK  A  LETTER  ?  U
U  IS  NOT  IN  THE  WORD
   PICK  A  LETTER  ?  I
I  IS  IN  POSITION  5
   .
   .
   .

CONGRATULATIONS,  YOU  HAVE  GOT  ALL  THE  LETTERS
YOU  HAD  _____  INCORRECT  LETTERS
```

Note that this program assumes the human will use pencil and paper to fill in blank dashes in order to visualize better what is known at each stage. Your program may assume that the human will not ask any letters twice.

★★   **16.** See Appendix C, Exercise 22, for a version of hangman in which the computer displays the letters that are known (filled into their proper positions) and also displays incorrect letters guessed.

ASCII NUMERIC CODE

17. What will the printout be?

```
10  PRINT CHR$(68);PRINT CHR$(32);PRINT CHR$(82)
20  PRINT ASC("F")
```

18. What is the value of CHR$(ASC("R"))?

19. Write a program using the statement FOR J=65 TO 90 to print all the letters of the alphabet on one line.

20. Complete and run the three-shift encoding program of Section 22.4.

21. Write a program to five-shift encode.

22. Write a program that takes as input a message that has been encoded by a three-shift. The printout should be the message in ordinary English.

★★   **23.** See Appendix C, Exercise 12 (substitution encoding without using the INSTR function).

★   **24.** Also see Appendix B, Exercise 10.

23

Bubble Sort

Rearranging a list of numbers so they are in increasing (or decreasing) order is termed **sorting**. In this chapter we consider one particular sorting method known as the **bubble sort**. See Appendix E for the **Shell sort**, a more advanced sorting method.

23.1 Switching Values of Two Variables

PROBLEM **One Method of Switching**   Suppose that when the computer reaches line 50, A = 2 and B = 5. What values will A and B have after line 70?

```
50   TEMP=A
60   A=B
70   B=TEMP
```

ANSWER   A will be 5 and B will be 2. The above fragment switches the values of A and B.

SWAP Statement—Easier Method of Switching.   The statement SWAP A,B is an easier way to switch the values of A and B. The SWAP statement can be used to switch the values of any two variables of the same type. Thus, SWAP A$,J$ is legal and so is SWAP B(J),M. However SWAP B(J),M$ would be illegal, since B(J) is numeric and M$ is string.

23.2 Simple Bubble Sort Procedure

In the bubble sort, the smallest numbers of an array will "bubble" to the top as the larger ones are moved toward the end of the array.

One Pass in Bubble Sort.   Suppose that four numbers are stored in memory boxes A(1) through A(4).

*A **pass** consists of the following: Compare the contents of A(1) and A(2); if A(1) contains the larger number, swap the contents of these two cells. Next, compare the current contents of cell A(2) with that of cell A(3); swap their contents if necessary (that is, if A(2) has the larger number). Finally, compare the current contents of cell A(3) with that of A(4); swap their contents if necessary.*

At the end of the first pass, the largest number will be in A(4). Let us illustrate the first pass when A(1) through A(4) contain the numbers 6, 5, 8, and 3.

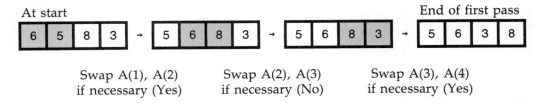

At start   End of first pass

Swap A(1), A(2)   Swap A(2), A(3)   Swap A(3), A(4)
if necessary (Yes)   if necessary (No)   if necessary (Yes)

Note that the two boxes with contents to be compared have been shaded.

QUESTION   Illustrate a first pass for | 6 | 5 | 9 | 2 | 4 | 8 |

ANSWER

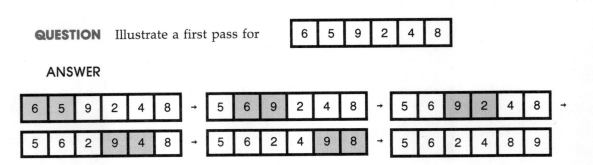

Program Segment for One Pass.   Let us suppose that N numbers are stored in boxes A(1) through A(N).

```
100  FOR K=1 TO N-1
110    IF A(K)>A(K+1) THEN SWAP A(K),A(K+1)
120  NEXT K
```

For each value of K, a pair of adjacent boxes will be compared and their contents switched if necessary. More specifically:

When K=1, the contents of A(1) and A(2) will be compared and switched if necessary.

When K=2, the contents of A(2) and A(3) will be compared and switched if necessary.

$\vdots$

When K=N−1, the contents of A(N−1) and A(N) will be compared and switched if necessary.

23.3 Complete Bubble Sort

In a complete bubble sort program the computer keeps performing passes until it makes a pass in which there are no further swaps. For example, consider

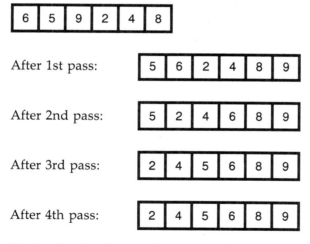

| 6 | 5 | 9 | 2 | 4 | 8 |

After 1st pass:

| 5 | 6 | 2 | 4 | 8 | 9 |

After 2nd pass:

| 5 | 2 | 4 | 6 | 8 | 9 |

After 3rd pass:

| 2 | 4 | 5 | 6 | 8 | 9 |

After 4th pass:

| 2 | 4 | 5 | 6 | 8 | 9 |

During the fourth pass there are no further swaps. This implies that the array is sorted.

REMARK: Each pass is guaranteed to put the next-largest number that is out of order in its proper place. Of course, a pass could accomplish more than this by chance, and also put other numbers in their proper places.

EXAMPLE Suppose 7,4,2,3,6 are in boxes A(1) through A(5). Consider the bubble sort.

1st pass: Start

| 7 | 4 | 2 | 3 | 6 | → · · · → | 4 | 2 | 3 | 6 | 7 |

Note that in this example the first pass put the largest number in its proper place and by chance it also put the second-largest number in its proper place. The next pass is guaranteed to put at least the next-largest number that is out of order in its proper place. In fact, it does even more; the numbers will be completely sorted after only two passes.

Complete Bubble Sort Program.   In this program we sort five numbers by the bubble sort. Pay particular attention to the use of the mock Boolean variable DONE$. (See Chapter 17.)

Each execution of the WHILE loop (lines 160–210) performs a pass. Note that in the *first line of the WHILE loop body, DONE$ is set at "YES"*. There are two possibilities for what will happen during the inner FOR-NEXT loop (lines 180–200).

1. If no swaps are made during the entire FOR-NEXT loop, DONE$ will remain at "YES". Thus, when the computer reaches the WHILE condition, it will not enter the WHILE loop again. This is what we would want, since if no swaps occurred, the array is in order.

2. If at least one swap is made during the FOR-NEXT loop, then DONE$ will become "NO", and will have the value "NO" when the computer reaches the WHILE condition. This means the array may still be out of order, and we would want to perform another pass.

PROBLEM   Fill in line 150.

```
95    REM BUBBLE SORT
96    REM ****
100   DATA _____,_____,_____,_____,_____
110   N=5 : REM SORT 5 NUMBERS
120   FOR J=1 TO N
130     READ A(J)
140   NEXT J
150   _____
160   WHILE DONE$="NO"
170     DONE$="YES"
180     FOR K=1 TO N-1
190       IF A(K)>A(K+1) THEN SWAP A(K),A(K+1):DONE$="NO"
200     NEXT K
210   WEND
220   REM NUMBERS ARE SORTED
230   FOR J=1 TO N
240     PRINT A(J);
250   NEXT J
260   END
```

ANSWER   Line 150 DONE$="NO" will ensure that the WHILE loop is entered a first time.

23.4 More Efficient Sorting

Improved Bubble Sort.   Exercise 12 of this chapter illustrates a more efficient bubble sort program. The program in Section 23.3 makes some unnecessary comparisons. Each pass is performed on *all* the boxes, even though more and more of the larger numbers become gradually fixed in their proper positions. For example, consider the bubble sort on eight numbers in boxes A(1) through A(8). After the first pass, the largest number will be in box A(8). Thus, in the second pass, the comparison of boxes A(7) and A(8) is not necessary; it would be sufficient to perform the second pass on boxes A(1) through A(7). Similarly, since at the start of the third pass the second-largest number will already be in box A(7), it would be sufficient to perform the third pass on boxes A(1) through A(6). Further unnecessary comparisons are also made in the remaining passes. See Exercise 12 for details.

Other Sorting Procedures.   The primary advantage of the bubble sort over all other sorting procedures is its easy comprehensibility. However, it is one of the slowest and most inefficient sorting procedures. In Appendix D we discuss the Shell sort, which is considerably faster than the bubble sort. The real benefit in more efficient sorting procedures is in sorting long lists of numbers. In sorting short lists of only 20 numbers there is not a noticeable difference in the amount of time used by the various sorting procedures. For sorting a list of 100 numbers, however, the Shell sort is almost twice as fast as the improved bubble sort; for even longer lists of numbers, the Shell sort is faster by a larger factor.

Measuring Procedure Efficiency.   One way of determining the procedure efficiency is to measure the amount of time used. A more instructive method is to count both the number of comparisons used and the number of switches made. Exercise 13 involves modifying the bubble sort program on 50 numbers so that in addition to printing the unsorted list and the sorted list, it will also print the number of comparisons used and the number of switches made.

Exercises

1. Apply the first pass procedure to

5	9	8	3	10	4

   What will be the contents of the memory boxes at the end of this first pass?

2. Apply by hand the bubble sort procedure of Section 23.3 to the numbers in Exercise 1.

3. Write and run a program that arranges any list of six DATA numbers in increasing order. Run it for DATA 7,9,3,15,8,2.

★ 4. Write a program that arranges any list of six DATA numbers in decreasing order.

5. Write a program that will print the median score for any DATA line giving the grades of seven students.

★ 6. Write a program to sort a list of 10 DATA numbers. In addition to printing a sorted list, the program should indicate whether there is a tie for the largest. If there is a tie, the printout should also state how many numbers are tied.

7. Write a program to alphabetize any DATA line of six last names.

★★ 8. The *Backward* # of an arrangement of the integers 1, 2, 3, 4, 5 is defined as the number of pairs that are not in the usual order. For example, the arrangement 1, 3, 5, 2, 4 has Backward # three, because there are three pairs out of order, namely: (3,2), (5,2), and (5,4). The arrangement 5, 4, 3, 2, 1 has Backward # ten because there are 10 pairs not in order. Write a program so that if the DATA line is an arrangement of the integers 1–5, the printout will be the Backward # of that arrangement. Run it with DATA 1,3,5,2,4. Then rerun it with DATA 5,4,3,2,1.

★★ 9. Suppose each pair of DATA values gives a salesperson's name and number of sales for the month.

    DATA   "FOY",176,"POE",341,"LEE",154,"KOHN",128,"DIAZ",180

Write a program that will list the salespeople in increasing order of sales. Format the printout so that it will be the following. Your program can assume there will be five salespeople. (*Hint:* Use parallel arrays.)

SALESPERSON	NUMBER OF SALES
KOHN	128
LEE	154
FOY	176
DIAZ	180
POE	341

★ 10. Write a program that generates a list of 50 random integers between 1 and 100, prints the list, sorts it, and then prints the sorted list.

★ 11. (a) Give an example of a list of eight numbers in boxes A(1) through A(8) that would not be sorted after the first pass but would be sorted after the second pass.

    (b) How many passes would the program of Section 23.3 actually perform in sorting that list?

★ 12. Regarding the improved bubble sort discussed in Section 23.4, use the variable PASSES to keep track of the number of passes performed. Three modifications in the program of 23.3 need to be made. PASSES should be initialized at 0. At the start of each pass, the variable PASSES should be incremented by 1, and line 180 should be changed to FOR K = 1 TO N − PASSES. Write the improved bubble sort program.

★ **13.** Modify the bubble sort procedure so that it also prints both the number of comparisons used and the number of switches made.

★★ **14.** Write a program that will generate and store 50 random integers from 1 to 100, print the unsorted list, and sort the list first by the bubble sort and then by the improved bubble. The printout should give the number of comparisons used and the number of switches made, first for the bubble sort and then for the improved bubble sort.

★ **15.** Also see Appendix B, Exercise 23.

CHAPTER 24

Binary Search

In a linear search of a list of items, you start with the first item and examine them one after another until you find a particular searched-for item or reach the end of the list. The linear search method works well enough for a fairly short list; for example, a list of approximately 50 items.

However, if you wished to look up William Timmerman in the Manhattan telephone directory, it would be unproductive to start with the first name and continue searching one by one. A more efficient method would take advantage of the alphabetical ordering of the names to jump immediately toward the end of the book.

Binary search is similar in nature to your automatic method of looking up a name in a telephone directory. It must be emphasized, however, that a binary search can only be used on an ordered list; for example, either a sorted list of numbers or an alphabetized list of names.

24.1 Binary Search Procedure

EXAMPLE 1 Let us suppose the number searched for is X = 57.

Starting array

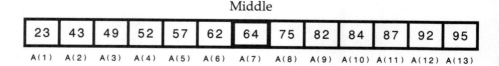

Middle

23	43	49	52	57	62	64	75	82	84	87	92	95
A(1)	A(2)	A(3)	A(4)	A(5)	A(6)	A(7)	A(8)	A(9)	A(10)	A(11)	A(12)	A(13)

First compare the searched-for number, 57, to the contents of the middle box

238

A(7). Since 57 is less than 64, we can conclude that if 57 is in the array at all, it must be in the left-half, that is, among boxes A(1)–A(6).

Segment still under consideration

Next, compare the searched-for number, 57, to the contents of the current middle box, A(3). (*When there is an even number of boxes, we take as the middle box the one just to the left of the midline.*) Since 57 is greater than 49, we can narrow the search to the remaining right-half; that is, boxes A(4)–A(6).

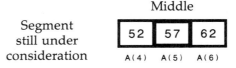

Segment still under consideration

This time the searched-for number, 57, is equal to the contents of the middle box. It has been located in box A(5).

Binary Search Program Variables.   The variables FIRST, LAST, and MD will keep track of the subscripts for the first, last, and middle boxes for the segment still under consideration.

NOTE: We abbreviate middle as MD, because MID is a reserved word.

EXAMPLE 2   Let us suppose that the searched-for number is 87, and the array is the same as in Example 1. At the start, FIRST will be 1, LAST will be 13, and MD will be 7.

After comparing the searched-for number, 87, to the contents of A(7), we can narrow the search to the right-half; that is, boxes A(8)–A(13).

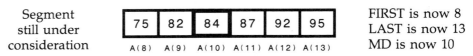

Segment still under consideration

FIRST is now 8
LAST is now 13
MD is now 10

After comparing 87 to the contents of the current middle box, A(10), we can further narrow the search to the right-half, boxes A(11)–A(13).

Segment still under consideration

FIRST is now 11
LAST is now 13
MD is now 12

After comparing 87 to the contents of the current middle box, A(12), we can further narrow the search to the left-half, box A(11).

Segment FIRST is now 11
still under A(11) LAST is now 11
consideration MD is now 11

This time a match is found between the searched-for number and the contents of the current middle box.

24.2 Program Fragment to Perform Binary Search for X in Array A(1)–A(N)

PROGRAM IDEAS FOR BINARY SEARCH

Let us suppose that the array is A(1) through A(13), that is, LAST = 13. The program will use a loop to keep cutting the segment under consideration in half until X is located or there no longer exists a segment under consideration.

During First Execution of Loop Body.   Compare X to the contents of A(7), the middle box of the array A(1)–A(13). If they are equal, exit from the loop, since the search is over. If they are not equal, use another IF-THEN test to determine in which side of A(7), the *left*-side or the *right*-side, we should continue to search. Use that *half* as the segment still under consideration during the next loop execution.

During Further Execution of Loop Body.   Compare X against the contents of the middle box of the segment still under consideration. If they are equal, exit; otherwise determine the appropriate half from the segment still under consideration, and go on to the next execution of the loop body.
:
:

Eventually either the position of X in the array will be located, or, if X is not in the array, the segment still under consideration will diminish to nothing.

The Program.   In line 120 of the program, MD is set equal to the average of FIRST and LAST by the statement MD = INT((FIRST + LAST)/2). Note how the use of INT works on an even number of boxes. It will determine MD to be the box just to the left of the midline. Line 130 tests for a match.
      A key test in the loop body is in line 140. This line tests whether the search is to be narrowed to the left-half or the right-half of the current segment. Let us suppose that X is less than A(MD) and so the search should be

narrowed to the left-half. The way to narrow the search to the left-half of the current segment is to change the value of LAST to MD − 1. The value of FIRST should not be changed.

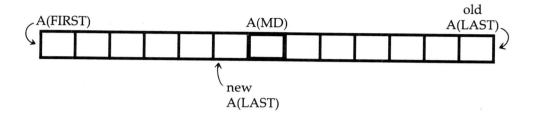

QUESTION   Fill in the ELSE branch of line 140.

```
10    REM BINARY SEARCH
20    REM ****
30    DATA 23,43,49,52,57,62,64,75,82,84,87,92,95
40    N=13 : DIM A(N)
50    FOR J=1 TO N
60       READ A(J)
70    NEXT J
80    INPUT "SEARCHED-FOR NUMBER";X
90    FIRST=1 : LAST=N
100   FOUND$="NO"
110   WHILE FIRST<=LAST AND FOUND$="NO"
120     MD=INT((FIRST+LAST)/2)
130     IF X=A(MD) THEN FOUND$="YES"
140     IF X<A(MD) THEN LAST=MD-1
                   ELSE _____
150   WEND
160   IF FOUND$="YES" THEN PRINT "ON LIST IN POSITION";MD
                   ELSE PRINT "NOT ON LIST"
170   END
```

ANSWER   The ELSE branch is to be taken when the search should be further narrowed to the right-half. To do so, we must change the value of FIRST so that it represents the box just to the right of the middle box. (The value of LAST should not be changed.) The ELSE branch should be ELSE FIRST = MD + 1.

When Number X Not on List.   When the number X is not on the list, the subscript FIRST will eventually exceed the subscript LAST. Consider the array from Example 1, with X = 90. The segment under consideration will be narrowed down to:

87 92 95   with FIRST = 11, LAST = 13, MD = 12.

A(11) A(12) A(13)

Then it will be narrowed to

87   with FIRST = 11, LAST = 11, MD = 11.

A(11)

Then since 90 is not less than 87, FIRST will become 12 and LAST will remain 11. Note what will then happen in line 110 of the preceding program.

24.3 Measure of Efficiency

For a linear search on a list of size N:

1. If the item is on the list, it would require, on the average, N/2 comparisons to locate its position.
2. If the item is not on the list, it would always require *exactly* N comparisons.

For a binary search on a list of size N, whether or not the item is on the list, it would require at most $INT[\log_2 N] + 1$ comparison pairs. Thus, for a list of size 128 with an item not on the list, it would take 128 comparisons by the linear search to ascertain that the item is not on the list; it would take only eight executions of the loop by the binary search method (each time the loop body is executed, the current segment is cut in half).

Exercises

1. For the array

| 38 | 43 | 49 | 52 | 57 | 59 | 64 | 77 | 82 | 85 | 94 |

and X = 64, here is a list of the successive values for the variables FIRST and LAST: FIRST = 1, LAST = 11; FIRST = 7, LAST = 11; FIRST = 7, LAST = 8. Then 64 is located.

Give that type of list for FIRST and LAST when
(a) X=52   **(c)** X=85
(b) X=53   **(d)** X=72

2. Use the array below.

21	25	28	30	34	36	38	50	52	53	58	59	60	62	65	68

As in Exercise 1, give the listing for all the values of FIRST and LAST when
(a) X=38   **(b)** X=65   **(c)** X=44

3. For a binary search of 500 items, what is the maximum number of times the loop body will be executed?

4. What changes would be needed to have the program of Section 24.2 search for X$ in the array A$(1) to A$(N)?

5. Also see Appendix B, Exercises 44–46.

25

Matrices: Two-Dimensional Arrays

So far, all the arrays we have considered have been one-dimensional, that is, only one index was necessary to specify the desired element. However, when information fits naturally into a rectangular table, it is often advantageous to store it in a two-dimensional array, also called a **matrix**. For a matrix, two indexes are necessary to specify any one element; namely, a row index and a column index.

For example let P be the following matrix with three rows and four columns:

	col. 1	col. 2	col. 3	col. 4
row 1	9	5	14	1
row 2	7	3	−6	6
row 3	2	0	10	4

For this matrix, P(1,1) denotes the value in row 1, column 1, namely 9. P(1,2) denotes the value in row 1, column 2, namely 5. In general, P(I,J) denotes the value in row I, column J. What is the value of P(2,1)? *Answer:* 7 (the value in the second row and first column). What are the values of P(2,3), P(3,2), and P(1,4)? *Answer:* −6, 0, and 1, respectively.

25.1 DIM Statements

In a BASIC program that uses two-dimensional matrices, there should be DIM statements to tell the computer how many rows and columns each matrix is to have. For example, DIM P(3,4) tells the computer that the matrix P is to have three rows and four columns. Similarly DIM Q(2,5) tells the computer that the matrix Q is to have two rows and five columns. A single DIM statement can dimension several matrices, as in DIM A(4,7),B(5,5),C(16,3). Since DIM statements should precede the first use of the matrices involved, DIM statements are usually given toward the beginning of the program.

NOTE: Although a zero row and a zero column of a matrix are also created by a DIM statement, none of the following programs uses this feature.

25.2 Reading DATA Numbers into Matrix

Note the use of nested loops to read DATA values into a matrix. In the following program DIM Q(2,3) creates memory space for a matrix with two rows and three columns. You may envision that each time READ Q(ROW,COL) is executed, the next DATA number will be read into the box occupying the row and column of the table, corresponding to ROW and COL.

```
100  DIM Q(2,3)
110  FOR ROW=1 TO 2
120    FOR COL=1 TO 3
130       READ Q(ROW,COL)
140    NEXT COL
150  NEXT ROW
160  PRINT Q(2,1)
170  PRINT Q(1,2)
180  DATA 6,3,5
190  DATA 8,7,9
200  END
```

While ROW = 1, the first value of COL will be 1, then 2, then 3. Line 130 becomes READ Q(1,1), then READ Q(1,2), and then READ Q(1,3). Thus, while ROW = 1, DATA numbers are read into the first row of Q.

While ROW = 2, DATA numbers are read into the second row of Q. Hence, by the time the computer has finished the nested loop, the memory box picture will be

6	3	5
8	7	9

REMARK: If DATA lines 180 and 190 had been written as a single line DATA 6,3,5,8,7,9, the same memory matrix would have been created. However, it is usually better style to format DATA lines to resemble the matrix that will be created in memory.

PROBLEM   Draw a memory box picture for the matrix B in the following program; then give the printout.

```
100   DIM B(3,2)
110   FOR ROW=1 TO 3
120      FOR COL=1 TO 2
130         READ B(ROW,COL)
140      NEXT COL
150   NEXT ROW
160   PRINT B(2,1)
170   PRINT B(3,2)
180   PRINT B(3,1) + B(3,2)
190   DATA 5,8
200   DATA 7,12
210   DATA 11,29
220   END
```

ANSWER   The memory box picture will be

5	8
7	12
11	29

The printout will be

```
7
29
40
```

PROBLEM   Fill in the blanks in lines 110, 120, and 130 from this program fragment that will read DATA values into the matrix A.

```
100   DIM A(3,4)
110   FOR ROW=1 TO _____
120      FOR COL=1 TO _____
130         READ _____
140      NEXT COL
150   NEXT ROW
160   DATA 37,45,52,72
170   DATA 44,85,62,60
180   DATA 39,28,51,45
```

ANSWER The upper limit for the outer loop gives the number of rows. When ROW = 1, the first four DATA values are read into the first row of A. When ROW = 2, the second row is read. When ROW = 3, the third row is read.

Line 110   FOR ROW = 1 TO 3
Line 120   FOR COL = 1 TO 4
Line 130   READ A(ROW, COL)

25.3 Summing Columns

Summing Single Column of Matrix.   Suppose the matrix Q contains the following values:

1	4	2
3	6	4
9	9	5

Complete lines 230 and 250 so that the program fragment below will compute and then print out the sum of the numbers in the second column of Q. Thus, the printout should be ☐ 19 ☐, since 4 + 6 + 9 = 19.

```
200   REM SUM OF COLUMN 2
210   COL=2
220   SUM=0
230   FOR _____
240      SUM=SUM+Q(ROW,COL)
250   NEXT _____
260   PRINT SUM
```

ANSWER You want to add Q(1,2) + Q(2,2) + Q(3,2). While COL = 2, the row index ROW should be 1, then 2, then 3. Thus, line 230 should be FOR ROW = 1 TO 3 and line 250 NEXT ROW. Note also that this program could have been written with line 210 omitted and line 240 changed to SUM = SUM + Q(ROW,2). The printout would still be ☐ 19 ☐.

Summing Columns of Table Separately.   Suppose that a basketball team consisting of five players has played three games and that the players' scoring is given in the table below.

	Game 1	Game 2	Game 3
Player 1	16	23	21
Player 2	15	30	18
Player 3	7	6	10
Player 4	12	11	16
Player 5	8	10	15

PROBLEM   Complete lines 180, 210, 230, and 260 of the following program, which computes the total number of points scored in each game.

```
95   REM SUMMING COLUMNS (GAME POINT TOTALS)
96   REM ****
100  DIM PTS(5,3) : DIM SUM(3)
110  FOR PLAYER=1 TO 5
120    FOR GAME=1 TO 3
130      READ PTS(PLAYER,GAME)
140    NEXT GAME
150  NEXT PLAYER
160  '
170  PRINT "GAME","PT. TOTAL"
180  FOR _____
190    REM SUM EACH GAME
200    SUM(GAME)=0
210    FOR _____
220      SUM(GAME)=SUM(GAME)+PTS(PLAYER,GAME)
230    NEXT _____
240    REM POINT TOTAL FOR GAME
250    PRINT GAME,SUM(GAME)
260  NEXT _____
270  DATA 16,23,21
280  DATA 15,30,18
290  DATA 7,6,10
300  DATA 12,11,16
310  DATA 8,10,15
320  END
```

The printout should be

GAME	PT. TOTAL
1	58
2	80
3	80

ANSWER   You must find the sum of column 1, then the sum of column 2, and then the sum of column 3. Thus, the outer loop should be FOR GAME = 1 TO 3.

> (line) 180   FOR GAME = 1 TO 3
> (line) 210   FOR PLAYER = 1 TO 5
> (line) 230   NEXT PLAYER
> (line) 260   NEXT GAME

25.4 Summing Rows

To sum each of the rows of a table separately you would use a nested loop similar to the one in lines 180–260 of the previous program.

QUESTION   Assuming ROW is the row variable and COL is the column variable, should the outer loop be FOR COL = 1 TO _____ or FOR ROW = 1 TO _____?

ANSWER   The outer loop should be FOR ROW = 1 TO _____. Exercise 4(b) covers this topic in more detail.

25.5 Printing Matrix Contents

PROBLEM   Suppose A is the 3 × 3 matrix with values as depicted:

Matrix A

$$\begin{bmatrix} 12 & 14 & 13 \\ 15 & 18 & 19 \\ 22 & 16 & 21 \end{bmatrix}$$

We wish to write a program fragment to print out the contents of A in the format

```
12    14    13
15    18    19
22    16    21
```

1. What printout will be produced by program fragment (a)? (It is not in the desired format.)

2. Complete lines 240 and 250 for program fragment (b) so that the desired printout will be produced.

(a)

```
200  FOR ROW=1 TO 3
210     FOR COL=1 TO 3
220        PRINT A(ROW,COL);
230     NEXT COL
240  NEXT ROW
```

(b)

```
200  FOR ROW=1 TO 3
210     FOR COL=1 TO 3
220        PRINT A(ROW,COL);
230     NEXT COL
240  _____
250  _____
```

ANSWER   (a)

| 12 | 14 | 13 | 15 | 18 | 19 | 22 | 16 | 21 |

(b) Line 240 should be PRINT and line 250 NEXT ROW. Here is why: While ROW = 1 the first row of matrix A is printed. Before going on to print the next row of A, we need to drop the printing carriage down to the next line—this is accomplished by the blank PRINT statement.

Printing Headings and Matrix Contents.   The program below will produce the following printout. (It uses the TAB function instead of commas in the PRINT statements, because there are *six* tightly spaced columns.)

SALESPERSON	MON	TUE	WED	THU	TOTAL
SMITH	15	10	12	10	47
CHAN	12	18	20	15	65
ORTIZ	14	17	12	10	53

```
95    REM  SALESMEN'S WEEKLY REPORT
96    REM ****
100   DIM HRS(3,4)  :  DIM NAM$(3),SUM(3)
110   FOR SALESMAN=1 TO 3
120     READ NAM$(SALESMAN)
130     SUM(SALESMAN)=0
140     FOR DAY=1 TO 4
150       READ HRS(SALESMAN,DAY)
160       SUM(SALESMAN)=SUM(SALESMAN)+HRS(SALESMAN,DAY)
170     NEXT DAY
180   NEXT SALESMAN
190   '
200   PRINT "SALESMAN"; TAB(11)"MON"; TAB(16)"TUE";
210   PRINT TAB(21)"WED"; TAB(26)"THU"; TAB(31)"TOTAL"
220   FOR SALESMAN=1 TO 3
230     PRINT NAM$(SALESMAN);
240     FOR DAY=1 TO 4
250       PRINT TAB(11+(DAY-1)*5)HRS(SALESMAN,DAY);
260     NEXT DAY
270     PRINT TAB(31)SUM(SALESMAN)
280   NEXT SALESMAN
290   DATA "SMITH",15,10,12,10
300   DATA "CHAN",12,18,20,15
310   DATA "ORTIZ",14,17,12,10
320   END
```

REMARKS:

1. Note the formula TAB(11 + (DAY − 1)*5) used in line 250.
2. Note that line 250 has trailing punctuation whereas line 270 does *not*.

Exercises

1. **(a)** What DIM statement would be needed for each of these matrices

$$A = \begin{bmatrix} 1 & 2 & 1 & 4 & 5 \\ 2 & 1 & 6 & 7 & 8 \end{bmatrix} \quad B = \begin{bmatrix} 3 \\ 5 \end{bmatrix} \quad C = \begin{bmatrix} 1 & 2 & 1 \\ 5 & 4 & 4 \\ 1 & 1 & 1 \end{bmatrix}$$

(b) B(M,N) is the number in the Mth _____ and Nth _____ of the table B.

(c) In using the loop method to read in matrix entries, it is standard to read in the entries row by row. Thus, to read into a 5×3 matrix, the outer loop should be FOR _____ =1 TO _____.

2. What will the printouts be?

(a)

```
10  DIM A(2,4)
20  FOR ROW=1 TO 2
30    FOR COL=1 TO 4
40      READ A(ROW,COL)
50    NEXT COL
60  NEXT ROW
70  PRINT A(2,2)
80  DATA 4,5,6,7,8,1,2,3
90  END
```

(b)

```
10   DIM EV(3,2)
20   FOR ROW=1 TO 3
30     FOR COL=1 TO 2
40       READ EV(ROW,COL)
50     NEXT COL
60   NEXT ROW
70   PRINT EV(3,1)+1
80   PRINT EV(3,1)+EV(3,2)
90   DATA 2,4,6,8,10,12
100  END
```

(c)

```
10   DIM W(4,3)
20   COUNT=1
30   FOR ROW=1 TO 4
40     FOR COL=1 TO 3
50       COUNT=COUNT+1
60       W(ROW,COL)=COUNT
70     NEXT COL
80   NEXT ROW
90   PRINT W(1,3);W(2,3)
100  END
```

3. What will the printout be?

```
10   DIM X(4,3)
20   FOR ROW=1 TO 4
30     FOR COL=1 TO 3
40       READ X(ROW,COL)
50     NEXT COL
60   NEXT ROW
70   FOR COL=1 TO 3
80     PRINT X(4,COL)
90   NEXT COL
100  DATA 1,2,3,1,1,1,5,6,7,8,9,10
110  END
```

4. (a) Write a program to read three lines of DATA into the 3 × 4 matrix A, so that

$$A = \begin{bmatrix} 3 & 1 & 5 & 8 \\ 2 & 0 & 0 & 4 \\ 9 & 11 & 2 & 9 \end{bmatrix}$$

(This program will produce no printout.)
(b) Extend the program in part (a) so that it gives the printout

```
ROW              SUM OF  ENTRIES
 1                    17
 2                    6
 3                    31
```

(c) Extend the program so that it also gives the printout

```
COLUMN           SUM OF  ENTRIES
 1                    14
 2                    12
 3                    7
 4                    21
```

5. Modify the basketball scoring program so that the printout gives the point average for each player separately.

6. Write a program that prints which students had an average above 90 and then on which exams the class average was above 90.

Student	Exam 1	Exam 2	Exam 3
1	90	85	90
2	95	87	93
3	100	80	92

Use as DATA

    DATA 90,85,90
    DATA 95,87,93
    DATA 100,80,92

Printout

```
STUDENTS WITH OVER 90 AVERAGE
   STUDENT 2
   STUDENT 3
EXAMS WITH OVER 90 CLASS AVERAGE
   EXAM 1
   EXAM 3
```

★★   **7. (a)** Write a program that will print out the total vote for each candidate separately. Use as DATA

DATA 60,100,40

DATA 30,90,30

DATA 90,90,90

	Precinct 1	**Precinct 2**	**Precinct 3**
Cane	60	30	90
Hund	100	90	90
Wolff	40	30	90

(b) Modify the program so that it will also give the percentage of the vote received by each candidate in each district. Format the printout as follows:

```
PERCENT OF VOTE
PRECINCT    CANE        HUND        WOLFF
   1         30          50          20
   2         20          60          20
   3        33.3333     33.3333     33.3333
```

★   **8.** Suppose for each pair of DATA numbers, the first number (1, 2, or 3) tells whether the vote is for Washington, Jefferson, or Lincoln, and the second number tells whether the voter was female or male (1 for female and 2 for male).

DATA 1,2,3,2,1,2,3,1,3,2,1,1,2,1,1,1,3,2,1,1,2,1,1,1,999,999

Using the above DATA line, run a program that will tabulate the votes in the following form. (You may use commas in PRINT statements rather than TAB.)

CANDIDATE	FEMALE VOTES	MALE VOTES
WASHINGTON	4	2
JEFFERSON	2	0
LINCOLN	1	3

(*Hint:* Use T(1,1), T(1,2), T(2,1), T(2,2), T(3,1), T(3,2) as counters.)

★   **9.** Write a program for the previous problem, this time using subscripted string variables, so that the three printout lines containing the results are handled by a FOR-NEXT loop.

★   **10.** Here is a price schedule for three items.

	No Discount	Student Price	Member Price
TV	400	340	310
Stereo	300	250	190
Radio	175	150	115

Write an interactive program that reads the table into a matrix, and includes the lines

```
30  PRINT  " I AM READY TO TAKE YOUR ORDER "
40  PRINT  " TYPE 1 FOR TV, 2 FOR STEREO, OR 3 FOR RADIO"
60  PRINT  "TYPE 1 FOR NO DISC. 2 FOR STUD. 3 FOR MEMB. "
80  PRINT  "HOW MANY ARE YOU ORDERING"
```

so that if the user inputs 2, then 3, then 5, the printout should be

```
YOUR TOTAL IS 950 DOLLARS
```

since he has ordered five stereos at member's price. Run it also inputting 1, 2, 4. The printout should be

```
YOUR TOTAL IS 1360 DOLLARS
```

★★   **11.** Each triple of numbers in the following DATA line gives the item, discount status, and how many were ordered, with the same coding and pricing as in Exercise 10:

DATA 2,1,5,1,1,6,3,1,8,2,2,15,1,2,7,3,2,9,1,2,6,

DATA 2,1,6,999,999,999

(a) Write a program that computes the total bill.

(b) Write a program that prints separately the total bills for TVs, stereos, and radios.

★ 12. (a) For the following program fragment, what will the printout be on a system that has five zones to a line?

(b) Insert one blank PRINT statement so that the printout will be formatted as a 3 × 3 matrix.

```
30   FOR ROW=1 TO 3
40      FOR COL=1 TO 3
50         PRINT AM(ROW,COL),
60      NEXT COL
70   NEXT ROW
```

When line 30 is reached, the contents of the 3 × 3 matrix AM is as follows:

1	2	3
4	5	6
7	8	9

★ 13. Modify the three salespeople program of Section 25.5, so that for the given DATA the printout will be

SALESPERSON	MON	TUE	WED	THU	TOTAL
SMITH	15	10	12	10	47
CHAN	12	18	20	15	65
ORTIZ	14	17	12	10	53
TOTALS	41	45	44	35	165

★ 14. For the following DATA lines

DATA "FRESHMEN",50,40,10

DATA "SOPHOMORES",40,60,10

DATA "JUNIORS",30,70,10

DATA "SENIORS",50,40,8

write a program that will produce as printout the table

YEAR	DEM	REP	IND	TOTAL
FRESHMEN	50	40	10	100
SOPHOMORES	40	60	10	110
JUNIORS	30	70	10	110
SENIORS	50	40	8	98

15. Each of the following DATA lines represents the scores for a student on three exams:

DATA "SMITH",40,80,91

DATA "JONES",40,80,95

DATA "DIAZ",50,90,91

DATA "CHAN",50,70,91

Using a one-dimensional array for names and a two-dimensional array for grades, write a program so that for the four students listed above, the printout is

```
SMITH       40    80    91
JONES       40    80    95
DIAZ        50    90    91
CHAN        50    70    91
***CLASS AVERAGE FOR EACH EXAM***
AVERAGE ON EXAM 1:  45
AVERAGE ON EXAM 2:  80
AVERAGE ON EXAM 3:  92
HIGHEST INDIVIDUAL SCORE WAS 95
OBTAINED BY JONES ON EXAM 3
```

16. Also see Appendix B, Exercise 42.

CHAPTER
26

Sequential Files

All the methods for entering data that have been discussed until now have involved typing and using data as part of a single program. With these methods, if the data used in one program are later needed for another program, it is necessary to retype those data completely. Clearly, this is undesirable when large amounts of data are involved. For example, it would be extremely time consuming for a large company to retype all employee data each time it had a program written that put this information to a particular use.

Files provide an efficient means for storing data that can later be used by any number of programs. Files are stored on an external storage device such as a **diskette** or **hard disk**. Each file is assigned an access name for referral.

26.1 Type of Files

There are two different types of files: **sequential files** and **random access files**. For each of these types of files, the data are grouped together in records.

Sequential files, though simpler to learn, are not nearly as flexible as random access files. As you will see *sequential files* have the following two *limitations*:

1. In order to access a particular record from a sequential file, all the records preceding it must be read through first.
2. In order to update a particular record in a sequential file, it is not possible to rewrite that *one* record alone. The whole file must be copied again.

Random access files (discussed in Chapter 27) *do not have these two limitations*.

File Is Collection of Records.   Each record in a file should consist of a group of associated data. Frequently, a record will contain information concerning a single individual or item. In the first example of the next section, we consider a file consisting of four records, in which each record contains a person's name, birth year, and hourly pay rate.

File Names.   Files of records are given names so that they can be accessed by referring to their names.

26.2   Creating New File

There are three steps to creating a new file: (1) opening the file, (2) writing the data onto the file, and (3) closing the file.

OPEN Statement.   A file is opened by using the OPEN statement. The syntax for opening a sequential file is

OPEN mode, #filenumber,filename

For example, OPEN "O",#1,"BIRTH" would open the file named BIRTH in mode "O", with #1 reserved for referring to this open file. The letter "O" specifies that the file is to be opened for Output from the computer, that is, for writing onto the file. (Section 26.3 deals with OPEN statements for files to be read from.) An alternative form for the previous OPEN statement is

OPEN "BIRTH" FOR OUTPUT AS #1

WRITE # Statement.   The WRITE # statement is used to write data onto an open file. The syntax for the WRITE statement is

WRITE #filenumber, list of items

in which the list of items consists of variables separated by commas. For example, in the first program of this chapter we use WRITE #1,NAM$,YR,RATE.

CLOSE Statement.   After your program has finished using a file, that file *must* be closed. (Failure to close can lead to errors.) The syntax for CLOSE is

CLOSE #filenumber

Creating File for Four Employees.   We wish to create the following file in which each record contains an employee's *name, birth year*, and *hourly pay rate*.

"JONES",1960,4.00
"COHN",1959,8.50
"CHAN",1963,12.00
"POE",1964,5.50

We will now consider two programs, either of which could be used to create the preceding file. One program uses a FOR-NEXT loop, the other is interactive.

Creating File Using FOR-NEXT Program

```
10  OPEN "O",#1,"EMPLOY"
20  FOR J=1 TO 4
30    READ NAM$,YR,RATE
40    WRITE #1,NAM$,YR,RATE
50  NEXT J
60  CLOSE #1
70  DATA "JONES",1960,4.00,"COHN",1959,8.50
80  DATA "CHAN",1963,12.00,"POE",1964,5.50
90  END
```

REMARK: When J = 1, the first group of DATA values in line 30 is assigned to the variables NAM$, YR, and RATE. In line 40 these values are written onto the file as its first record. Similarly, for J = 2,3, and 4, the second, third, and fourth records are written.

Creating File Using Interactive Program.   In this program the data will be entered by the user in response to INPUT prompts.

```
10   OPEN "O",#1,"EMPLOY"
20   INPUT "TYPE NAME OR XYZ TO STOP";NAM$
30   WHILE NAM$ <> "XYZ"
40     INPUT "  BIRTH YR";YR
50     INPUT "  HOURLY RATE";RATE
60     WRITE #1,NAM$,YR,RATE
70     INPUT "TYPE NAME OR XYZ TO STOP";NAM$
80   WEND
90   CLOSE #1
100  END
```

Here is the run that would create the file for the four employees JONES, COHN, CHAN, and POE.

```
RUN
TYPE NAME OR XYZ TO STOP?  JONES
   BIRTH YR?  1960
   HOURLY RATE?  4.00
TYPE NAME OR XYZ TO STOP?  COHN
   BIRTH YR?  1959
   HOURLY RATE?  8.50
TYPE NAME OR XYZ TO STOP?  CHAN
   BIRTH YR?  1963
   HOURLY RATE?  12.00
TYPE NAME OR XYZ TO STOP?  POE
   BIRTH YR?  1964
   HOURLY RATE?  5.50
TYPE NAME OR XYZ TO STOP?  XYZ
```

REMARK: This program uses *pump priming* through the INPUT statement in line 20 that requests the employee's name. The input for each employee's record is split into two stages. The first employee's name is input before the loop, and his birth year and hourly rate are input at the beginning of the loop body.

26.3 Using Existing File

When an existing file is opened so that information can be retrieved, the file is said to be opened for Input, that is, so that data can be input to the computer.

End Of File Marker and EOF Function. In any file created, the computer automatically writes an **end of file marker** after the last record. The End Of File (EOF) function can be used to test whether the end of the file has been reached. Note that EOF(1) becomes true once the last record of file #1 has been retrieved. Thus, the condition WHILE NOT EOF(1) can be used to have the computer continue to enter a loop as long as the end of file marker has not been reached.

EXAMPLE   Using EMPLOY File   The following program will print out the names of anyone from the EMPLOY file who earns more than $7.00 per hour. The printout will be

```
MAKES OVER $7.00 PER HOUR
COHN
CHAN
```

```
10   OPEN "I",#1,"EMPLOY"
20   PRINT "MAKES OVER $7.00 PER HOUR"
30   WHILE NOT EOF(1)
40      INPUT #1,NAM$,YR,RATE
50      IF RATE>7 THEN PRINT NAM$
60   WEND
70   CLOSE #1
80   END
```

REMARKS

1. Line 10 opens the EMPLOY file for Input. When a file is open for input, the program can *only retrieve* information from it, that is, input data into the computer's memory.
2. In line 40, the statement INPUT #1,NAM$,YR,RATE has the computer retrieve the next record from the file and assign those three values to NAM$, YR, and RATE respectively.

EOF in Preceding Program.   The preceding program did not use any *pump-priming* because the WHILE condition in line 30, WHILE NOT EOF(1), causes the computer to continue entering the WHILE loop as long as the end of the file has *not* been reached.

INPUT PAST END Error Message.   Note that a file INPUT statement attempting to retrieve information beyond the last record will cause the computer to stop execution with the error message INPUT PAST END .

26.4 Updating Records from Existing File

Now we will consider a program that allows the owner of an auto parts store to modify a file that keeps track of how many of each item he has in stock.

For the sake of simplicity, suppose he has only five items with ID numbers 400, 402, 407, 408, 413. Each block in the file below gives an item ID number and the quantity in stock.

File before update:

| 400,36 | 402,25 | 407,84 | 408,24 | 413,6 |

Suppose that the store receives a shipment containing 10 of item 407, and 20 of item 413. Suppose also that the store has just sold four of item 400. During an update, run the following ID numbers and changes as input.

```
PART  ID  OR  999?  407
   CHANGED  BY?  10
PART  ID  OR  999?  413
   CHANGED  BY?  20
PART  ID  OR  999?  400
   CHANGED  BY?  -4
PART  ID  OR  999?  999
```

File after update:

| 400,32 | 402,25 | 407,94 | 408,24 | 413,26 |

In studying the next program, note the following important limitation of a sequential file: *when a file is opened for output (i.e., for writing onto), any previous contents of the file are erased.* Accordingly, if we want to update some of the items in an existing file we can (1) first retrieve all the file information and store it in an array, (2) perform the update on the contents of the array, and (3) finally write the modified array contents onto the file. Fill in the blanks in the following program.

NOTE: There is another method for updating a file that should be used if the file is too large to fit in memory. That method is to write directly to a new file and then kill the old file.

Program Summary. The following program allows the owner of an auto parts store to modify the file that keeps track of how many of each part is in stock. Any given part's stock might increase (as a result of a new shipment) or decrease (through a sale).

PROBLEM   Fill in lines 170, 210, and 230.

```
5     REM AUTO PARTS INVENTORY
6     REM *****
10    OPEN "I",#1,"PARTS"
20    FOR ITEM=1 TO 5
30      INPUT #1,ID(ITEM),QUANT(ITEM)
40    NEXT ITEM
50    CLOSE #1
60    '
70    REM MAKE CHANGE ON ARRAY
80    INPUT "PART ID OR 999";NUM
90    WHILE NUM <> 999
100     INPUT "  CHANGED BY";AMT
110     REM SEARCH FOR INPUT ID
120     ITEM=1
130     WHILE ID(ITEM)<>NUM AND ITEM<5
140        ITEM=ITEM+1
150     WEND
160     IF ID(ITEM)=NUM
           THEN QUANT(ITEM)=QUANT(ITEM)+AMT
           ELSE PRINT "INVALID ID"
170    _____
180   WEND
190   '
200   REM WRITE ONTO FILE
210   OPEN _____
220   FOR ITEM=1 TO 5
230     WRITE _____
240   NEXT ITEM
250   CLOSE #1
260   END
```

Lines 10–50 store all the file data in arrays.

Each execution of the loop body in lines 90–180 has the user input a change. That change is then made on the array.

Lines 220–250 write the modified array contents onto the file.

ANSWER   Line 170   INPUT "PART ID OR 999";NUM
Line 210   OPEN "O",#1,"PARTS"
Line 230   WRITE #1,ID(ITEM),QUANT(ITEM)

REMARK: Note that in line 130 we test for ITEM<5, not ITEM<=5, because if the input part number is incorrect, ITEM will eventually become 6. That would cause a problem since ID only has elements ID(1) through ID(5).

26.5 Appending New Input Items

Suppose that for an existing file, we need to append some completely new items to the end of the file (as opposed to modifying information about items already in the file). On most implementations of IBM BASIC and MBASIC, we can use the **append-file-opening statement**. The statement OPEN "A",#1,"GROUP" would open the file named GROUP for appending. This statement does not erase the previous contents of the file. Instead, it opens the file for writing onto so that the file pointer is just past the last item on the existing file.

A program to interactively append records to the file EMPLOY would be identical to the program to create EMPLOY, given in Section 26.2, with one change: line 10 would be OPEN "A",#1,"EMPLOY". The A stands for Append.

26.6 Programs with Several Files

If a program uses more than one file, we would use different #file numbers for the different files. The next program provides an example of the method for appending one file to the end of another.

EXAMPLE Suppose GROUPA and GROUPB are separate files of names. The program below will create a file GROUPC with names from GROUPB appended to those of GROUPA.

```
10    OPEN " I ",#1, "GROUPA"
20    OPEN " I ",#2, "GROUPB"
30    OPEN "O",#3, "GROUPC"
40    WHILE NOT EOF(1)
50        INPUT #1, NAM$
60        WRITE #3, NAM$
70    WEND
80    CLOSE #1
90    WHILE NOT EOF(2)
100       INPUT #2, NAM$
110       WRITE #3, NAM$
120   WEND
130   CLOSE #2
140   CLOSE #3
150   END
```

In Exercise 12 you are to merge two alphabetized files so that the resulting file is also alphabetized.

■ 26.7 Redirecting Printout

Sequential files are also convenient for printing output to the printer rather than to the screen. The previously illustrated method for doing this was to use the Ctrl-PrtSc key. Ctrl-PrtSc has two disadvantages: it always prints to the screen as well as to the printer, and it can only go to other devices. In this section, we discuss procedures for opening a file for output to the printer and for using the PRINT # statement to print to that file.

Opening Sequential Files.   Before we can print to a sequential file, we have to use the OPEN statement to open it. Recall that the syntax of the OPEN statement for output is

> OPEN "O", #filenumber, filename

In the syntax above, filename is a string expression that contains the name of the file to be opened. Certain file names are special to BASIC. For instance, the file name "SCRN:" refers to the computer screen. The file name "LPT1:" refers to the computer printer. If the file name is not a special name, it is assumed to refer to a disk file.

QUESTION   What does the following program segment do?

```
10  OPEN  "O", #1, "SCRN:"
20  OPEN  "O", #2, "LPT1:"
30  OPEN  "O", #3, "OUTFILE"
```

ANSWER   Line 10 opens the screen as file number 1. Line 20 opens the printer as file number 2. Line 30 opens the file "OUTFILE" on disk. From now on, filenumber 1 refers to the screen, filenumber 2 refers to the printer, and filenumber 3 refers to the disk file. When you have finished using a file, you must CLOSE it.

QUESTION   Assuming the preceding OPEN statements, what does the following program segment do?

```
970  CLOSE #1
980  CLOSE #2
990  CLOSE #3
```

ANSWER   Line 970 closes file #1, which was opened to the screen. Line 980 closes file #2, which was opened to the printer. Finally, line 990 closes the disk file, "OUTFILE", which was opened as file #3.

PRINT #. To print something to the file itself, we use the PRINT # statement. The syntax of the PRINT # statement is

PRINT #filenumber, value list

The filenumber must be the number of a currently open (that is, open and not yet closed) file. The value list is a list of string or numeric variables or expressions that are to be printed. The rules governing the expressions that the value list may contain are exactly the same as for the PRINT statement. In fact, the only difference between PRINT # and PRINT are that PRINT always prints on the screen, but PRINT # prints to whatever file was opened. The printing formats are *exactly the same* for both.

QUESTION What is printed by the following programs?

(a)
```
10  OPEN  "O",#1,"SCRN:"
20  PRINT #1,"HELLO THERE","FRED";"*JONES"
30  CLOSE #1
40  END
```

(b)
```
20  PRINT  "HELLO THERE","FRED";"*JONES"
40  END
```

ANSWER Both programs print

```
HELLO THERE     FRED*JONES
```

on the *screen*.

The second program is simpler than the first, but the first program is more flexible, in that it can direct the output to the screen, to the printer, or to any desired file. In order to redirect the output, we merely change the file name in line 10. This is especially convenient if there are many PRINT statements in a program.

QUESTION How would you change program (a), above, so that output will go to the printer rather than the screen? How would you need to change program (b)?

ANSWER For program (a), change line 10 to

10   OPEN "O",#1,"LPT1:"

For program (b), change the PRINT statement to LPRINT.

REMARK: It would be easier to change the first program than the second if there were many PRINT statements.

To change a program that uses PRINT or LPRINT into a program that uses PRINT #, follow these steps:

Step 1. Insert OPEN statements into the program near the beginning. If you have only PRINT or only LPRINT statements, you will need only one OPEN statement. If you have *both* PRINT and LPRINT, you will need two OPEN statements. If you have more than one OPEN statement, be sure to use different file numbers and to remember which file number is for PRINT and which one is for LPRINT.

Step 2. Change all the PRINT and LPRINT statements into PRINT # statements. Make sure that the file number in each of the PRINT # statements matches the file number in the appropriate OPEN statement. (Compare line 20 in the two preceding programs.)

Step 3. Finally, remember to close the file before the program ends. (See line 30 in program (a).)

Experienced programmers never use PRINT or LPRINT because PRINT and LPRINT make it difficult to redirect the output. PRINT #, on the other hand, enables them to write PRINT statements in almost the same way as usual and to redirect screen output to a printer. This is useful for establishing a permanent record of the printouts for debugging purposes or for handing in assignments. Printer output may also be directed to the screen, should there be no printer available to the computer at that particular time. It is also possible to PRINT # output to a disk file that may be printed later, but that procedure involves more advanced programming techniques. In order to make any of these changes, all that requires changing is the file name in the OPEN statement—just *one line*.

Exercises

1. For each of the following OPEN statements state whether it will be used to create the named file or to retrieve information from it.
   (a) OPEN "I",#1,"EMPLOY"
   (b) OPEN "O",#1,"EMPLOY"
   (c) OPEN "O",#1,"ROSTER"
2. Explain the syntax error for each of the following:
   (a) OPEN "O",1,"EMPLOY"
   (b) CLOSE "0",#1,"EMPLOY"
   (c) INPUT "EMPLOY",#1,N$

3. Write a program to create interactively a file named PAYROLL so that it will contain

   "FOY",5.00,42

   "POE",6.00,40

   "BOND",7.50,30

   "SIMMS",5.50,41

   (Each record contains an employee's name, pay rate, and hours worked.)

4. Write a program that will print out the contents of the file EMPLOY in the following form:

   ```
   NAME        BIRTH YR      HOURS
   JONES        1960          4.00
   COHN         1959          8.50
   CHAN         1963         12.00
   POE          1964          5.50
   **** NUMBER OF RECORDS  4
   ```

5. Write a program to print out for PAYROLL of Exercise 3. The amount each employee is to be paid and also the total paid should be printed.

6. Write a program to create a file named TELE with the information

   "FOY","482-7316"

   "HALL","482-5512"

   "POE","482-5132"

   "NYE","482-5411"

   (Use a string variable for the telephone number.)

★ 7. Run a program to create a file with the information

   "JONES","05/30/1960"

   "COHEN","07/02/1959"

   "POE","11/22/1960"

   "FOY","04/30/1958"

   Run a second program that will print out the names of all the people born in 1960. (See the chapter on substring manipulations.)

8. Suppose we have a file named ROSTER for which the statement WRITE #1,N$,G1,G2 was used to write onto the file. Suppose, in addition, we do not know how many records there are in the file. Write a program that will give as printout

   ```
   FILE CONTAINS_____RECORDS
   ```

9. Insert additional statement(s) to the program (Section 26.4) to modify the PARTS file so that if the user inputs an ID number not included in the file, the computer will print back the message

```
INVALID ID NUM. TRY AGAIN
PART ID NUM?
```

★ 10. Suppose the file, ADDRESSES, contains twelve addresses in the form

```
AL JONES,     13 APPLE ST.,      ALBANY, N.Y.

ED BROWN,     5 MAIN ST.,        BOSTON, MA.

LOU BOND,     4 OWL AVE.,        DALLAS, TX.

    :             :                  :
```

Write a program that will prepare mailing labels three across in the form

```
AL JONES        ED BROWN        LOU BOND
13 APPLE ST.    5 MAIN ST.      4 OWL AVE.
ALBANY, N.Y.    BOSTON, MA.     DALLAS, TX.
    :               :               :
```

11. Write a program to read from two files, ROSTERA and ROSTERB, and create a new file, ROSTERC, containing all names common to ROSTERA and ROSTERB.

★ 12. Suppose ROSTERA and ROSTERB are two alphabetized files. Write a program to create a file, ROSTERC, that contains the combined contents of ROSTERA and ROSTERB in alphabetical order. ROSTERC is called the **merge** of ROSTERA and ROSTERB.

13. Also see Appendix C, Exercises 15 and 16.

CHAPTER 27

Random Access Files

27.1 Random Access Files versus Sequential Files

One advantage of **random access files** is that a single record can be accessed directly. For example, in a random access file of 1000 records, if you wish to access just the record in position 800, you can have the computer skip directly to this record. By contrast, in a sequential file, to access the 800th record it would be necessary for the computer to access the first 799 records—a much more time consuming procedure than skipping directly to the 800th record.

Even when you do not know the numerical position of the particular record you wish to access, ordered random access files allow the possibility of a binary search (see Chapter 24), whereas sequential files only permit linear searches.

Another advantage of random access files is that it is much easier to make changes in data stored in the files. Recall that to change data in a sequential file it was necessary to temporarily store the file in an array, make the changes on the array, and then copy over the whole file. With a random access file it is possible to make the changes directly on the file.

The flexibility of random access files is made possible by the more rigid way their records are structured. Two points are worth mentioning in this connection:

1. All records of a random access file must be of the same length. (This is what makes it feasible for the computer to jump directly to a particular record or to update a single record without copying over the file.)

2. All data, even the numerical values, are stored in string form. This ensures uniform record length and helps speed up execution time. This feature does complicate the programmer's task, however, since

it requires converting numerical values back and forth between numerical and string values.

27.2 Files without Header Record

MKS$, MKI$, and MKD$ Functions.   All data (including numerical values) in a random access file are stored in string form. The make string, MKS$, function converts a single precision number into a four-byte string. The MKI$ and MKD$ functions are also available. MKI$ converts an integer into a two-byte string and MKD$ converts a double precision number into an eight-byte string.

Opening Random Access File.   In a random access file, each record must have the same total length. Moreover, each record is subdivided into *fields* of specified lengths.

Opening a random access file requires a pair of statements: (1) an OPEN statement gives the name of the file and the total length for each record, and (2) a FIELD statement defines the fields into which each record is subdivided. For example,

```
10  OPEN  "R",#1,"ROSTER",12
20  FIELD #1,8 AS PERSON$,4 AS YEAR$
```

opens the file named ROSTER, in which each record has a total length 12 and is subdivided into a PERSON$ field of length 8 and a YEAR$ field of length 4. (The "R" in line 10 informs the computer that the file is R̲andom access.) Note the use of a string variable for a year.

Suppose for the sake of simplicity that we want the file ROSTER to contain the three records as given below. (Note that each record has a name field and a birth-year field.)

ROSTER FILE

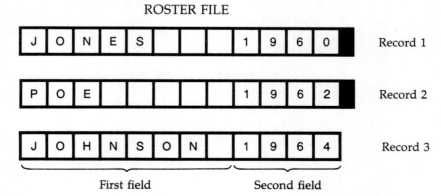

| J | O | N | E | S | | | | 1 | 9 | 6 | 0 | Record 1

| P | O | E | | | | | | 1 | 9 | 6 | 2 | Record 2

| J | O | H | N | S | O | N | | 1 | 9 | 6 | 4 | Record 3

First field   Second field

LSET and RSET.   The only way to assign a value to a field variable is by using an LSET or RSET statement. *Ordinary LET statements must not be used.*

When the LSET statement is used to assign a string value to a field variable it left justifies the string. For example, if PERSON$ is a field of length 8, the statement LSET PERSON$ = "POE" will position POE starting at the left and then pad the remaining field spaces with blanks:

PERSON$

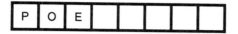

Although LSET is much more common, the RSET statement may be used when you wish the strings to be right justified.

PUT.   The LSET and RSET statements only store the string values in a buffer for field variables. In order to *write* the buffer contents onto the appropriate file as a record, you need to use the PUT statement. For example, the statement PUT #1,3 will take all the strings previously assigned by LSET and RSET and write them as the *third* record of file #1.

Program to Create ROSTER File.   Lines 10 and 20 open the file and field it. Let us consider what is involved in writing a single record onto the file, such as to write the record JOHNSON 1964 into position 3 of the file. First, LSET statements are used to assign the values "JOHNSON" and "1964" to the field variables PERSON$ and YEAR$. Then the record as a whole is written into position 3 by the statement PUT #1,3.

Here is a complete program to create the ROSTER file with the three records:

```
10   OPEN "R",#1,"ROSTER",12
20   FIELD #1,8 AS PERSON$,4 AS YEAR$
30   FOR REC=1 TO 3
40     READ NAM$,YR
50     LSET PERSON$=NAM$
60     LSET YEAR$=MKS$(YR)
70     PUT #1,REC
80   NEXT REC
90   DATA "JONES",1960,"POE",1962,"JOHNSON",1964
100  CLOSE #1
110  END
```

REMARKS:
1. Note that for each REC, the statement PUT #1,REC writes the current values of the field variables as record REC in the files.
2. Use LSET statements (and never LET statements) to assign values to field

variables. Using a LET statement would cause the pointer for that variable to point to a string space instead of the file buffer. In the above program, PERSON\$ is a field variable of length eight. Thus, PERSON\$ is expecting as values strings of length *exactly* eight. A statement like LSET PERSON\$ = "POE" assigns "POE" as an eight-character string by left justifying (using "POE" as the first three characters, and *using blanks as the remaining five characters*). It is stored as "POE   ".

3. Note that line 60 was not simply LSET YEAR = YR. This is because all field variables must be string variables. The make string function, MKS\$, converts a number (single precision) into a string.

Retrieving Record from File: CVS, CVI, and CVD Functions.   Recall that numerical data is stored in a file in string form. Thus, before this data can be used, it must be converted back into numerical form. The CVS (ConVert Single precision) function converts the four-byte string form of a number into a numerical value. Similarly, CVI (ConVert Integer) and CVD (ConVert Double precision) are used to convert string forms of integers and double precision numbers, respectively, into numerical values.

GET Statement.   The GET statement is used to assign a record from the file, as values to the field variables. For example, GET #1,2 would assign the values in record number 2 to field variables.

In the program below, the record in position two of the ROSTER file will be accessed. The printout will specify in what year the person in record two was born, and also in what year he will turn 30. Thus, the printout will be

```
POE        WAS BORN IN 1962
HE WILL BE 30 IN 1992
```

```
10  OPEN "R",#1,"ROSTER",12
20  FIELD #1,8 AS PERSON$,4 AS YEAR$
30  GET #1,2
40  PRINT PERSON$;" WAS BORN IN";CVS(YEAR$)
50  PRINT "HE WILL BE 30 IN";CVS(YEAR$)+30
60  CLOSE #1
70  END
```

REMARKS

1. The CVS (convert string) function is used to convert the four-byte string form of a number into numerical form. This conversion is necessary even

to print the number. Try replacing line 40 by PRINT PERSON$;"WAS BORN IN";YEAR$ (this would not work); the computer would not print 1962.

2. In the printout, note that there are six spaces between POE and WAS. This is because POE was stored in the eight-place field with five trailing blanks. The sixth space comes from ;"   WAS . . ." in line 40.

Drawback of Files without Headers.   Recall that when we wished to access each of the records from a sequential file, we could use the EOF function to prevent the computer from reading past the last record. However, *there is no EOF well suited to random access files.*

In the next section we introduce the technique of using the first record to keep track of the number of records in the file—a **header record**—enabling a program to access each of the records in the file by using a FOR-NEXT loop.

27.3 Creating File with Record 1 Header

Using First Record as Header.   Two different programs to create the furniture store STOCK file for *four* items are discussed in this section. Note that record 1 gives the count for the number of actual furniture records to follow. A furniture record uses the variables ITEMNAME$,PRICE$,SUPPLY$.

Furniture STOCK file

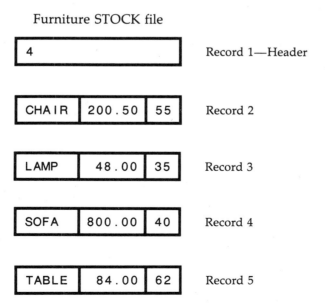

4			Record 1—Header
CHAIR	200.50	55	Record 2
LAMP	48.00	35	Record 3
SOFA	800.00	40	Record 4
TABLE	84.00	62	Record 5

Multiple Field Statements for Same File.   It is permissible to have two or more different field statements for the same file. The only use that we will make of this feature is in creating the header record as record 1.

```
100   OPEN  "R" , #1 , "STOCK" , 15
110   FIELD  #1 , 2  AS  NUMITEMS$
120   FIELD  #1 , 7  AS  ITEMNAME$ , 4  AS  PRICE$ , 4  AS  SUPPLY$
```

Line 110 creates the field with variable NUMITEMS$. This variable will be used for the header record.

Creating File Using Data from DATA Lines

```
95    REM CREATING FURNITURE FILE FROM DATA
96    REM ****
100   OPEN  "R" , #1 , "STOCK" , 15
110   FIELD  #1 , 2  AS  NUMITEMS$
120   FIELD  #1 , 7  AS  ITEMNAME$ , 4  AS  PRICE$ , 4  AS  SUPPLY$
130   FOR REC=2 TO 5
140     READ NAM$ , COST , QUANT
150     LSET  ITEMNAME$=NAM$
160     LSET  PRICE$=MKS$ ( COST )
170     LSET  SUPPLY$=MKS$ ( QUANT )
180     PUT #1 , REC
190   NEXT REC
200   LSET NUMITEMS$=MKI$ ( 4 )
210   PUT #1 , 1
220   CLOSE #1
230   DATA  "CHAIR" , 200.50 , 55 , "LAMP" , 48.00 , 35
240   DATA  "SOFA" , 800.00 , 40 , "TABLE" , 84.00 , 62
250   END
```

REMARKS
1. The *four* records for the individual furniture items are contained in records 2 through 5. Note the use of the statement FOR REC = 2 TO 5.
2. Record 1 is reserved for the number of items. Note that in the LSET statement in line 200, the number of items (4) is converted into a two-byte integer string using MKI$. Line 210 writes this number as the first record of the file.

Creating Furniture STOCK File Interactively

PROBLEM   The following program could also be used to create the previous STOCK file. Complete lines 170, 190, 240, and 250.

```
95    REM CREATING FURNITURE FILE INTERACTIVELY
96    REM ****
100   OPEN "R",#1,"STOCK",15
110   FIELD #1,2 AS NUMITEMS$
120   FIELD #1,7 AS ITEMNAME$,4 AS PRICE$,4 AS SUPPLY$
130   COUNT=0          ' SET RECORD COUNTER AT 0
140   INPUT "TYPE NAME OF ITEM OR XYZ";NAM$
150   WHILE NAM$<>"XYZ"
160     INPUT "TYPE PRICE AND QUANTITY IN STOCK";COST,QUANT
170     LSET ITEMNAME$=_____
180     LSET PRICE$=MKS$(COST)
190     LSET SUPPLY$=_____
200     PUT #1,COUNT +2        'FIRST ITEM AS RECORD 2
210     COUNT=COUNT +1
220     INPUT "TYPE NAME OF ITEM OR XYZ";NAM$
230   WEND
240   LSET _____
250   PUT _____
260   CLOSE #1
270   END
```

ANSWER   In line 170 the make string function is not needed, since NAM$ is already a string. Line 170 should be LSET ITEMNAME$ = NAM$. In line 190, however, QUANT must be converted to string form. Line 190 should be LSET SUPPLY$ = MKS$(QUANT).

   Lines 240 and 250 write the count for the number of items onto the file as record 1. Line 240 should be LSET NUMITEMS$ = MKI$(COUNT). Line 250 should be PUT #1,1.

■■■ **27.4** Retrieving Records from File with Header

PROBLEM   **Accessing Each Record from File**   The program below will read through the furniture STOCK file and print out the names of any items for which the supply has dropped below 50. Fill in the blanks in lines 150 and 180. (Note that SUPPLY$ is in string form.)

```
95    REM PRINTING SUPPLIES<50
96    REM ****
100   OPEN "R",#1,"STOCK",15
110   FIELD #1,2 AS NUMITEMS$
120   FIELD #1,7 AS ITEMNAME$,4 AS PRICE$,4 AS SUPPLY$
130   GET #1,1      'GET NUMBER OF ITEMS
140   PRINT "ITEMS WITH SUPPLY LESS THAN 50"
150   FOR REC=_____ TO CVI(NUMITEMS$)+1
160      GET #1,REC
170      NAM$=ITEMNAME$
180      QUANT=_____
190      IF QUANT<50 THEN PRINT NAM$;QUANT
200   NEXT REC
210   CLOSE #1
220   END
```

ANSWER The blank in line 150 should be 2, since record 1 will hold the leader. Line 180 should be QUANT=CVS(SUPPLY$).

REMARK: Remember that the record number of the last record is the numerical value of NUMITEMS$, plus 1 for the header record. Hence the limit value in line 150 above.

PROBLEM Fill in line 80.

```
5     REM PRICE CHANGING
6     REM ****
10    OPEN "R",#1,"STOCK",15
20    FIELD #1,7 AS ITEMNAME$,4 AS PRICE$,4 AS SUPPLY$
30    INPUT "TYPE RECORD POSITION OF ITEM";REC
40    GET #1,REC
50    PRINT ITEMNAME$;" OLD PRICE $";CVS(PRICE$)
60    INPUT "TYPE NEW PRICE";COST
70    LSET PRICE$=MKS$(COST)
80    _____
90    CLOSE #1
100   END
```

ANSWER Line 80 will replace the old record in position REC with the current values of the field variables. Line 80 should be PUT #1,REC.

REMARK: Note that this program did not have to use a second field Statement, because it did not need to know the number of items. However, the user must be careful not to input a record position of 1, the header position.

Program to Modify Record When Position Unknown. Suppose that the clerk in the furniture store wants to update the STOCK file with the new price for sofas, but does not know the record position for sofas. The following program allows the user to input the name of the item. After the computer performs a linear search to locate the record position for that item, it asks the clerk for the new price. Here is a typical run:

```
TYPE ITEM IN QUOTES WITH LENGTH 7? "SOFA    "
OLD PRICE OF SOFA $800
TYPE NEW PRICE? 859.88
```

```
5     REM FIND AND REPLACE RECORD
6     REM *****
10    OPEN "R",#1,"STOCK",15
20    FIELD #1,2 AS NUMITEMS$
30    FIELD #1,7 AS ITEMNAME$,4 AS PRICE$,4 AS SUPPLY$
40    GET #1,1
50    INPUT "TYPE ITEM IN QUOTES WITH LENGTH 7";NAM$
60    REC=2
70    GET #1,REC
80    WHILE NAM$<>ITEMNAME$ AND REC<CVI(NUMITEMS$)+1
90       REC=REC+1
100      GET #1,REC
110   WEND
120   IF NAM$=ITEMNAME$ THEN 140 ELSE 200
130   REM THEN
140      PRINT "OLD PRICE OF ";NAM$;" $";CVS(PRICE$)
150      INPUT "TYPE NEW PRICE";COST
160      LSET PRICE$=MKS$(COST)
170      PUT #1,REC
180   GO TO 210
190   REM ELSE
200      PRINT "NO SUCH ITEM"
210   CLOSE #1
220   END
```

REMARK: Of course, for a larger file it would make more sense to use a binary search instead of a linear search (see Exercise 10).

■■■ 27.5 Maintaining Membership File

Assume that we have a random access file containing data about the members of the John Doe Society. Each record contains a member's name, city, and status as active or inactive member. A member's record will thus have four fields: NAM$, CITY$, and STATUS$ ("ACTIVE   " or "INACTIVE"). As before, we will reserve record 1 as a header to keep track of the number of member records.

Using the above information, let us write a program that will allow someone to select from the following menu: (1) add a new member, (2) delete a current member (by changing his status to "INACTIVE"), (3) list all active members, or (4) exit.

```
95    REM MEMBERSHIP FILE
96    REM *****
100   OPEN "R",#1,"MEMBERS",43
110   FIELD #1,2 AS NUMREC$
120   FIELD #1,20 AS NAM$,15 AS CITY$,8 AS STATUS$
130   GET #1,1            'FETCH COUNT
140   NUMREC=CVI(NUMREC$)
150   CHOICE=0
160   WHILE CHOICE<>4
170     PRINT "ENTER 1) TO ADD"
180     PRINT "      2) TO DELETE"
190     PRINT "      3) TO LIST"
200     PRINT "      4) TO EXIT"
210     INPUT CHOICE
220     ON CHOICE GOSUB 400,700,900
230   WEND
240   LSET NUMREC$=MKI$(NUMREC)
250   PUT #1,1        'WRITE COUNT
260   CLOSE #1
270   END
280   '
400   REM **** ADD A MEMBER
410   PRINT "ADDING A MEMBER"
420   INPUT "ENTER NAME IN QUOTES WITH LENGTH 20";N$
430   REM SEARCH
440   REC=2
450   GET #1,REC
460   WHILE NAM$<>N$ AND REC<NUMREC+1
470     REC=REC+1
480     GET #1,REC
490   WEND
500   IF NAM$=N$ THEN 520 ELSE 550
510   REM THEN
```

```
520    IF STATUS$=" INACTIVE"
          THEN LSET STATUS$="ACTIVE"  :  PUT #1,REC
          ELSE PRINT "ALREADY ACTIVE"
530    GO TO 610
540  REM ELSE
550    INPUT "ENTER CITY, UP TO LENGTH 15";C$
560    LSET NAM$=N$
570    LSET CITY$=C$
580    LSET STATUS$="ACTIVE"
590    NUMREC=NUMREC+1
600    PUT #1,NUMREC+1
610  RETURN
620  '
700  REM **** DELETE A MEMBER
710  PRINT "DELETING A MEMBER"
720  INPUT "ENTER NAME IN QUOTES WITH LENGTH 20";N$
730  REM SEARCH
740  REC=2
750  GET #1,REC
760  WHILE NAM$<>N$ AND REC<NUMREC+1
770    REC=REC+1
780    GET #1,REC
790  WEND
800  IF NAM$=N$ THEN 820 ELSE 850
810  REM THEN
820    IF STATUS$="ACTIVE   "
          THEN LSET STATUS$=" INACTIVE"  :  PUT #1,REC
          ELSE PRINT "ALREADY INACTIVE"
830  GO TO 860
840  REM ELSE
850    PRINT "NO SUCH MEMBER"
860  RETURN
879  '
900  REM **** LIST ACTIVE MEMBERS
910  FOR REC=2 TO NUMREC+1
920    GET #1,REC
930    IF STATUS$="ACTIVE   "
          THEN PRINT NAM$ : PRINT CITY$ : PRINT
940  NEXT REC
950  RETURN
```

Creating Membership File Using Previous Program.   The preceding program can be used to create a membership file as well. Suppose that there is no file named "MEMBERS" already in existence, prior to the run of this program. Line 140 might seem to be a possible trouble spot. However, an OPEN statement for a nonexistent random access file creates a null file. Thus, the net effect of lines 130 and 140 is to assign the value 0 to NUMREC.

Exercises

1. **(a)** Suppose PRICE\$ and NUM\$ are field variables, P is a single precision number, and N is an integer. Fill in each of the blanks with the appropriate function.

   LSET PRICE\$ = _____(P)

   LSET NUM\$ = _____(N)

   (b) Suppose PRICE\$ is the string form of a single precision number and NUM\$ is the string form of an integer. Fill in each of the blanks with the appropriate function.

   P = _____(PRICE\$)

   N = _____(NUM\$)

2. When we use the first record as a header,
   (a) What function do we use to convert the *integer* number of records to string form?
   (b) How many bytes are there in the field variable for the string form of an integer?

3. For the ROSTER file of Section 27.2 write a program to print out each of the records. Your program should use the fact that the file contains three records with no header.

4. **(a)** Write a program to create a random access file (with header as record 1) and with the fields PERSON\$, YRHIRED\$, PAYRATE\$. Have the file contain the following information: SMITH,1980,6.00,COHN, 1982, 6.50, BOTZ, 1978, 5.00, CANE, 1985, 4.00, PARKER, 1983, 7.00, LUPO, 1980, 7.00.
   (b) Write a program to print the names of all the employees that were hired before 1983. (Make sure your program retrieves the number of items from record 1.)
   (c) Write a program to print out each of the records of the file.

5. For the file in Exercise 4,
   (a) Write a program that prompts the user to input record position. The printout will give the contents of that record.
   (b) Write a program that uses a loop to prompt the user to input a record position for a printout of its contents or to input the word DONE to stop.

6. For the file in Exercise 4, write a program that prompts the user to input the name of the employee whose hourly rate is to be updated. The program should use a linear search to locate the record and then prompt the user for the new hourly rate.

★ 7. Modify the furniture stock program to update a record, when the position of the record is unknown, so that the user could input the name of the item without quotes or padding with trailing blanks. Thus, the user could input SOFA instead of "SOFA   ". (Use concatenation and the LEFT$ function.)

★ 8. Write a program that will print out the names of all the members of the John Doe Society who owe money (the amount owed should also be printed). In the field OWES$, a zero means the member does not owe anything and a positive number means the member owes that amount.

★ 9. Modify the Membership File program of Section 27.5 so that the user has a fourth option in the menu: listing all active members of a given input city.

10. Suppose a file, ALPHAB, contains the following alphabetical list of 13 names and pay rates. ALOU, 4.00, COHN, 5.00, FALL, 3.00, KENT, 5.00, MOTT, 6.00, NATT, 7.50, OHM, 2.50, POE, 5.50, ROE, 7.00, YALE, 4.50, WANG,5.00,WONG,6.00,ZORN,5.00. Write a program that will prompt the user to input the name of the employee whose pay rate is to be modified. The program should locate this employee's record by using a binary search. (Let the variable MD keep track of a record position.)

CHAPTER 28

GET SMART: A Program That Learns

This chapter deals with different types of programs in which the computer plays a match game against a human opponent. In the first type of program, the computer moves at random. Even a weak human opponent should win most of the time. A second type of program is dependent on the writer of the program knowing the perfect strategy. With a program of this type, the computer will play perfectly on every attempt. Writing this program is Exercise 4.

The most difficult type of program to write is one in which the computer plays badly at first but has the capability of *learning* to play well. Against a good player it will learn quickly how to play a perfect game. Interestingly, this third program could be written by a programmer who does not even know how to play perfectly.

The rules for the 10-match game are the following:

1. There are 10 matches at the start.

2. The player may remove 1 or 2 matches per turn.

3. The loser is the person who takes the last match.

Here is a sample game.

Player I takes 2 matches leaving 8.

Player II takes 2 matches leaving 6.

Player I takes 1 match leaving 5.

Player II takes 2 matches leaving 3.

Player I takes 2 matches leaving 1.

Player II loses (must take the last match).

You should play this game at least three times against a human opponent. (In the following computer programs for match games, the human always makes the first move.)

28.1 Program with Random Computer Moves

In the following program, the computer moves at random. Try playing against the computer using this program—it will be easy to beat. To play, just type the program into the computer and RUN the program. The computer will tell you when it is your turn.

The following is a typical run, after a seed has been entered:

```
START GAME.   THERE ARE 10 MATCHES
HUMAN GOES FIRST
HOW MANY MATCHES DO YOU LEAVE? 8
     COMPUTER LEAVES 6
HOW MANY MATCHES DO YOU LEAVE? 5
     COMPUTER LEAVES 4
HOW MANY MATCHES DO YOU LEAVE? 3
     COMPUTER LEAVES 2
HOW MANY MATCHES DO YOU LEAVE? 1
     COMPUTER LEAVES 0
*** HUMAN WON ***
```

PROBLEM Fill in the blank in line 180.

```
95    REM PLAYING MATCH GAME RANDOMLY
96    REM ****
100   RANDOMIZE
110   PRINT "START GAME.   THERE ARE 10 MATCHES"
115   PRINT "HUMAN GOES FIRST"
120   HUM=10 : COMP=10
130   WHILE (HUM<>0) AND (COMP<>0)
140      INPUT "HOW MANY MATCHES DO YOU LEAVE";HUM
150      IF HUM=0 THEN 200
160      REM COMPUTER'S TURN
170      K=INT(2*RND)+1
180      IF HUM-K<0 THEN COMP=0
                     ELSE COMP=_____
190      PRINT "   COMPUTER LEAVES";COMP
200   WEND
210   IF HUM=0 THEN PRINT "*** YOU LOSE, HUMAN ***"
                 ELSE PRINT "*** HUMAN WON ***"
220   END
```

ANSWER The blank in line 180 should be HUM−K. (When it is the computer's turn to move, line 170 randomly determines whether the computer will remove 1 or 2 matches. The IF-THEN-ELSE test in line 180 ensures that toward the end of the game, the computer will not leave a negative number of matches.)

REMARK: In Exercise 3, you are asked to insert some additional lines to prevent the human from cheating.

28.2 Drill

QUESTION Before proceeding to GET SMART, of Section 28.3, give the printouts for the following two programs.

(a)
```
10  FOR I=1 TO 10
20    V(I)=I*I
30  NEXT I
40  N=5
50  V(N)=V(N)+1
60  PRINT V(N)
70  PRINT V(N+1)
80  END
```

(b)
```
10  FOR I=1 TO 10
20    V(I)=I*I
30  NEXT I
40  FOR J=1 TO 3
50    A(J)=2*J
60  NEXT J
70  PRINT A(1)
80  PRINT V(A(1))
90  PRINT V(A(3))
100 END
```

ANSWER Printouts

(a)
```
26
36
```

(b)
```
2
4
36
```

In program (a), in line 50, V(5) becomes 26. Line 50 does *not* affect the contents of box V(6). In line 70, the content of box V(6) is printed. In program (b), in line 80, note that V(A(1)) means the same thing as V(2) since A(1)=2. Similarly, V(A(3)) means the same thing as V(6).

28.3 GET SMART

In the next program, GET SMART, the computer improves as it plays. Opposing a good player, it learns how to play a perfect game very quickly. The main principle of this program is that the computer keeps a record of the success of various positions in previous games. On its turn, the computer moves so that it leaves the position that has previously been more successful. For example, suppose its human opponent has just left 7 matches. The computer has a choice between leaving 6 or 5 matches. It will check which of

```
95    REM PLAYING MATCH GAMES INTELLIGENTLY
96    REM ****
100   FOR I=1 TO 8
110     V(I)=0
120   NEXT I
130   MORE$="YES"
140   WHILE MORE$="YES"
150     PRINT "START GAME. THERE ARE 10 MATCHES"
160     C=0          ' C COUNTS COMPUTER'S MOVES DURING GAME
170     HUM=10 : COMP=10
180     WHILE HUM<>0 AND COMP<>0
190       INPUT "HOW MANY MATCHES DO YOU LEAVE";HUM
200       IF HUM=0 THEN 250
210       GOSUB 400        ' COMPUTER SELECTS ITS MOVE
220       PRINT "COMPUTER LEAVES";COMP
230       C=C+1
240       MOVE(C)=COMP
250     WEND
255     REM GAME OVER--SEE WHO WON
260     IF COMP=0 THEN PRINT "COMPUTER LOSES" : ADJUST=-1
                    ELSE PRINT "COMPUTER WINS" : ADJUST=1
270     GOSUB 510        ' UPDATE DESIRABILITY VALUES
280     INPUT "SHALL WE PLAY AGAIN.TYPE YES OR NO";MORE$
290   WEND
300   END
310   '
320   '
400   REM **** COMPUTER SELECTS ITS MOVE
410   IF HUM=1 THEN COMP=0 : GOTO 440
420   IF HUM=2 THEN COMP=1 : GOTO 440
430   IF V(HUM-1)>=V(HUM-2) THEN COMP=HUM-1
                            ELSE COMP=HUM-2
440   RETURN
450   '
500   REM *** UPDATE DESIRABILITY VALUES
510   REM ADJUST VALUES OF POSITIONS COMPUTER LEFT
520   FOR J=1 TO C
530     V(MOVE(J))=V(MOVE(J))+ADJUST
540   NEXT J
550   RETURN
```

these moves has worked better in previous games. (If leaving 5 has worked better in previous games, the computer will leave 5.)

Since the human goes first, the computer will never have a chance to leave 9 matches. It will use the memory boxes V(8), V(7), V(6), V(5), and so on, to keep track of the desirability values of leaving 8, 7, 6, 5, and so on. At the start of the program (during the first game of a run), all positions will have desirability value 0. Whenever the computer wins a game, it adds 1 to the desirability values of those positions that the computer left during that game. For example, if the computer won a game in which it left positions 8, 4, and 1, it will add 1 to the contents of memory boxes V(8), V(4), and V(1). Whenever the computer loses a game, it subtracts 1 from the desirability values of the positions it left during that game.

Suppose the computer has already played several games during a run of the program and it is now playing another game. If the human opponent has just left 8, the computer must decide whether to leave 7 or 6. It does so by comparing V(7) with V(6) in line 430 to see which position has greater desirability value. (Note that in the event that two positions have the same desirability value, the computer will leave the larger number of matches.)

Note that at the start of each game, C is reset at 0. C will count how many moves the computer makes during that game. Observe how lines 230–240 work. Suppose the computer has left 7 for its first move of a game. C becomes 1 and MOVE(1) becomes 7. Suppose the computer has left 5 for its second move. C becomes 2 and MOVE(2) becomes 5, etc. The computer is keeping a record of its moves during that game so it will be able to add or subtract 1 from the memory boxes V(7), V(5), and so on.

Exercises

1. Suppose the program Get Smart has just played the first game of a run and the game went as follows: Human 8, Computer 7, Human 6, Computer 5, Human 4, Computer 3, Human 1, Computer Loses. What positions at the start of the second game will have desirability value −1?

2. Suppose that the computer has already played a number of games during a run and, so far, in the games in which the computer has left 4, it has won five times and lost twice. What will be the desirability value of leaving 4 for the next game? What will be the contents of memory box V(4)?

3. A drawback of the Moving-at-Random program and also the program Get Smart is that the human could cheat by making an illegal move. Insert some additional lines in the Moving-at-Random program so that if the human makes an illegal INPUT the computer will print out

> HUMAN LOSES, ILLEGAL MOVE

★★ **4.** Write a program for the 10-match game so that the computer plays perfectly from the start. This is a much simpler program than Get Smart, but you *do* have to know the perfect strategy yourself.

★ **5.** In the Get Smart program, could a clever human player prevent the computer from learning to play perfectly by the hundredth game of a run? The answer is either yes or no. Explain your answer.

★★ **6.** Consider the following game: There are 13 matches at the start. The player can take 1, 2, or 3 matches per turn. The loser is the person who takes the last match. Write a program similar to Get Smart for this game. (*Note:* For many computers the subscript for a subscripted variable can never be negative; you will get an error message.)

★★ **7.** How could a human play the Get Smart program 100 games on a single run of the program with the human winning at least 50 games?

CHAPTER 29

Graphics

The details of graphics features vary widely from computer to computer. This chapter concentrates on graphics in the *Apple* and *IBM PC* systems. The *Apple* system is simpler and easier to comprehend.

The topics discussed in this chapter include the following:

1. Plotting individual points
2. Drawing a line
3. Sketching a figure
4. Animation—moving a point or figure (by using plot-erase)
5. Detecting collisions

29.1 Introduction to *Apple* Graphics

***Apple* Low Resolution Graphics.** The statement GR puts the computer in the **low-resolution graphics** mode. In this mode the graphics area consists of the first 20 lines of the screen; the remaining 4 lines comprise the text window.

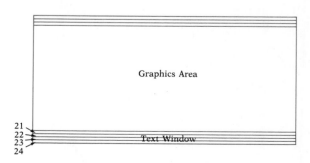

The graphics area uses a 40-by-40 grid of rectangular blocks called **pixels*** (for *picture elements.*) An individual pixel can be referred to by giving its coordinates. The coordinates are based on labeling both the columns and rows from 0 to 39, with the upper left-hand pixel having coordinates 0,0. The *x*-coordinate, that is, the column number, is always given first. Thus the pixel with coordinates 8,2 would in column 8 and row 2.

In the illustration below the locations of the pixels (0,0), (8,2), (1,38) and (39,1) have been indicated.

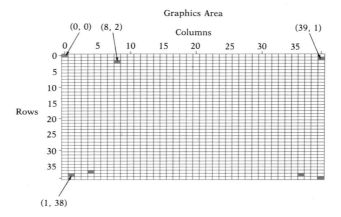

QUESTION   What are the coordinates of the other three pixels that have been shaded in?

ANSWER   The pixel near (1,38) has coordinates (4,37). The other two have coordinates (36,38) and (39,39).

REMARK: The height of each pixel is one half of a line; thus there are 40 rows of pixels in the 20-line graphics area. Also note that the pixels are not square—their widths are greater than their heights.

COLOR Statements.   In low resolution color graphics there are 16 colors numbered from 0 to 15 as follows:

0 Black	5 Dark Gray	10 Gray
1 Magenta	6 Medium Blue	11 Pink
2 Dark Blue	7 Light Blue	12 Green
3 Purple	8 Brown	13 Yellow
4 Dark Green	9 Orange	14 Aqua
		15 White

The general form of a COLOR statement is

COLOR = number

* Note: These rectangular blocks are in turn composed of tiny dots. Sometimes, the word *pixel* is used to mean these tiny dots rather than the rectangular blocks.

For example, COLOR = 3 would specify that purple is to be the current color value for plotting individual pixels or drawing lines. It should be noted that black is the color of the unlit screen. The GR statement clears the graphics area and causes it to be unlit (i.e., colors it black).

PLOT Statements.   In executing the statement PLOT X,Y, the computer will use the current color value to light up the pixel with coordinates X,Y. Let us consider the following program:

```
10  GR
20  COLOR=3
30  PLOT 1,4 : PLOT 39,39
40  PLOT 2,38
50  END
```

The three pixels in the graphics area that would be lit in purple have been indicated by shading.

QUESTION   On a color screen, how would the graphics display from the following program differ from that displayed by the previous program?

```
10  GR
20  COLOR=3
30  PLOT 1,4 : PLOT 39,39
40  COLOR=7
50  PLOT 2,38
60  END
```

ANSWER   The pixel at 2,38 would be colored in light blue instead of purple. (Note that on a black and white screen, assigning COLOR a different value will only result in different degrees of brightness.)

Getting Out of GR Mode

Method 1.   Include the TEXT and HOME statements at the end of the graphics portion of your program:

```
10  GR
20  PLOT, PLOT . . . . . . . .
30  TEXT
40  HOME : REM OPTIONAL IF YOU WANT TO CLEAR SCREEN
```

Method 2.   After you have run a program that produces a graphics display, and you want to clear the screen, you can hit the CTRL and RESET keys and then type HOME.

More on PLOT

1. PLOT X,Y truncates the fractional parts of X and Y. Thus, PLOT 3.7,5.9 would have the same effect at PLOT 3,5.

2. Each of the coordinates in PLOT X,Y must be less than 40 and greater than or equal to 0. For example, PLOT 3,40 would result in an error message.

HLIN and VLIN—Drawing Horizontal and Vertical Lines

HLIN 5,8 AT 1 produces a horizontal line in row 1 extending from X = 5 to X = 8. VLIN 0,39 AT 37 produces a vertical line in column 37 extending from Y = 0 to Y = 39.

These lines would appear as follows:

PROBLEM   Give a rough sketch of the graphics display that would be produced by the segment below:

```
10  GR : COLOR=3
20  VLIN 0,39 AT 0
30  VLIN 0,39 AT 35
40  HLIN 0,39 AT 39
50  VLIN 35,20 AT 3
```

ANSWER

X = 0   X = 35

Y = 39

REMARK: VLIN 35,20 AT 3 produces the same result as the PLOT statements PLOT 3,20; PLOT 3,21; . . . ; PLOT 3,35

PROBLEM   **Sketching Figures**   Determine the letter produced by program (a) and the animal produced by program (b).

(a)

```
10   GR  :  COLOR=3
20   Y=10
30   HLIN 3,7 AT Y
40   HLIN 3,5 AT Y+2
50   HLIN 3,7 AT Y+4
60   VLIN 10,14 AT 3
```

(b)

```
10   GR  :  COLOR=3
20   X=1  :  Y=10
30   PLOT X+3,Y
40   HLIN X,X+2 AT Y+1
50   HLIN X,X+2 AT Y+2
60   PLOT X,Y+3  :  PLOT X+2,Y+3
```

ANSWER   The letter E and a dog. (We have indicated the individual pixels that will be lit.)

29.2 Printing in Text Window

All PRINT or INPUT statements in a program in the GR mode will have their contents appear in the 4-line text window. First consider the following drill program.

```
10   GR  :  COLOR=3
20   PLOT 0,0  :  PLOT 1,1
30   PLOT 2,2
40   HLIN 0,39 AT 39
50   HLIN 0,24 AT 38
60   PRINT "SO LONG"
```

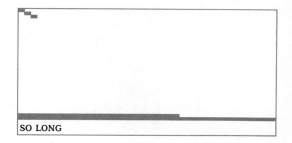

SO LONG

GR : HOME.   From now on, the first program line will be GR : HOME. This ensures that the text window is cleared during the beginning of program execution. For example, for a long program with program lines occurring in the text window, GR would only clear the graphics area whereas GR : HOME would clear the entire screen.

PROBLEM   **Histogram**   Suppose that during the years 1981, 1982, 1983, 1984, 1985, and 1986, a company's sales in millions are 7, 12, 18, 28, 26, and 29, respectively. The following program will produce the histogram given below.

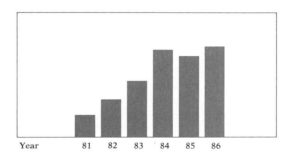

Fill in lines 70 and 80.

```
5       REM HISTOGRAM
6       REM ****
10      GR : HOME : COLOR=3
20      X=9
30      FOR J=1 TO 6
40         READ S
50         VLIN 39,40-S AT X
60         VLIN 39,40-S AT X+1
70         VLIN _____
80         X=_____
90      NEXT J
100     REM ****************** NOW PRINT IN TEXT WINDOW
110     PRINT "YEAR";TAB(10);81;TAB(14);82;TAB(18);83;
120     PRINT TAB(22);84;TAB(26);85;TAB(30);86
130     DATA 7,12,18,28,26,29
140     END
```

ANSWER   Line 70 should be VLIN 39,40−S AT X+2. Lines 50, 60, and 70 give the vertical bar *triple* thickness, by sketching three vertical lines with the same height. Line 80 should be X=X+4 so the next vertical bar will start four pixels to the right.

REMARKS

1. Note that the year 81 is printed in alignment with the vertical bars for 1981. On the *Apple*, TAB(10) is the same column as those pixels with X-coordinate 9. (This is because the left margin PRINT position is labeled column 1, whereas the left margin pixels have X-coordinate equal to 0.)
2. Note that we use VLIN 39,40 − S in lines 60–80, to produce a vertical bar S units high. To see this, consider for example, if S = 2, VLIN 39,38 AT X will produce a vertical line with height two in column X, since it would light up the pixels at X,39 and X,38.

In this example, sales numbers were all less than 40. In Exercise 6, we consider a *scaling* technique for situations in which we do not assume each value is less than 40.

■■■ 29.3 Animation

The following program will cause a dot to move across the screen in a horizontal path along row 20. The illusion of motion is created by lighting up and then erasing a sequence of pixels.

```
10  GR
20  Y=20
30  FOR X=1 TO 35 STEP 2
40     COLOR=3 : PLOT X,Y
50     FOR J=1 TO 100 : NEXT J : REM TIME DELAY
60     COLOR=0 : PLOT X,Y : REM ERASE DOT
70  NEXT X
80  END
```

When X = 1, the pixel at (1,20) will light up. Then after the time delay created by the FOR J = 1 TO 100 : NEXT J loop, the pixel at (1,20) will be turned off. When X = 3, the pixel at (3,20) will light up, and then after a time delay it will be turned off. The dot will appear to move continuously across the screen occupying positions (1,20), (3,20), (5,20), and so on, finally stopping at (35,20). To speed up the motion of the dot, line 50 could be changed to shorter time delay, such as FOR J = 1 TO 50 : NEXT J.

Walking Dog   Complete lines 50 and 60 in this program that causes a dog to walk (i.e., glide) across the screen.

```
5      REM  ANIMATED  DOG
6      REM  ****
10     GR  :  HOME
20     Y=20
30     FOR  X=1  TO  35  STEP  2
40        COLOR=3  :  GOSUB  200
50        FOR  J=1  _____
60        _____  :  GOSUB  200
70     NEXT  X
80     GOTO  300
200    REM  LIGHT  UP  OR  ERASE  DOG
210    PLOT  X+3,Y
220    HLIN  X,X+2  AT  Y+1
230    HLIN  X,X+2  AT  Y+2
240    PLOT  X,Y+3  :  PLOT  X+2,Y+3
250    RETURN
300    END
```

ANSWER Line 50 is a time delay. For a slowly walking dog it might be FOR J = 1 TO 200 : NEXT J. For a faster dog, use FOR J = 1 TO 100 : NEXT J. Line 60 should be COLOR = 0 : GOSUB 200. This sets the color equal to black so that this execution of the subroutine turns off the pixels just lit up by the dog.

EXAMPLE **Bouncing Ball in Box** The box in the next program has four walls. In lines 120–150 of the following program, the walls of the box are drawn. This program introduces two new features: (1) the dot will move in a slanting line path instead of horizontally, and (2) when it reaches a wall it will "bounce" off the wall. Line 160 gives the starting position (1,38) for the dot. Line 170, DX = 1 : DY = −3 sets the angle for the slanting line path; for every one unit to the right in the X direction, there should be three units up in the Y direction. (Note that the y-coordinate *decreases* as you move *up* on the screen.)

The "bouncing off the wall" is caused by lines 370–400. These lines keep the coordinates X,Y within the confines of the box and reverse the direction of the dot.

On the diagram below we have indicated the path of the dot for the first few seconds of the running of the program. Of course, the program contains an infinite loop, and therefore the dot (ball) will keep moving until the program is stopped manually by hitting the CTRL/C keys.

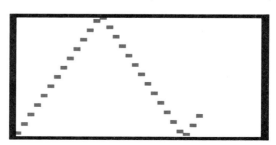

```
95    REM BOUNCING BALL
96    REM ****
100   GR  :  HOME
110   COLOR=7
120   HLIN 0,39 AT 0
130   HLIN 0,39 AT 39
140   VLIN 0,39 AT 0
150   VLIN 0,39 AT 39
160   X=1  :  Y=38
170   DX=1  :  DY=-3
300   WHILE 1=1
310      COLOR=3  :  PLOT X,Y
320      FOR J=1 TO 30  :  NEXT J  :  REM TIME DELAY
330      COLOR=0  :  PLOT X,Y  :  REM ERASE DOT
340      REM CALCULATE NEXT POSITION
350      X=X+DX  :  Y=Y+DY
360      REM IF AT OR BEYOND WALL CHANGE DIRECTION
370      IF X>=38 THEN X=38  :  DX=-DX
380      IF X<=1 THEN X=1  :  DX=-DX
390      IF Y>=38 THEN Y=38  :  DY=-DY
400      IF Y<=1 THEN Y=1  :  DY=-DY
410   WEND
500   END
```

Draw walls of box.

(1,38) will be starting position.

NOTE: The ball in this program does not always take a true bounce off the wall. See Exercise 10.

SCRN Function. In the low resolution graphics mode, SCRN(X,Y) returns the color value of the pixel X,Y. The SCRN function can be used to detect when a bullet hits the target.

PROBLEM In the example below, a target pixel is lit up in color 7. A bullet starts in the bottom left corner of the screen and travels in an angular path. Before each position of the bullet is plotted in color 3, the program uses the SCRN function to detect if the target is in that position. What will the printout be?

```
5    REM COLLISION DETECTION
6    REM ****
10   GR
20   COLOR=7 : PLOT 5,30 : REM TARGET PIXEL
30   X=1 : Y=38 : REM INITIAL POSITION OF BULLET
40   DX=1 : DY=-2
50   COLOR=3 : PLOT X,Y
60   C=1
70   WHILE SCRN(X,Y)=7
80      FOR J=1 : TO 20 : NEXT J : REM TIME DELAY
90      COLOR=0 : PLOT X,Y
100     X=X+DX : Y=Y+DY
110     COLOR=3 : PLOT X,Y
120     C=C+1
130  WEND
140  PRINT "HIT TARGET. BULLET OCCUPIED";C;"POSITIONS"
150  END
```

ANSWER

```
HIT TARGET. BULLET OCCUPIED 5 POSITIONS
```

29.4 Introduction to IBM PC Graphics

IBM PC Graphics.   One key difference between *Apple* and *IBM* computers is that *Apple* computers have built-in graphics hardware, whereas *IBM* computers include graphics only as an optional add-on. The syntax in *IBM* graphics is also quite different from that of *Apple* Graphics. The following table compares several similar statements in *IBM* and *Apple* graphics:

IBM Statement	Similar Apple Statement
SCREEN 1	GR
PSET (X,Y), color #	COLOR=color # : PLOT X,Y
PRESET (X,Y)	COLOR=0 : PLOT X,Y
COLOR background #, palette #	No similar statement
LINE (X1,Y1)–(X2,Y2)	More flexible than HLIN or VLIN (Can draw a slanted line as well as horizontal and vertical lines)

SCREEN 1.   The statement SCREEN 1 puts the computer in the **medium resolution graphics** mode. In this mode the entire screen (there is no separate

text window) is subdivided into a 320-by-200 grid of rectangular blocks called pixels (for *pic*ture *el*ements.) An individual pixel can be referred to by giving its coordinates: columns are labeled from 0 to 319, and rows are labeled from 0 to 199, with the upper left pixel having coordinates (0,0). As usual, the X coordinate (the column number) is always given first.

COLOR Background #, Palette #.

An *IBM* statement such as COLOR 2,1 has no similar statement in *Apple* graphics. COLOR 2,1 will select green as the background color and restrict the colors for lighting up individual pixels to those colors in palette 1.

Background Colors		Palette 0	Palette 1
0 Black	8 Gray	0 Background	0 Background
1 Blue	9 Light Blue	1 Green	1 Cyan
2 Green	10 Light Green	2 Red	2 Magenta
3 Cyan	11 Light Cyan	3 Brown	3 White
4 Red	12 Light Red		
5 Magenta	13 Light Magenta		
6 Brown	14 Yellow		
7 White	15 Bright White		

PSET.

A statement such as PSET(5,5),2 will light up pixel (5,5) in color 2 from the current palette; that is, it will light up (5,5) either red or magenta depending on whether the current palette is 0 or 1.

KEY OFF.

The statement KEY OFF turns off the function key display at the bottom of the screen, as illustrated here.

(a)
```
5    KEY OFF
10   SCREEN 1
20   COLOR 8,0
30   PSET (5,5),2
40   PSET (5,10),3
```

(b)
```
5    KEY OFF
10   SCREEN 1
20   COLOR 2,1
30   PSET (5,5),2
40   PSET (5,10),3
```

In program (a), line 20, COLOR 8,0, sets the background color as gray, and palette 0 as the palette to be used. Thus PSET (5,5),2 lights up in red the pixel at (5,5), and PSET (5,10),3 lights (5,10) in brown. The rest of the screen is the background color gray.

In program (b), pixel (5,5) will be lit up in magenta, and pixel (5,10) will be lit up white (since palette 1 was selected). The rest of the screen will be green.

LINE (X1,Y1)–(X2,Y2), COLOR #. The statement LINE (0,0)–(0,39),2 will light up a horizontal line from pixel (0,0) to pixel (0,39) using color 2 from the current palette. The line statement can also be used to light up a slanted line. For example, LINE (5,5)–(25,30),2 would light up the line of pixels connecting (5,5) and (25,30).

29.5 Mixing Text and Graphics: Histograms

LOCATE. The LOCATE command in the form LOCATE *row,column* moves the cursor to the designated position. It is generally used before a PRINT statement.

Drawing Unfilled-in Box. The command

LINE (X1,Y1)–(X2,Y2),color #,B

causes the computer to draw a rectangular box boundary with (X1,Y1) as the lower left-hand corner and (X2,Y2) as the upper right-hand corner. The boundary is drawn in the specified color.

Drawing Filled-in Box. The command

LINE (X1,Y1)–(X2,Y2),color #,BF

causes the computer to draw a *solid* rectangular box in the specified color.

PROBLEM The following program produces a histogram graph showing a company's sales in millions during the years 1981, 1982, 1983, 1984, 1985, and 1986. It uses the LOCATE function and the BF-option of the LINE statement.

Line 70 draws and fills in the bars of the histogram using the input data to determine the height of the bars. Line 100 positions the cursor to print the year headings.

Fill in line 80, so that there will be 5 pixels between each bar.

```
5      REM HISTOGRAM
6      REM ****
10     KEY OFF
20     SCREEN 1 : CLS
30     COLOR 0,1
40     X=70
50     FOR J=1 TO 6
60       READ S
70       LINE (X,160)-(X+25,160-S),1,BF
80       _____
90     NEXT J
100    LOCATE 22,1
110    PRINT "YEAR"TAB(9)81;82;83;84;85;86
120    DATA 7,12,18,28,26,29
130    END
```

ANSWER   Line 80 should be $X = X + 30$.

29.6   *IBM* Animation: Using PSET and PRESET

IBM animation is quite similar to *Apple* animation. The basic idea for creating the appearance of motion is the lighting up and erasing of a sequence of pixels.

PRESET Statement.   PRESET(X,Y) will cause pixel (X,Y) to have the background color. Thus, the PRESET statement enables us to erase a pixel that was lit up in another color.

EXAMPLE   Moving a Dot across the Screen in a Horizontal Path

```
5    KEY OFF
10   SCREEN 1 : COLOR 1,0
15   CLS
20   Y=100
30   FOR X=1 TO 199 STEP 2
40     PSET (X,Y),2
50     FOR J=1 TO 10 : NEXT J : REM TIME DELAY
60     PRESET (X,Y) : REM ERASE DOT
70   NEXT X
80   END
```

PROBLEM **Bouncing Bit** In this program, walls for a box are drawn in brown around the edge of the screen and the background is blue. A red bouncing bit starts at pixel (1,198); its horizontal velocity component is 1 and its vertical velocity component is 3. Note the use of the infinite loop. To stop this program press CTRL-C. *For more details see the similar Apple program in Section 29.3.*

Complete lines 150 and 390.

```
95   REM BOUNCING BIT
96   REM ****
100  KEY OFF
110  SCREEN A : CLS
120  COLOR 1,0
130  REM DRAW WALLS
140  LINE(0,0)-(319,0),3 : LINE(0,199)-(319,199),3
150  LINE (0,0)-(0,199),3 : _____
160  X=1 : Y=198
170  DX=1 : DY=-3
300  WHILE 1=1
310     PSET (X,Y),2
320     FOR J=1 TO 20 : NEXT J : REM TIME DELAY
330     PRESET (X,Y) : REM ERASE DOT
340     REM CALCULATE NEXT POSITION
350     X=X+DX : Y=Y+DY
360     REM CHECK IF AT OR BEYOND WALL
370     IF X>=318 THEN X=318 : DX=-DX
380     IF X<=1 THEN X=1 : DX=-DX
390     IF Y>= _____
400     IF Y<=1 THEN Y=1 : DY=-DY
410  WEND
500  END
```

ANSWER The blank in line 150 should be LINE(319,0)–(319,199),3. Line 390 should be IF Y>=198 THEN Y=198 : DY=-DY.

29.7 Animation Using GET and PUT

GET and PUT statements allow us to move an *entire object* from one location on the screen to another, as opposed to moving a *single pixel* across the screen.

GET Statement. The GET statement is used to store in memory an object, namely, the current screen image from a rectangular "boxed" or "windowed" portion of the screen. The syntax for the GET statement is

GET (X1,Y1)–(X2,Y2), arrayname

The points (X1,Y1) and (X2,Y2) specify the rectangular "box" by giving diagonally opposite corners. The array is used to store a numerical representation of that object, that is, screen image. Thus, GET (20,30)–(60,45), A would store in the array A a representation for the current screen image of the rectangle with opposite corners (20,30) and (60,45).

EXAMPLE   House with a Chimney

```
5    REM DRAW HOUSE
6    REM ****
10   SCREEN 1
20   CLS : KEY OFF
30   COLOR 1,0
40   LINE (0,5)-(30,25),3,BF     'HOUSE
50   LINE (20,0)-(24,4),3,BF     'CHIMNEY
60   DIM A(53)
70   GET (0,0)-(30,25), A
```

The preceding program fragment will store in memory the current image of the rectangle with opposite corners (0,0) and (30,25).

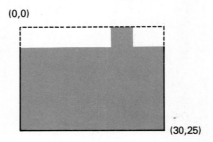

(0,0)

(30,25)

PUT Statement.   The PUT statement displays a stored rectangular image on the screen. The PUT statement must specify not only the array in which the image is stored but also where on the screen the image should be displayed. PUT does so by giving the screen position for the upper-left corner of the rectangle. The syntax for the PUT statement is

PUT (X,Y), array

(X,Y) are the coordinates of the upper-left corner of the rectangular region of the screen on which the stored image is to be displayed.

Using PUT as On–Off Switch.   Two successive, identical PUT statements will have the effect of first displaying the stored image on the screen and then erasing it. Thus

    PUT (50,80),A

    PUT (50,80),A

will first display the stored image in the specified rectangle and then erase it. In animation it is advisable also to include a time delay.

EXAMPLE   Moving House with Chimney across the Screen

```
95   REM ANIMATE HOUSE
96   REM ****
100  SCREEN 1 : KEY OFF
110  COLOR 1,0
120  DIM A(53)
130  GOSUB     ' DRAW HOUSE
140  GET (0,0)-(30,25),A      'STORE HOUSE IN ARRAY A
150  CLS     'CLEAR SCREEN
160  X=0 : Y=50
170  FOR J=1 TO 200
180     PUT (X,Y),A
190     FOR K=1 TO 25 : NEXT K      'DELAY
200     PUT (X,Y),A
210     X=X+1
220  NEXT J
230  END
300  REM **** DRAW HOUSE ****
310  LINE (0,5)-(30,25),3,BF      'HOUSE
320  LINE (20,0)-(24,4),3,BF      ' CHIMNEY
330  RETURN
```

Calculating Dimension Needed in Array.   Obviously, the larger the rectangular "window", the larger the array needed to store a numerical representation of its screen image. The dimension D can be calculated as follows: First compute B, the number of bytes needed

$$B = 4 + X*INT((2*Y + 7)/8)$$

Then, since each cell of a single precision array can store 4 bytes, we calculate the dimension $D = INT(B/4)$.

EXAMPLE For the 30 by 25 rectangle

$$B = 4 + 30*INT((2*25+7)/8)$$
$$= 4 + 30*7 = 214$$

Thus, $D = 53$

If you wish, you may insert several lines of code in the program, so that the computer determines the dimension needed for the array.

PROBLEM Fill in the blanks in this program to move a boat across the screen.

```
95    REM ANIMATE BOAT
96    REM ****
100   SCREEN 1 : KEY OFF
110   COLOR 1,0
120   DIM A(5)
130   GOSUB 300 ' DRAW BOAT
140   _____ ' STORE BOAT IN ARRAY A
150   CLS ' CLEAR SCREEN
160   X=0 : Y=50
170   FOR J=1 TO 200
180      _____
190      _____
200      _____
210      X=X+1
220   NEXT J
230   END
240   '
300   REM *** DRAW BOAT ***
310   LINE (0,6)-(7,6),3,BF
320   LINE (0,5)-(8,5),3,BF
330   LINE (0,4),(9,4),3,BF
340   LINE (2,3)-(4,3),3,BF
350   PSET (3,2) : PSET (3,1) : PSET (3,0) : PSET (4,0)
360   RETURN
```

ANSWER The boat is drawn originally in the rectangle with opposite corners (0,0) and (9,7). Thus, line 140 should be GET (0,0)–(9,7),A

Line 180 PUT (X,Y),A

Line 190 FOR K = 1 TO 25 : NEXT K   'DELAY

Line 200 PUT (X,Y),A

EXAMPLE **Bouncing Ball** We now give a GET-PUT version of the bouncing ball program of Section 29.3. Note that the ball is not completely round.

```
100  SCREEN 1
110  KEY OFF
120  COLOR 1,0
130  DIM A(5001)
140  GOSUB 400     'DRAW A BALL
150  GET (0,0)-(5,5),A    'STORE BALL
160  CLS' CLEAR THE SCREEN
170  REM *** DRAW WALLS
180  LINE (0,0)-(319,0),3 : LINE (0,199)-(319,199),3
190  LINE (0,0)-(0,199),3 : LINE (319,0)-(319,199),3
200  X=1 : Y=194
210  DX=1 : DY=-3
220  WHILE 1=1
230    PUT (X,Y),A
240    FOR J=1 TO 5 : NEXT J     'TIME DELAY
250    PUT (X,Y),A
260    REM CALCULATE NEXT POSITION
270    X=X+DX : Y=Y+DY
280    REM CHECK IF AT OR BEYOND WALL
290    IF X>=314 THEN X=1 : DX=-DX
300    IF X<=1 THEN X=1 : DX=-DX
310    IF Y>=194 THEN Y=194 : DY=-DY
320    IF Y<=1 THEN Y=1 : DY=-DY
330  WEND
340  END
350  '
360  REM *** DRAW BALL
370  LINE (2,0)-(3,0) : LINE (1,1)-(4,1) : LINE (0,2)-(5,2)
380  LINE (1,3)-(4,3) : LINE (2,4)-(3,4)
390  RETURN
```

Exercises

APPLE GRAPHICS

1. Give the graphics display that each of the following programs will provide:

(a)
```
10  GR : COLOR=3
20  PLOT 2,5 : PLOT 0,38
30  HLIN 0,20 AT 15
40  VLIN 0,20 AT 15
50  END
```

(b)
```
10  GR : COLOR=3
20  HLIN 0,38 AT 20
30  COLOR=0
40  HLIN 0,38 AT 23
50  END
```

(c)

```
10  GR  :  COLOR=3
20  FOR  X=0  TO  39
30      PLOT  X,39-X
40  NEXT  X
50  END
```

(d)

```
10  GR  :  COLOR=3
20  X=5  :  Y=39
30  VLIN  Y,Y-1  AT  X
40  VLIN  Y,Y-1  AT  X-1
50  VLIN  Y,Y-5  AT  X+2
60  END
```

2. Write a program to produce a striped display, by coloring every other row purple, that is, alternate between coloring one row purple and leaving the next unlit.

3. Write a program to spell out the name J O E in large letters in the graphics area.

4. Write a program (using the INPUT statement) asking which rectangle the user would like colored and what color it should be. The program should then color the specified rectangle in the requested color.

5. In a class of 80 students, 12 received an A, 28 B, 30 C, 7 D, and 3 F. Write a program to produce a histogram.

★ 6. In a class of 300 students, the number of students receiving grades of A, B, C, D, and F, respectively, were 45, 90, 100, 35, and 30. Since some of these numbers exceed 39, we should scale them down. One way to do this is to set up a scale so that the maximum data number, 100, will have a height of less than 39. Thus, each data number could be scaled down by dividing it by 3. Write a program to produce a histogram on this scaling.

7. (a) Write a program to have a ball move back and forth in a *horizontal* path at Y = 10 between two vertical walls (at X = 0 and at X = 39). Initialize with DX = 1 and have the ball reverse its direction when it reaches the wall.

   (b) Modify the previous program so that DX is initialized with the value 3.

★★ 8. Modify the Walking Dog program of Section 29.3 so that the dog keeps walking back and forth between the left and right edges of the screen. The dog should turn around each time it reaches a wall.

★★ 9. *Arcade Game.*

   (a) Write a program in which a duck target occupies pixels at (0,20), (1,20), (2,20), and (3,19). The bullet is set at initial position (1,38). The user is also asked to input values for DX between 1 and 4 and for DY between −1 and −4. The user is to try to hit the target before the bullet hits *six* walls.

   (b) Modify the program so that the user is also asked to input the initial bullet position from the choices (1,38), (1,37), (1,36), and (1,35).

** **10.** Explain why the ball in the bouncing ball program does not always take a true bounce off a wall. (*Hint:* You might focus on what happens when the ball is at pixel (13,2) and will hit the wall on the next step.)

IBM GRAPHICS

11. What will the screen display be by the end of each of the following programs?

(a)

```
10  SCREEN 1 : KEY OFF
20  COLOR 8,0 : CLS
30  PSET (5,5),3
40  LINE (0,0)-(0,39),1
50  END
```

(b)

```
10  SCREEN 1 : KEY OFF
20  COLOR 2,1 : CLS
30  PSET (5,5),3 : PSET (10,10),3
40  FOR J=1 TO 1000 : NEXT J
50  PRESET (5,5) : PRESET (30,30)
60  END
```

12. Write a program to spell out JOE in large letters.

13. Write a program to have a ball move back and forth in a horizontal path between two vertical walls.

14. Write a program to have a dog walk back and forth between the left and right edges of the screen. The dog should turn around each time it reaches a wall. (The dog sketched in the *Apple* program of Section 29.3 was composed of 9 pixels. You might wish to use more pixels for an *IBM* program, since the *IBM* pixels are so much smaller than the *Apple* pixels.)

A

Functions

BASIC contains two types of functions; built-in functions and user-defined functions.

A.1 Built-in Functions

The accompanying table describes 11 standard built-in functions.

Function	Description
SIN(X)	Sine of X ⎤
COS(X)	Cosine of X angle of X in radians
TAN(X)	Tangent of X ⎦
ATN(X)	Arctangent of X
SQR(X)	Positive square root of X
ABS(X)	Absolute value of X
EXP(X)	e raised to the power of X
LOG(X)	Natural log of X
INT(X)	Integer part of X; for most systems this function truncates the fractional part of X.
SGN(X)	-1, 0, or $+1$, depending on whether X is negative, zero, or positive, respectively
RND	A random number (actually pseudorandom) between 0 and 1.

Note that the variable or expression to which you are applying the function must be enclosed in parentheses. Thus, INT(X) and SQR(A + 7) are valid expressions, whereas INT X and SIN X are not. It is permissible for the argument of a built-in function to contain a function. In BASIC, $|\sin(x)|$ is written ABS(SIN(X)).

All the trigonometric functions apply to angles in radians. To convert degrees into radians recall the following:

1 degree = $\pi/180$ radians

DEG degrees = DEGπ/180 radians.

Thus, in BASIC, RAD = DEG*3.14159/180 converts DEG degrees into RAD radians.

PROBLEM   Complete line 30 of this program, which computes the sine of an input number of degrees.

```
10   INPUT  "AN ANGLE IN DEGREES";DEG
20   RAD=DEG*3.14159/180
30   PRINT  "THE SINE OF";DEG;"DEGREES IS";_____
40   END
```

ANSWER   SIN(RAD). Note that SIN(DEG) is incorrect.

A.2 User-Defined Functions

Recall that in complex expressions, the computer will perform exponentiation before multiplication or division, and multiplication or division before addition or subtraction (unless, of course, parentheses indicate otherwise). Thus, when $\wedge$ is the symbol for exponentiation, $x^3 + 5x^2 - 6$ is written as X$\wedge$3 + 5*X$\wedge$2 − 6. How would you write $3x^4 + 7x$ in BASIC? *Answer:* 3*X$\wedge$4 + 7*X.

If you wish to define a function during a program, you may do so by use of a statement such as DEF FNB(X) = X$\wedge$3 + 1. The letter that follows FN is the name of the function. The previous statement defined the function B, which is $x^3 + 1$. In the following program, two functions are defined, namely, function B and function G. What will the printout be?

```
10   DEF  FNB(X)=X∧2+1
20   DEF  FNG(X)=X∧3+2*X+1
30   PRINT  FNB(3)
40   PRINT  FNG(2)
50   PRINT  FNB(2)
60   END
```

Printout

```
10
13
5
```

PROBLEM   Complete lines 10, 30, and 50 of the following program, which will print the following table of values for $G(x) = x^2 + 1$.

```
10   PRINT _____
20   PRINT "X","Y"
30   DEF _____
40   FOR X=1 TO 5
50      PRINT _____
60   NEXT X
70   END
```

```
G(X)=X^2+1
X              Y
 1             2
 2             5
 3            10
 4            17
 5            26
```

ANSWER   Line 10 PRINT "G(X)=X^2+1"
                  Line 30 DEF FNG(X)=X^2+1
                  Line 50 PRINT X,FNG(X)

Dummy Variable.   The letter in parentheses on the left side of a DEF statement is called a dummy variable. The right side of the DEF statement should be an expression involving the dummy variable. Although the expression on the right side of a DEF statement can contain other variables besides the dummy variable, each of these other variables should already have a value prior to the DEF statement. For example

```
10   DATA 3,5
20   READ A,B
30   DEF FNG(R)=2*A+R+B
40   PRINT FNG(7),FNG(10)
50   END
```

The printout will be

```
18                    21
```

Compound Interest Programs.   Complete lines 40 and 50 to give the following printout. The balance is for $400 invested for one year at 5%, 6%, and 7%, respectively.

```
10  DATA 400
20  READ PRINCIPAL
30  PRINT "AT 5%","AT 6%","AT 7%"
40  DEF FNB(_____)=PRINCIPAL*(1+RATE/100)
50  _____
60  END
```

```
AT 5%           AT 6%           AT 7%
 420             424             428
```

The dummy variable in line 40 is RATE

    40   DEF FNB(RATE) = PRINCIPAL*(1 + RATE/100)
    50   PRINT FNB(5),FNB(6),FNB(7)

If PRINCIPAL dollars are invested at the rate of RATE percent compounded annually, the balance after YRS years will be $PRINCIPAL(1 + RATE/100)^{YRS}$. Completing lines 40 and 50 to produce the printout shown below is exercise 5.

```
10  DATA 400,5
20  READ PRINCIPAL,RATE
25  PRINT _____
30  PRINT "AFTER 2 YEARS","AFTER 9 YEARS"
40  DEF FNB _____
50  PRINT _____
60  END
```

```
INITIAL BALANCE $ 400 INTEREST RATE 5%
AFTER 2 YEARS           AFTER 9 YEARS
 441                     620.526
```

Exercises

1. Identify the error in each of the following BASIC expressions:
   (a) SQR24
   (b) SQR(X + Y)/3 for $\sqrt{(X+Y)/3}$
   (c) SIN(60) for sine of 60 degrees

2. Write a program for which the lengths of the legs of a right triangle are input and the length of the hypotenuse is printed.

★ **3.** Write a program to print out a table that gives in steps of 10° each angle from 0° to 90°, its equivalent in radians, and its sine.

DEGREES	RADIANS	SIN
0	0	0
10	.174533	.173648
20	.349066	.34202
:		
:		

4. Use the computer to find $\sqrt{N^2 + 5N + 83}$ for $N=5$, $N=8$, and $N=14$.

5. **(a)** Complete lines 40 and 50 of the last program in this chapter.
   (b) Rerun this program to find the balance from $700 dollars at a rate of 6% after two years and nine years, respectively.

6. **(a)** For $G(x) = x^3 + 2x$, compute $G(x)$ in steps of $\frac{1}{2}$ on the intervals [2,4]. Format the printout in table form with a heading.
   (b) Do the same for $G(x) = x^5 - 3x^3 + 4x$.

7. Write a program that will print a table of the form

DEGREES	SIN	TAN	COTAN
30			
31			
32			
:			
:			
40			

★ **8.** Write a program that will compute and print out in table form the value of

$$\frac{SIN\ X}{X} \text{ for } X = \frac{1}{2}, \frac{1}{4}, \frac{1}{8}, \ldots, \frac{1}{2^{10}}$$

Also see Appendix B, Exercises 43–46 and see Appendix C, Exercise 7.

More Mathematical Problems

Integers and Their Digits (Chapters 5 and 8)

1. Complete lines 30–50 of the following program:

```
10  INPUT "TYPE ANY THREE DIGIT NUMBER";N
20  HUNS=N MOD 100
30  TENS= _____
40  ONES= _____
50  PRINT "THE DIGITS ARE _____
60  END
```

Here is a typical printout:

```
TYPE ANY THREE DIGIT NUMBER? 573
THE DIGITS ARE 5   7   3
```

2. Rewrite the preceding program using a FOR-NEXT loop.

    FOR EXPON = 2 TO _____ STEP − 1

★ 3. Write a program that converts an input number ranging from 1 to 100 to its equivalent in base 2. When 53 is input, the printout should be

```
0   1   1   0   1   0   1
```

since $53 = 1 \cdot 2^5 + 1 \cdot 2^4 + 0 \cdot 2^3 + 1 \cdot 2^2 + 0 \cdot 2^1 + 1 \cdot 2^0$. Rerun it inputting 76, then 55. The printouts should be

1	0	0	1	1	0	0

and

0	1	1	0	1	1	1

respectively.

★★ **4.** Write a program such that if the DATA line consists of the departure time and the arrival time (on a 24-hour clock), the printout will give the flight duration. The times 9:45 A.M. and 1:48 P.M. would be given as DATA 0945,1348. The printout would be

FLIGHT DURATION 4 HRS 3 MIN

Run it again with DATA 0625,1210 and then with DATA 2120,0205. You may assume that no flight lasts more than 24 hours.

Euclidean Algorithm (Chapter 11)

5. Write a program that reads and prints two input integers, and then finds their greatest common divisor (GCD). Use this algorithm: *Divide the smaller number into the larger number, obtaining a quotient and a remainder. If the remainder is not zero, divide the remainder into the quotient. Keep repeating this process until the remainder is zero. The last nonzero remainder is the GCD.* Example for 12 and 32:

$$32 = 12(2) + 8$$
$$12 = 8(1) + 4$$
$$8 = 4(2) + 0 \text{ stop}$$

The GCD is 4 since it was the last nonzero remainder.

Series for e^x (Chapter 11)

6. e^x can be represented as the infinite series

$$e^x = 1 + x + \frac{x^2}{2!} + \frac{x^3}{3!} + \cdots$$

Consider 1 as the 0th term, x as the first term, $x^2/2!$ as the second term, $x^3/3!$ etc., then the nth term is the previous term multiplied by x/n. Based on this series, run a program to find an approximation for $e^{2.5}$. The program should stop when the term just added is less than .0001. Rerun it to find an approximation for *e*. Compare results by also printing the values returned by the built-in function EXP (X).

(Chapter 12)

7. Write a program so that for three input numbers the printout will be $\boxed{\text{NONE EQUAL}}$, $\boxed{\text{TWO EQUAL}}$, or $\boxed{\text{ALL EQUAL}}$.

Prime and Other Interesting Numbers (Chapter 17 or 19)

An integer greater than 1 is called **prime** if its only positive divisors are 1 and itself. Thus for example 2, 3, 5, 7, and 11 are some primes; 4 is not a prime since it is divisible by 2. *Number Theory Fact: If an integer N has no divisors between 2 and $\sqrt{N}$, then we can conclude that N is prime.* Thus, to test whether 67 is prime it would be sufficient to check for a divisor between 2 and $INT(\sqrt{67})$, that is, between 2 and 8.

8. Write a program that will determine whether or not an input integer is prime. For input 67, the printout should be $\boxed{\text{67 IS PRIME}}$. For input 91, the printout should be $\boxed{\text{91 IS NOT PRIME}}$, since $91 = 7 \times 13$.

PROGRAM IDEAS

Recall that J divides N provided that N MOD J = 0. This program is somewhat similar to a linear search. Fill in the blanks in lines 40 and 70.

```
10   INPUT  "TYPE  NUMBER " ; NUM
20   J=2
30   UPPER= I NT ( SQR ( NUM ) )
40   WH I LE  J <=UPPER  AND  _____
50      J=J+1
60   WEND
70   I F  _____  THEN  PR I NT  NUM;  " I S  PR I ME "
                   ELSE  PR I NT  NUM;  " I S  NOT  PR I ME "
80   END
```

★ **9.** Write a program that will find and print the smallest prime divisor of an integer DATA number.

Since a number of the exercises in this section involve the idea of loops within loops, we give one such sample problem with a partial solution.

★ **10.** An integer N is called *perfect* if N is equal to the sum of all its divisors other than itself. For example, 6 is perfect, since $6 = 1 + 2 + 3$. Fill in line 70 of the preceding program, which prints the first two perfect integers.

PROGRAM IDEAS

Step 1. Let C be the counter for the number of perfect integers printed so far. Let N be the current integer being tested for perfectness.

Step 2. Initialize C and N.

Step 3. Generate next N.
Use FOR-NEXT loop to find the sum of the divisors of N.
Test whether N is perfect; Print N and increase C if so.
Test whether C is 2; if so, exit from loop; otherwise loop back.

Fill in the blanks in lines 70 and 90.

```
10   C=0
20   N=1
30   WHILE C<2
40      N=N+1
50      S=0
60      FOR D=1 TO N/2
70         IF _____ THEN S=_____
80      NEXT D
90      IF S=N THEN _____ : PRINT N; "IS PERFECT"
100  WEND
110  END
```

★   **11.** Write a program to list all the prime numbers <100. (The program will involve nested loops.)

★   **12. (a)** $x^2 - x + 41$ is a famous, faulty prime-generating formula. For $x = 1$, the formula gives 41, which is prime; $x = 2$ gives 43, which is prime; $x = 3$ gives 47, which is prime. Write a program to find the smallest positive integer x for which the formula fails to give a prime and to print a factorization for the number given by the formula.

★★   **(b)** Find the first three values of x for which the formula fails to give a prime.

★★   **13.** *Twin primes.* A pair of odd numbers that are both prime and differ by 2 is called a pair of twin primes. Some examples are 3,5 5,7 11,13 17,19. Write a program that prints all pairs of twin primes less than 100.

★   **14.** An integer N is called abundant if N is less than the sum of its divisors other than itself. For example, $12 < 1 + 2 + 3 + 4 + 6$. Thus, 12 is abundant. Even abundant numbers are numerous; however, odd abundant numbers are quite scarce. Write a program that will find and print all abundant *odd* numbers less than 1000. (On many microcomputers this program will run for well over five minutes.)

Mode (Chapter 14)

★★ **15.** Suppose a list of DATA numbers with flag 999 is in *increasing* order. Write a program to find the mode of the DATA list. The mode of the list is defined as the number having the largest number of occurrences in the list. Run with DATA 72,72,75,75,79,79,79,84,85,86,88,88,89,999. Rerun it with DATA 73,73,73,75,75,78,78,81,81,85,999. The printouts should be 79 and 73 respectively.

Approximation for π (Chapter 18 or Appendix A)

★★ **16.** Write a program that will randomly generate (but not print) 1000 points inside the square (shown in the diagram) counting how many of these points lie inside the circle with center (1/2, 1/2) and radius 1/2. Have the program print an approximation for π based on the fact that the area of the square is 1 and the area of the circle is π/4. (*Hint:* A point is inside the circle if its distance to (1/2, 1/2) is less than 1/2.)

Ulam's Conjecture (Chapter 19)

Start with any positive integer. If it is even, divide it by two; if it is odd, multiply it by three and add one. Obtain successive integers by repeating this process. The mathematician S. Ulam has conjectured that no matter what the starting integer is, eventually the number 1 will be obtained. For example, when 22 is the starting integer the procedure gives the following series:

22   11   34   17   52   26   13   40   20   10   5   16   8   4   2   1

★ **17.** Write a program to find an integer with longest Ulam length of all the integers between 2 and 100 (i.e., so that the number of steps for it to produce 1 is at least as large as for any other integer between 2 and 100). (Chapter 20)

Drunkard's Walk (Chapter 19)

★ **18.** A drunkard standing in the middle of an 8-foot-long bridge is trying to get off. Each step he takes is one foot long. Unfortunately, each step is just as likely to be in the backward direction as in the forward direction.

(a) Simulate the drunkard continuing to take random 1-foot-long steps until he reaches an end of the bridge; have the computer print out how many steps it took and which end he reached (left or right).

(b) Simulate 100 repetitions of the drunkard's-walk experiment. (Of course, for each new repetition the drunkard stands in the middle of the bridge.) Have as the only printout

```
ON  THE  AVERAGE  IT  TOOK  _____  STEPS  TO  REACH  AN  END
```

Nested Loops (Chapter 19)

★ **19.** *Square-producing pairs.* The pair of numbers 8 and 17 has a nice property: both their sum, 25, and their difference, 9, are perfect squares. Write a program that will print all pairs of integers less than 100 whose sum and difference are both perfect squares. (*Hint:* N is a perfect square, provided INT(SQR(N)) = SQR(N). Also, it is inefficient to use both FOR-NEXT loops from 1 to 100.)

★ **20.** Write a program to find the sum of all three-digit numbers that can be formed using the digits 1, 2, and 3:

$$111 + 112 + 113 + 121 + 122 + 123 + \cdots + 333$$

★ **21.** Write a program to find all integer pairs (X, Y) that satisfy both inequalities

$$3X - 2Y \leqslant 5$$
$$-X + 2Y \leqslant 6$$

with X and Y both in the interval [0,7].

Permutations (Chapter 19 or 21)

The set of all permutations of N objects consists of all arrangements with *no repetitions* allowed. For example, the set of all permutations of the numbers {1, 2, 3} consists of the six arrangements 123, 132, 213, 231, 312, and 321.

★ **22. (a)** Complete lines 30 and 50, so that the following program will produce the 6 permutations of {1, 2, 3} as formatted in printout (a).

(b) Modify the program so that if the system has four print zones, the printout will be formatted as in (b).

```
10    FOR  J=1  TO  3
20      FOR  K=1  TO  3
30        IF  K=J  THEN  _____
40        FOR  M=1  TO  3
50          IF  M=J  OR  M=K  THEN  _____
60            PRINT  J;K;M
70          NEXT  M
80        NEXT  K
90      NEXT  J
100   END
```

(a)

```
1  2  3
1  3  2
2  1  3
2  3  1
3  1  2
3  2  1
```

(b)

```
1  2  3        1  3  2        2  1  3        2  3  1
3  1  2        3  2  1
```

23. Write a program to list 27 arrangements of the numbers {1, 2, 3} with *repetitions* of the same number *allowed* in an arrangement. The list will consist of 111,112,113,121,122,123, and so on.

★★ **24.** Modify the program in Exercise 22 so that it produces all 24 permutations of the numbers {1, 2, 3, 4}.

★★ **25. (a)** Write a program to produce all 6 permutations of the letters {A, B, C}. (Use subscripted string variables.)
  (b) Write a program to produce all 24 permutations of the letters {A, B, C, D}.

Pythagorean Triples (Chapter 19)

A triple of positive integers *A, B, C* is called a Pythagorean triple if $C^2 = A^2 + B^2$. For example, 3, 4, 5 is called a Pythagorean triple. (*Note:* In some systems, IF $3\wedge2+4\wedge2=5\wedge2$ will test out as false as a result of numerical difficulties—logarithms are used for computing powers. Test your system for this possible difficulty. If your system has this difficulty, you can set $E = .001$ and use the test

$$\text{IF } \text{INT}(A\wedge 2 + E) + \text{INT}(B\wedge 2 + E) = \text{INT}(C\wedge 2 + E) \text{ THEN } \ldots$$

Another way around this difficulty is to use the test IF $A*A + B*B = C*C$.)

★   **26.** Write a program to list all Pythagorean triples with A, B, C each $\leqslant 25$. Do not allow any repetitions of the same three numbers in a different order. (Nested loops can have depth 3.)

★★   **27.** Write a program to list all the Pythagorean triples in reduced form with A, B, C each $\leqslant 25$. That is, do not allow duplications of similar triangles. Thus, 3, 4, 5 should appear on the list, but 6, 8, 10 should not.

Pascal's Triangle (Chapter 19)

★★   **28.** Here is a program fragment to print the binomial coefficient (N, R) where

$$(N, R) = \frac{N(N-1) \ldots (N-R+1)}{1\cdot 2\cdot \ldots \cdot R}$$

```
100   C=1
110   FOR  J=1  TO  R
120      C=C*(N-J+1)/J
130   NEXT  J
140   PRINT  C
```

Using triple-nested loops, write a program to print Pascal's triangle down to $N = 6$.

```
1  1
1  2  1
1  3  3  1
1  4  6  4  1
1  5  10  10  5  1
1  6  15  20  15  6  1
```

Guessing Computer's Number (Chapter 18)

★   **29.** Write a program in which the computer randomly selects an integer ranging from 1 to 16 and then requests that the human keep inputting guesses (which the computer assesses). Design your program so that a typical printout might be

```
COMPUTER HAS SELECTED AN INTEGER FROM 1 TO 16
TAKE A GUESS HUMAN ? 7
TOO LOW, GUESS AGAIN ? 12
TOO HIGH, GUESS AGAIN ? 9
TOO LOW, GUESS AGAIN ? 11
NOW YOU HAVE IT
```

Guessing Your Number (Chapter 24)

★★ **30.** Write a program in which the user thinks of an integer ranging from 1 to 64. The computer program first asks the question: IS YOUR NUMBER GREATER THAN 32? TYPE YES OR NO. After the user responds, the computer asks a second yes or no question. By the time the user has responded to a total of six yes or no questions, the computer prints

```
YOUR NUMBER IS _____
```

Running Five-Day Average (Chapter 20)

★ **31.** The DATA line gives the daily sales over a fifteen-day period.

DATA 10,60,20,20,35,40,10,34,37,56,34,45,33,26,20

Write a program to compute the current *five*-day average. Format the printout as follows:

DAY	SALES THAT DAY	TOTAL TO DATE	CURRENT FIVE, DAY AVERAGE
1	10	10	
2	60	70	
3	20	90	
4	20	110	
5	35	145	29
6	40	185	35
7	10	195	25
.	.	.	.
.	.	.	.
15	.	.	.

Goldbach's Conjecture (Chapter 20)

★★ **32.** It has been conjectured but never proved that every even integer greater than two can be represented as the sum of two primes. Write a program that will verify this for every even integer less than 100. (First load an array with primes.)

Multiplying Two Polynomials (Chapter 20)

** **33.** A polynomial of order N can be written in the form

$$a_0 + a_1 X^1 + a_2 X^2 + \cdots + a_n X^n$$

Write a program that multiplies two polynomials of order ≤ 5 and prints the coefficients of the product. For each polynomial, the data line gives the order of the polynomial followed by the coefficients.

Ex. DATA 2,5, -3,8 represents $5 - 3X + 8X^2$

DATA 1,7, -1 represents $7 - X$

(*Note:* If the order is 2, you must read 3 coefficients. It is convenient to read them into array A as A(0), A(1), A(2).)

Print the coefficients of the two polynomials and of the product. Give the coefficients of the terms in ascending order.

Prime Numbers and Sieve of Eratosthenes (Chapter 20)

In trying to determine whether an integer is prime, it is sufficient to test for factors from the set consisting of 2 and all *odd* integers $\leq$ the square root of the integer.* For example, to determine whether 97 is prime, it is sufficient to test whether 2, 3, 5, 7, or 9 divides 97; since none of them does, 97 is prime.

Here is a procedure for finding all the primes between 2 and 100. First cross out all multiples of 2 greater than 2. Then cross out all multiples of 3 greater than 3; then all multiples of 5 greater than 5; then all multiples of 7 greater than 7; and finally all multiples of 9 greater than 9. Stop, since $\sqrt{100} = 10$. Whatever has not been crossed out is prime.

2	3	~~4~~	5	~~6~~	7	~~8~~	~~9~~	~~10~~	11	~~12~~	13	~~14~~	~~15~~	~~16~~
17	~~18~~	19	~~20~~	~~21~~	~~22~~	23	~~24~~	25	~~26~~	~~27~~	~~28~~	29	~~30~~	31
~~32~~	~~33~~	~~34~~	~~35~~	~~36~~	37	~~38~~	~~39~~	~~40~~	41	~~42~~	43	~~44~~	~~45~~	~~46~~
47	~~48~~	~~49~~	~~50~~	~~51~~	~~52~~	53	~~54~~	~~55~~	~~56~~	~~57~~	~~58~~	59	~~60~~	61
~~62~~	~~63~~	~~64~~	~~65~~	~~66~~	67	~~68~~	~~69~~	~~70~~	71	~~72~~	73	~~74~~	~~75~~	~~76~~
~~77~~	~~78~~	79	~~80~~	~~81~~	~~82~~	83	~~84~~	~~85~~	~~86~~	~~87~~	~~88~~	89	~~90~~	~~91~~
~~92~~	~~93~~	~~94~~	~~95~~	~~96~~	97	~~98~~	~~99~~	100						

* The more efficient procedure of testing for factors from the set consisting of 2 and odd *primes* $\leq \sqrt{N}$ is employed in Exercise 36.

Here is a program based on the procedure just described:

```
10   DIM X(100)
20   FOR I=2 TO 100
30      X(I)=I
40   NEXT I
45   REM CROSS OUT ALL MULTIPLES OF 2 BIGGER THAN 2
50   FOR J=4 TO 100 STEP 2
60      X(J)=_____
70   NEXT J
80   REM USE A NESTED LOOP TO CROSS OUT MULTIPLES OF 3,5,7,9
90   FOR K=3 TO 9 STEP 2
95      REM CROSS OUT MULTIPLES OF K BIGGER THAN K
100     FOR L=2*K TO 100 STEP _____
110        _____
120     _____
130  NEXT K
140  REM PRINT ONLY THE PRIMES
150  FOR M=2 TO 100
160     _____
170     _____
180  NEXT M
190  END
```

34. Complete lines 60, 100, 110, 120, 160, 170. (*Hint:* You must devise a procedure for crossing out the nonprimes.)

35. Revise the previous program so that it will print all the primes between 2 and 500.

★ **36.** Same as Exercise 35, only design your program so that it omits the inefficient step of crossing out multiples of 9 (since they were already crossed out as multiples of 3), and so that for all nonprime odd numbers less than $\sqrt{500}$, the program omits the step of crossing out their multiples.

★ **37.** Use the computer to find the 77th prime. (2 is the first prime.)

★★ **38.** *Twin primes revisited.* A pair of *odd* numbers that are both prime and differ by 2 is called a pair of twin primes. Some examples are 3,5 5,7 11,13 17,19. Write a program using the sieve that prints all pairs of twin primes less than 1000.

Bridge Hand (Chapter 21 or 23)

★★ **39.** Write a program to deal a bridge hand at random with the cards arranged according to suit and in decreasing order within each suit. (*Note:* An ace is the highest card in a suit.)

Twenty–Ninety (Chapter 21)

** **40.** Using the following DATA lines:

DATA "ONE","TWO","THREE","FOUR","FIVE"
DATA "SIX","SEVEN","EIGHT","NINE"
DATA "TWENTY","THIRTY","FORTY","FIFTY","SIXTY"
DATA "SEVENTY","EIGHTY","NINETY"

write a program that will print TWENTY through NINETY as follows:

```
TWENTY         TWENTY ONE    TWENTY TWO      TWENTY THREE   TWENTY FOUR
TWENTY FIVE    TWENTY SIX         .               .              .
   .              .               .               .              .
   .              .               .               .              .
NINETY FIVE    NINETY SIX    NINETY SEVEN    NINETY EIGHT   NINETY NINE
```

Printing Triangle of Stars (Chapter 19)

* **41.** Write a program to produce the triangle below so that it is centered on the screen. The base has 7 stars. (Use TAB and nested loops.)

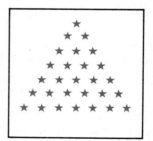

Matrix Row Interchange (Chapter 25)

** **42.** Write a program that reads 16 DATA numbers into a 4×4 matrix, A, and then forms and prints a new 4×4 matrix, B, in which the 2nd and 3rd rows of A are interchanged.

Area under Curve (Chapter 17 or Appendix A)

43. Consider the problem of finding the area under the curve $g(x) = x^2$ between $x = 0$ and $x = 1$. An approximation to the exact area can be obtained by subdividing [0,1] into four subintervals of width 1/4 and then, over each subinterval, taking the rectangle whose height is the value of $g(x)$ at the *midpoint* of that subinterval. The approximation is the sum of the areas of these rectangles.

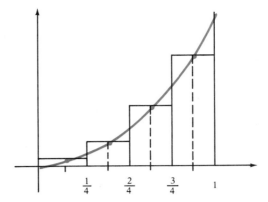

(a) Below is a program for approximating the area based on subdividing [0, 1] into ten subintervals, each of width 1/10, and using as rectangle heights the values of $g(x)$ at the midpoints of the subintervals. Fill in line 60.

```
10    DEF FNG(X)=X∧2
20    H=.1
30    S=0
40    FOR K=1 TO 10
50      X=(K-1)*H
60      REM X IS THE LEFT ENDPT OF CURRENT SUBINTERVAL
70    NEXT K
80    PRINT "AREA IS APPROXIMATELY";S
90    END
```

The printout will be ⎹ AREA IS APPROXIMATELY .332499 ⎸

(b) Rerun the program using subintervals of width .01. You will get a better approximation to the actual area, which we know from calculus is 1/3.

(c) Write an area under a curve program so that line 10 will contain the definition of the function and line 20 will give the endpoints of the interval. Line 30 should prompt the user to input how many subintervals should be used for the approximation. Run it several times for $g(x) = x^3$ over [0, 2] with different subinterval widths. Then run it for $g(x) = x^4 + 1$ over [1, 3].

Finding Approximate Roots by Binary Chopping (Chapter 25 or Appendix A)

Suppose G is a continuous function on [1, 2] such that G(1) is negative and G(2) is positive. Here is a procedure for finding an approximate root. First compute G at 1.5, the midpoint of [1, 2]. Let us suppose, for this G, that $G(1.5)$ is *positive*. Then G must have a root somewhere on $[1, 1.5]$, because $G(1)$ is negative and $G(1.5)$ is positive. Then using $[1, 1.5]$ as the new interval, computer G at 1.25, the midpoint. If $G(1.25)$ is positive, the next interval to use will be $[1, 1.25]$. If $G(1.25)$ is negative, the next interval to use will be $[1.25, 1.5]$. Continuing in this fashion, at each stage we find a smaller interval such that G is negative at the left endpoint and positive at the right endpoint and hence has a root somewhere on that interval.

★ **44.** Below is a program for finding an exact root or an x-value that is within a distance of .01 of an exact x that is a root. The program assumes that $G(1)$ is negative and $G(2)$ is positive. The last line in the printout table should be ⎣ APPROX. ROOT AT X = 1.75781 ⎦. Complete line 80.

```
10   DEF FNG(X)=X^5-6*X^2+X
20   PRINT "LEFT PT","RIGHT PT","MIDPT","VALUE AT MIDPT"
30   LPT=1
40   RPT=2
50   MPT=(LPT+RPT)/2
60   PRINT LPT,RPT,MPT,FNG(MPT)
70   WHILE MPT-LPT>.01 AND FNG(MPT)<>0
80      IF FNG(MPT)>0 THEN _____
                      ELSE _____
90      MPT=(LPT+RPT)/2
100     PRINT LPT,RPT,MPT,FNG(MPT)
110  WEND
120  IF FNG(MPT)=0 THEN PRINT "EXACT ROOT AT X=";MPT
                   ELSE PRINT "APPROX. ROOT AT X=";MPT
130  END
```

★ **45.** Write a program that will find an approximate root (within .01) for any continuous function G on $[1, 2]$ with $G(1)$ positive and $G(2)$ negative. Run it with $G(x) = x^3 - 6x^2 + 9$.

★★ **46.** Write a *single* program that will find an approximate root for any continuous function G on $[1, 2]$ for which $G(1)$ and $G(2)$ have opposite signs; that is, G at one of the endpoints is positive and at the other, negative. Run it first for $G(x) = x^5 - 6x^2 + x$. Then, changing only line 10, which defines the function, run the program for $G(x) = x^3 - 6x^2 + 9$.

Business and General Problems

(Chapter 4)

1. John Doe's federal tax rate is 30% and his state tax rate is 10%. Write a program so that when John Doe's weekly income is input, the printout will give the weekly deductions for federal and state tax and will also give the weekly net pay. (Assume state tax is deductible.)

> ENTER WEEKLY INCOME? 1000
> > STATE TAX $ 100
> > FEDERAL TAX $ 270
> > WEEKLY NET PAY $ 630

2. Rewrite the program from the previous exercise so that the user inputs not only the weekly income, but also the state and federal tax rates.

(Chapter 9)

3. Write a looping version of the program in Exercise 1, so that the first prompt is

> ENTER WEEKLY INCOME OR −1 TO QUIT

4. In a certain course, the final exam counts 50% and the hour exams average counts 50%.

In the following DATA line the first grade is the final exam grade and the other grades are hour-exam grades (−1 is a flag). Write a program that will print out the numerical grade for the course. For DATA 70, 90,

329

85, 95, 90, −1, the printout would be

```
FINAL NUMERICAL AVERAGE 80
```

(Chapter 8)

5. Write a program that will print the name, occupation, and income for the person that is in the fourth group of data from a given set of DATA lines. For

   DATA "FOY","LAWYER",40000,"DIAZ","DOCTOR",70000
   DATA "MUNSON","TEACHER",21000,"DAVIS","BARBER",28000
   DATA "BOND","PLUMBER",24000,"KUHN","DENTIST",50000

   the printout should be DAVIS BARBER 28000

6. Write a program that simulates using an automatic teller at a bank as follows: The program asks the user to enter the ID number. (This action corresponds to a customer inserting the card into the slot.) Then the program asks the user to input the five-character password. The program, after checking whether the password matches the user's ID number, prints whether the password is correct. Although the information on ID numbers and passwords would actually be stored in files, let us assume for this simplified program that all this information is contained in the *five* data groups in DATA lines 10 and 20.

   10   DATA 835214,"AB17X",835215,"BABEX",835216,"PEP14"
   20   DATA 835217,"HORSE",835218,"TAX55"

   Here are three sample printouts:

   (a)
   ```
   WHAT IS YOUR ID NUMBER ? 835217
   WHAT IS YOUR PASSWORD ? HORRS
   SORRY, PASSWORD DOES NOT MATCH
   ```

   (b)
   ```
   WHAT IS YOUR ID NUMBER ? 835217
   WHAT IS YOUR PASSWORD ? HORSE
   PASSWORD MATCHES
   ```

   (c)
   ```
   WHAT IS YOUR ID NUMBER ? 422984
   SORRY, YOUR ID NUMBER IS INVALID
   ```

(Chapter 13)

7. **(a)** Write a program that produces a table of five payment plans for purchasing a new car. The data line will contain the car make, the price, and the annual interest rate. For example, DATA "SAAB",10000,0.15. The printout, with payments truncated by the INT function to the nearest dollar, will look like this:

```
MONTHLY PAYMENTS FOR $10000 SAAB
AT 15% ANNUAL INTEREST
#YRS.        #PMTS       EACH PMT      TOTAL COST
  1           12           902           10824
  2           24           484           11606
  3           36          _____         _____
  4           48          _____         _____
  5           60          _____         _____
```

Use commas or TAB.

For payments made at the end of each month use this formula:

$$PMT = A \times \frac{I}{1-(1+I)^{-N}}$$

where A = original amount of loan (e.g. 10000)

I = interest rate per *month*

N = number of months (payments) of loan

(*Hint:* In line 1 of the table, $N=12$; in line 2, $N=24$, and so on. Make your program sufficiently general to handle any DATA line in the above form.)

(b) Rewrite the program using PRINT USING so that each payment is given to two decimal places.

(Chapter 11 or Appendix A)

8. **(a)** Write a program to produce a table of effective interest rates:

ANNUAL RATE %	EFFECTIVE RATES COMPOUNDED		
	QUARTERLY	MONTHLY	DAILY
6	.	.	.
7	.	.	.
8			
9			

(*Hint:* The effective rate E is given by the formula

$$E = \left(1 + \frac{R}{N}\right)^{N} - 1$$

where R is the annual rate and N the number of conversions per year.)

(b) If you did not do so in part (a), write the program so that it uses a single user-defined function for computing all the effective interest rates.

(Chapter 13)

9. Write a program that updates an investor's bank balance. DATA gives investor's name and present bank balance (Example: "SUSAN PRATT",21500). This is followed by information about 6 stock transactions. Each transaction has four items of information: company, price per share, buy or sell, number of shares. (Example: "I.B.M.",90.40,"BUY",12) This means Pratt wants to buy 12 shares of I.B.M. at 90.40/share.

The program will update the investor's bank balance. In the example above, the balance decreases by $1084.80. (When stock is sold, the balance will increase.) For each transaction, you must also deduct the broker's commission as follows: $100 for 10 or fewer shares. For more than 10 shares, add 5% of the value of the shares above 10. (Example: For 12 shares the commission is $100 plus 5% of the value of 2 shares.)

In the printout, start with the investor's name and original balance (Example: SUSAN PRATT ORIGINAL BALANCE 21500). For each transaction print information as below:

```
CO  :  IBM BUY SHARES  :  12 PER  :  90.40
COST  :  1084.80 COMM  :  109.04 BAL  :  20306.16
```

If balance goes below zero, print IN ARREARS. Use the following data to make up 3 more sets:

DATA "IBM",90.40,"BUY",12

DATA "NABISCO",28,"SELL",10

DATA "G.M.",72.75,"SELL",8

(Chapter 13)

10. Use this simplified method to compute income tax. DATA are wages, interest, expenses, dependents. Use the following method:

(a) Find the taxable interest. Take the portion of interest that exceeds 1% of the wages. Add the result to the wages.

(b) Deduct $1200 for each dependent.

(c) Take additional deductions according to the following:

if income $<=10000$, then deduct 15% of expenses from wages

if $10000 <$income<25000, deduct 25% of expenses

if income $>=25000$ or dependents >8, deduct 50% of expenses

(d) On resulting taxable income, INC, use this formula:

$$TAX = .000005(INC)^2 + .125(INC) - 405$$

Note: If the tax computed is negative, then make it zero. The printout should include a table showing

```
WAGES   INTR.   EXP.   #DEP   DEDUC   INC.    TAX
20000   600     5000   3      4850    15550   2747.76
```

For this example, the taxable interest is 400 and the deductions are $3600 + 1250 = 4850$. Total taxable interest is $20400 - 4850 = 15550$.

(Chapter 14)

11. Forty artists work in a studio painting ceramic plates. Each artist finishes 350 plates per season. The owner wants to hire more workers, but the studio is already crowded. An industrial psychologist warned that for each new worker hired, productivity per worker would decrease by 7 plates. Write a program to produce a table of productivity for staff sizes of 40 to 50 workers. Find the number of workers that produces the maximum productivity. The printout should look like this:

```
#WORKERS        #PLATES        TOTAL
  40             350           14000
  41             343           14063
  42             336           14112
  .               .              .
  .               .              .
  .               .              .
  50            _____        _____
MAXIMUM PRODUCTION: _____ WORKERS _____ TOTAL PLATES
```

Hangman (Chapter 22)

** **12.** Write a hangman program involving 7-letter words similar to Exercise 14 of Chapter 22, so that the computer will display what is known at each stage. A typical printout (assuming that the twelfth word is HEAVIER) might be

```
A SEVEN LETTER WORD WILL BE SELECTED
PICK AN INTEGER BETWEEN 1 AND 20 ?   12
   PICK A LETTER ?   E
SO FAR HAVE:  _ E _ _ _ E _
   PICK A LETTER ?   U
U IS NOT IN THE WORD
INCORRECT LETTERS GUESSED SO FAR: U
  PICK A LETTER ?   I
SO FAR WE HAVE:  _ E _ _ I E _
   :
   :

CONGRATULATIONS, YOU HAVE THE WORD
YOU HAD _____ INCORRECT LETTERS
```

Substitution Encoding (Chapter 22)

★★ **13.** Write a program that will perform a letter substitution coding based on the following:

ABCDEFGHIJKLMNOPQRSTUVWXYZ

HJAZKQYBFDPWTVSCUXLGINOEMR

Thus, A will be replaced by H, B by J, C by A, D by Z, E by K, and so on. Use the ASC function. Also, use a numeric array with memory cells L(65) through L(90), or, to save memory space, use cells L(1) through L(26).

For an input of "AT THE ZOO!", the printout should be

```
HG GBK RSS!
```

(Chapter 22 or 26)

14. (a) The ACME Computer Co. is developing a secret project, and security is very tight. Each employee is given a password, and the employee must enter that password into a computer at the door before he/she will be permitted to enter the premises. The formula for determining the person's password is the letters of his/her name spelled backwards. The computer thus takes the password, determines the employee's name, and validates it against the DATA lines that contain the names of all ACME employees. Write a program to do this. Some sample executions follow:

```
┌─────────────────────────────────┐              ┌─────────────────────────────────┐
│ ENTER PASSWORD:  EOD NHOJ       │      or      │ ENTER  PASSWORD:   AXWRD        │
│ YOU MAY ENTER,  JOHN DOE        │              │ SORRY,  PASSWORD  INVALID       │
└─────────────────────────────────┘              └─────────────────────────────────┘
```

(b) Write a version of the program in which all the employees' names are contained in a file named "EMPLOYEES".

(Chapter 26)

15. Using the formula given in Exercise 4, write a program to create a file containing the effective rates (for interest rates 5% to 25%) compounded quarterly, monthly, weekly, and daily. The file should have the same format as the table in Exercise 4.

(Chapter 23 or 26)

★ 16. **(a)** It is payday at the HO-HUM Harmonica Co., and the payroll fund is low. The board of directors has decided to begin paying the highest-paid employees first and gradually to work down to the lesser-paid employees (or until the money runs out, whichever comes first). The data is stored in DATA lines with the employees' names in alphabetical order. Each line contains an employee's name and monthly salary. Assuming that the company has 10 employees and that they have $15,000 to give these employees, write a program to print the names of all the employees that are paid (in the order that they are paid) and the amount of money left. No employee who is paid should receive less than full salary. (Use a bubble sort to put the employees in the order that they are paid.)

(b) Write a version of the program in which the data is contained in a file instead of in DATA lines.

Statistics

Many computer installations have a statistical package consisting of a collection of statistical programs (on file at the computer center) and a manual with instructions on how to call and use any of these programs. Essentially all the user does is call the particular program desired and then types DATA according to the format specified in the manual. The user does not write the programs. However, you will feel more comfortable if you have some idea of how statistical programs are written. The purpose of the following material is to provide some familiarity with basic statistical programs. See Chapters 1 through 9 and 19 for the programming concepts used in this appendix.

D.1 Computing Mean

The mean of a list of n numbers $x_1 \ldots x_n$ is $\frac{1}{n}(x_1 + \cdots + x_n)$. Here is a program for computing the mean. See Chapter 9 for a more complete explanation of FOR-NEXT loops.

```
10    DATA 5
20    DATA 13,8,24,11,19
30    REM THE # OF TERMS
40    READ N
50    SUM=0
60    FOR K=1 TO N
70      READ X
80      SUM=SUM+X
90    NEXT K
100   MEAN=SUM/N
110   PRINT "MEAN IS";MEAN
120   END
```

The printout will be

```
MEAN IS 15
```

D.2 Computing Standard Deviation

If $x_1, x_2 \ldots x_n$ are n sample values of a random variable and m is their mean, the variance V is defined as

$$V = \frac{1}{n-1} \sum_{i=1}^{n} (x_i - m)^2$$

and the standard deviation $D = \sqrt{V}$.

One way to find the standard deviation is first to compute the mean and then compute the variance.

PROBLEM Fill in line 100 so that this program will compute the standard deviation when $n = 5$. (Recall that the symbol for exponentiation is either $\wedge$ or ** or $\uparrow$.)

```
10    N=5
20    DATA 13,8,24,11,19
30    SUM=0
35    Q=0
40    FOR K=1 TO N
50       READ X(K)
60       SUM=SUM+X(K)
70    NEXT K
80    MEAN=SUM/N
90    FOR K=1 TO N
100      Q= _____
110   NEXT K
120   V=Q/(N-1)
130   STDEV=SQR(V)
140   PRINT "THE STANDARD DEVIATION IS";STDEV
150   END
```

ANSWER $Q = Q + (X(K) - \text{Mean})\wedge 2$.

There is a second and better formula for computing the variance V. It is

$$V = \frac{1}{n-1} \left[\left(\sum x_i^2 \right) - nm^2 \right]$$

Exercise

★ 1. Write a standard deviation program using the second formula for variance. Use only *one* FOR-NEXT loop in your program.

D.3 Chi Square

The following formula gives the method of calculating the chi-square of a body of data.

$$\chi^2 = \sum_{i=1}^{N} \frac{(P_i - E_i)^2}{P_i}$$

where P_i is the predicted number of occurrences of category i and E_i is the experimentally observed number of occurrences of category i. For example, a certain genetic theory might predict that in a sample of 50 rats there should be 20 black, 20 gray, and 10 spotted. If an actual sample of 50 rats had 15 black, 30 gray, and 5 spotted, then

$$\chi^2 = \frac{(20 - 15)^2}{20} + \frac{(20 - 30)^2}{20} + \frac{(10 - 5)^2}{10} = \frac{175}{20} = 8.75$$

PROBLEM Fill in line 70, so that this program computes chi square.

```
10   N=3
20   REM FOR EACH PAIR OF DATA #'S EXPERIMENTAL # IS FIRST
30   DATA 15,20,30,20,5,10
40   CHI.SQ=0
50   FOR K=1 TO N
60     READ E(K),P(K)
70     CHI.SQ= _____
80   NEXT K
90   PRINT "CHI SQUARE EQUALS";CHI.SQ
100  END
```

ANSWER Line 70 should be CHI.SQ = CHI.SQ + (E(K) − P(K))∧2/P(K).

Exercise

2. Run the chi square program when the predicted results in a sample of 100 are 30,30,30,10, and the experimental observations are 27,28,34,9.

D.4 Least Squares Method

Suppose that (X_1,Y_1), (X_2,Y_2), (X_3,Y_3) . . . (X_N,Y_N) is a set of N points. The least squares method gives the straight line that comes closest (in a certain technical sense) to fitting the N points. Let $\overline{X}$ and $\overline{Y}$ be the respective means;

that is, $\overline{X} = (\Sigma X_i)/N$ and $\overline{Y} = (\Sigma Y_i)/N$. The following statistical formulas are well known:

1. The corrected sum of X squares $= (\Sigma X_i^2) - N\cdot\overline{X}^2$.

2. The corrected sum of cross products $= (\Sigma X_iY_i) - N\cdot\overline{X}\cdot\overline{Y}$. Then, let

$$b = \frac{\text{corrected sum of cross products}}{\text{corrected sum of } X \text{ squares}}$$

$$a = \overline{Y} - b\overline{X}$$

It can be shown that $Y = a + bX=$ is the line given by the least squares method.

PROBLEM   Fill in lines 140, 160, and 200 of the following program, which computes a and b of the line given by the least squares method for the 4 points (1, 3), (2, 4), (3, 5), and (4, 8). (Look at the definitions given above. What values will X1 and Y1 have by the end of the FOR-NEXT loop?)

```
10     READ N
20     X1=0
30     Y1=0
40     X2=0
50     P=0
60     FOR J=1 TO N
70       READ X,Y
80       X1=X1+X
90       Y1=Y1+Y
100      X2=X2+X^2
110      P=P+X*Y
120    NEXT J
130    REM M1 FOR X MEAN
140    M1= _____
150    REM M2 FOR Y MEAN
160    M2 _____
170    REM C1 FOR CORRECTED X SQUARES SUM
180    C1=X2-N*M1*M1
190    REM C2 FOR CORRECTED CROSS PRODUCTS
200    C2 _____
210    B=C2/C1
220    A=M2-B*M1
230    PRINT "A EQUALS";A
240    PRINT "B EQUALS";B
250    DATA 4
260    DATA 1,3
270    DATA 2,4
280    DATA 3,5
290    DATA 4,8
300    END
```

ANSWER   By the end of the FOR-NEXT loop, X1 will equal the sum of the X_i. Thus, line 140 should be M1 = X1/N. Similarly, line 160 should be M2 = Y1/N. Line 200 should be C2 = P − N*M1*M2.

Exercises

3. **(a)** Run the Least Squares program for the given data.
   (b) Run it for the three points (1,2), (3,6), and (6,12). (Note that these points lie on a single line.)
   (c) Run it for the five points (2,2), (3,5), (4,7), (6,9), and (7,11).
4. The corrected sum of Y squares = $(\Sigma Y_i^2) - N \cdot \bar{Y}^2$.
   The correlation coefficient

   $$= \frac{\text{corrected sum of cross products}}{(\text{corrected sum of } X \text{ squares})(\text{corrected sum of } Y \text{ squares})}$$

   Add several lines to the Least Squares program so that it will also compute and print out the correlation coefficient.

Insertion and Shell Sorts

Although the bubble sort (discussed in Chapter 23) is probably the easiest sorting procedure to understand, it is not one of the fastest (i.e., it tends to use more CPU time than other procedures). In this appendix we discuss two other sorting procedures: (1) the insertion sort, which is somewhat faster than the bubble sort, and (2) the Shell sort (named after its inventor, Donald Shell), which is considerably faster than the bubble sort. (Since the Shell sort is performed by doing a number of miniature insertion sorts, it is important that you first understand the insertion sort.)

The slowness of the bubble sort stems from the fact that switching within a bubble-sort pass moves a number only one box at a time (i.e., switching is only between adjacent boxes), and that each pass is too focused on putting *just one* number in its proper box. The Shell sort, by contrast, uses a much more overall approach in which numbers, more than one box apart, can be compared and switched.

For fairly small arrays, the bubble sort is quite adequate since the Shell sort is only slightly faster. However, as the size of the array increases so does the factor by which the Shell sort is faster. For example, for an array of 20 elements, both sorts take approximately the same time. For an array of 500 elements, the bubble sort usually takes at least 5 times as long; for an array of 1000 elements, the bubble sort usually takes at least 10 times as long. In Exercise 10, you are asked to compare sorting times on your particular computer.

E.1 Insertion Sort

The insertion sort on *six* numbers in boxes A(1) through A(6) would proceed in *five* stages:

Description of stages	Initial Order:	8	6	3	9	7	2
Stage 1. Put current contents of boxes A(1) and A(2) in order.	After *Stage 1:*	6	8	3	9	7	2
Stage 2. Put current contents of boxes A(1), A(2), and A(3) in order.	After *Stage 2:*	3	6	8	9	7	2
Stage 3. Put current contents of boxes A(1) through A(4) in order.	After *Stage 3:*	3	6	8	9	7	2
Stage 4. Put current contents of boxes A(1) through A(5) in order.	After *Stage 4:*	3	6	7	8	9	2
Stage 5. Put current contents of boxes A(1) through A(6) in order.	After *Stage 5:*	2	3	6	7	8	9

A detailed description of the way to achieve the sorting in Stage M appears below. (At the start of Stage M the contents of boxes A(1) through A(M) will already be in order. By the end of Stage M, the contents of boxes A(1) through A(M + 1) must be in order.) Any box whose contents is out of order with the original contents of box A(M + 1) should have its contents shifted one box to the right; then the original content of box A(M + 1) should be *inserted* into the leftmost box whose content was shifted to the right.

Illustration. Let us consider Stage 4 (that is, M = 4) from the previous example. At the start of Stage 4, the memory box picture is

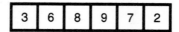

Note that the starting contents of boxes A(1) through A(4) are sorted. By the end of stage 4, boxes A(1) through A(5) must be sorted. We shall achieve this by shifting the 8 and 9 each one box to the right and then inserting the 7:

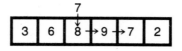

The following is an insertion sort program for six numbers (assuming the numbers are already in boxes A(1) through A(6):

```
100    FOR M=1 TO 5
110       J=M
120       B=A(M+1)
130       DONE$="NO"
140       WHILE DONE$="NO" AND J>=1
150          IF B>=A(J) THEN DONE$="YES"
                        ELSE A(J+1)=A(J) : J=J-1
160       WEND
170       A(J+1)=B
180    NEXT M
```

REMARK: While M = 1, Stage 1 is performed.
          While M = 2, Stage 2 is performed.
              ⋮

Procedure for Specific M, (e.g., M = 4—Stage 4).   Using the previous example, the relevant boxes at stage 4 will be A(1)–A(5):

3	6	8	9	7

B is fixed as the contents of box A(5). Boxes A(1)–A(4) are in order.

The computer search starts from the right at box A(4). The computer must locate the proper box for the contents of B. If $B >= A(J)$ then the search is over; otherwise if $B < A(J)$, the contents of A(J) should be shifted one box to the right. This is accomplished by $A(J + 1) = A(J)$.

Exercises

1. Modify the above program segment so that it will sort eight numbers stored in boxes A(1) through A(8).

2. By hand perform the insertion sort on

4	2	15	8	3

3. Explain why line 170 of the above program is $A(J + 1) = B$ and not $A(J) = B$.

▬ E.2 Shell Sort on N Elements

As previously discussed, a major disadvantage of both the bubble sort and insertion sort is that a number can be shifted only one box at a time. In the Shell sort, boxes S-units apart have their contents compared and shifted (if necessary); S starts out large. The variable S, standing for *shift size*, has initial value INT(N/2). During each successive pass the value of S is halved, until during the last pass, S has the value 1.

EXAMPLE Let us consider the Shell sort on

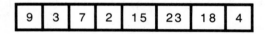

During Pass 1. The shift size S is equal to INT(8/2) = 4. There will be 4 *separate* insertion sorts on the following 4 pairs of boxes 4 units apart:

A(1),A(5)   A(2),A(6)   A(3),A(7)   A(4),A(8)

By the end of Pass 1 we will have

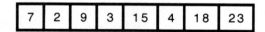

During Pass 2. The shift size S is equal to 4/2 = 2. There will be 2 *separate* insertion sorts on 2 sets of boxes, 2 units apart:

sort A(1), A(3), A(5), A(7)

sort A(2), A(4), A(6), A(8)

By the end of pass 2 we will have

```
7  2  9  3  15  4  18  23
```

During Pass 3. The shift size S = 2/2 = 1. There will be a single ordinary insertion sort on the entire array. By the end of Pass 3, the array will be sorted.

QUESTION Why not perform a single insertion sort at the very beginning, if the very last pass of the Shell sort is a single insertion sort on the entire array?

ANSWER An insertion sort on a totally unsorted array (for large N) is extremely slow, whereas it is much faster for an array that is almost sorted. In the Shell sort by the time S = 1, the array is nearly sorted.

Here is a program to perform a Shell sort. Note that it only sorts; it does not produce any printout. In Exercise 7 you are asked to extend this program so that it prints out both the original array and the sorted array.

```
95    REM SHELL SORT
96    REM ****
100   DATA __, __, __, __, __, __, __, __
110   N=8
120   FOR J=1 TO N
130     READ A(J)
140   NEXT J
150   S=INT(N/2)
160   WHILE S>=1
110     GOSUB 200        'PERFORM S SEPARATE INSERTION SORTS
120     S=INT(S/2)
130   WEND
140   REM ARRAY IS SORTED
150   '
160   '
200   REM *** S SEPARATE INSERTION SORTS
210   FOR K=1 TO S
220     FOR M=K TO N-S STEP S
230       J=M
240       B=A(M+S)
250       DONE$="NO"
260       WHILE DONE$="NO" AND J>=K
270         IF B>=A(J) THEN DONE$="YES"
                       ELSE A(J+S)=A(J) : J=J-S
280       WEND
290       A(J+S)=B
300     NEXT M
310   NEXT K
320   RETURN
```

Exercises

4. In sorting 16 numbers by the Shell sort, how many passes would there be? Same question for 20 numbers. Same question for 34 numbers.

5. Perform by hand the Shell sort on

7	28	13	29	10	21	8	4

6. Modify the Shell sort program segment so that it will print the DATA numbers both in their original order and also in sorted order. Run the program for the data in Exercise 5.

7. Which lines would you need to change to Shell sort 25 numbers?

★ 8. Apply the Shell sort to a list of 25 names.

★★ 9. Write a program to generate 100 random integers and sort them first by the bubble sort and then by the Shell sort. Note the time it takes by each method. Rerun your program several times, using different random integers. Then repeat, using 200 random integers.

Solutions to Selected Exercises

Chapter 1 Exercises

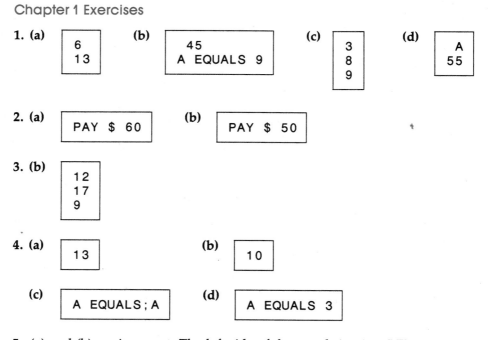

1. (a)
```
6
13
```
(b)
```
45
A EQUALS 9
```
(c)
```
3
8
9
```
(d)
```
A
55
```

2. (a) `PAY $ 60`   (b) `PAY $ 50`

3. (b)
```
12
17
9
```

4. (a) `13`   (b) `10`

(c) `A EQUALS ; A`   (d) `A EQUALS 3`

5. (a) and (b) are incorrect. The left side of the equal sign in a LET statement must be a single variable.
(c) is incorrect. The computer does not understand the word EQUAL.

6. (a)

```
HOWDY
  9
 16
```

(b)

```
3
```

7.

```
SO  LONGJONES
SO  LONG  JONES
```

8. 30   PRINT X$; " EXAM SCORE";G

9.

```
JOHNSMITH
JOHN  SMITH
```

Chapter 2 Exercises

3.

```
10  DATA 1,2
20  READ YDS,FT
30  LET INS=YDS*36+FT*12
40  PRINT YDS;"YARDS AND";FT;"FEET EQUALS";INS;"INCHES"
50  END
```

4.

```
10  DATA 8,23,14
20  READ A,B,C
30  LET AVG=(A+B+C)/3
40  PRINT "AVERAGE IS";AVG
50  END
```

5. Version (a) would appear. You would have to break from AUTO mode after line number 30 is given.

6. HELLO   would be printed on the screen.
SO   LONG   would be printed by the printer.

9.

```
KAREN
SMITH
GOOD  EVENING
```

10.

```
JAMES
```

Chapter 3 Exercises

1. **(a)** Under the 1 of the line number 10.
   (b) The right-arrow key.
2. **(a)** As a box in place of the letter "P".
   (b) The space bar.

Chapter 4 Exercises

2.
```
10   INPUT  "TYPE  TWO  NUMBERS" ; A , B
20   SUM=A+B
30   PRINT "THE  SUM OF " ; A ; "AND " ; B ; " I S " ; SUM
40   END
```

3. What follows the semicolon in an INPUT statement must be a variable.

7.
```
WHAT  IS  YOUR  NAME?  JOE
HELLOJOE
```

8. **(a)** IS 180 INCHES
   (b) Change line 20 to

   20   LPRINT YARDS;"YARDS IS";YARDS*36;"INCHES"

9.
```
10   INPUT  "WHAT  IS  YOUR  F IRST  NAME " ; F IRST$
20   PR INT  "WELL,  " ; F IRST$ ;
30   INPUT  "  WHAT  IS  YOUR  LAST  NAME " ; LAST$
```

11. **(a)**
```
10   INPUT  "ENTER  NUMBER  OF  YARDS " ; YDS
20   LPR INT  "ENTER  NUMBER  OF  YARDS" ; YDS
30   INS=YDS*36
40   LPR INT  YDS; "YARDS  EQUALS" ; INS; " INCHES"
50   END
```

   (b) Change line 20 to

   20   LPRINT "ENTER NUMBER OF YARDS?";YDS

Chapter 5 Exercises

1. **(a)** 10 **(b)** 19 **(c)** 5.5 **(d)** 13 **(e)** 19 **(f)** 20
2. **(a)** $(A+B)/2$ **(b)** $5*A\wedge 2 + B$ **(c)** $(A+B)/(C+D)$

3. **(a)** $5.3E+7$ **(b)** $7.92E+8$ **(c)** $1.34E-8$ **(d)** $2.56897E-4$

4. **(a)** 472.157   **(b)** 5,813,340   **(c)** 0.531461

5. **(a)** Legal.
   (b) Legal. The # symbol represents double precision.
   (c) Illegal. The first character must be a letter.
   (d) Illegal. NAME is a keyword.

6. **(a)** 3   **(b)** 4   **(c)** 9   **(d)** 1.73205

7. **(a)** $SQR(A \wedge 2 + B \wedge 2)$

8. **(a)** 0   **(b)** 0   **(c)** 1   **(d)** 4   **(e)** 5.4

Chapter 6 Exercises

1. **(a)** 4   **(b)** 11   **(c)** 7   **(d)** 3

2.
```
10  INPUT  "TYPE A NUMBER" ; NUM
20  IF NUM>=9 THEN PRINT NUM; "IS AT LEAST NINE"
               ELSE PRINT NUM; "IS LESS THAN NINE"
30  END
```

4.
```
10  INPUT  "NUMBER OF BASKETBALLS" ; NUM
20  IF NUM<5 THEN COST=12*NUM
               ELSE COST=10*NUM
30  PRINT NUM; "BASKETBALLS COST $" ; COST
40  END
```

8. **(a)**
   (1)   GOOD LUCK
   (2)   HIRED

Chapter 7 Exercises

1. **(a)**

```
4               6               8
4    6
8
```

(b)

```
COL  A          COL  B
  4               16
  5               25
  6               36
```

2.

```
1                    2                    3                    4                    5
6                    7                    8
```

3. (a)

```
4   5   6  BING
```

(b)

```
4   5   6
BING
```

4.

```
COL  A            COL  B            COL  C
  5                  6                  7
                     8
                     9                 1 0
```

5.

```
ZONE ONE        ZONE TWO        ZONE THREE
ZONE ONE        IS THIS IN ZONE TWO?        ZONE  THREE?
```

Chapter 8 Exercises

2. (a)

```
1
GOOD  DAY
2
GOOD  DAY
3
GOOD  DAY
JOE
```

(b)

```
1
3
6
10
15
```

(c)

```
COL  A            COL  B
  1                  2
  4                  4
  9                  6
 16                  8
```

(d)

```
HOWDY  1
HOWDY  2
HOWDY  3
HOWDY  5
```

3.

```
10   FOR N=11 TO 15
20      PRINT N; "SQUARED EQUALS" ;N^2
30   NEXT N
40   END
```

5.
```
10  PRINT "CENTIGRADE","FAHRENHEIT"
20  FOR CELS=0 TO 100 STEP 10
30    FAHR=(CELS*9/5)+32
40    PRINT CELS,FAHR
50  NEXT CELS
60  END
```

8.
```
10  SUM=0
20  FOR N=1 TO 100
30    SUM=SUM+1/N
40  NEXT N
50  PRINT SUM
60  END
```

15. (a)
```
10  FOR J=5 TO 1 STEP -1
20    PRINT J;
30  NEXT J
40  PRINT "BLAST OFF"
50  END
```

(b)
```
10  FOR J=5 TO 1 STEP -1
20    PRINT J;
30  NEXT J
40  PRINT
50  PRINT "BLAST OFF"
60  END
```

Chapter 9 Exercises

1. 27

2. (a)
```
10  DATA "SMITH",75,93,"BOND",82,87
20  DATA "JONES",92,94,"PARK",85,96
30  DATA "XYZ",-1,-1
40  READ NAM$,G1,G2
50  WHILE NAM$,<>"XYZ"
60    IF G1+G2>=180 THEN PRINT NAM$
70    READ NAM$,G1,G2
80  WEND
90  END
```

6.

```
NAME                WAGE
SMITH                200
CHAN                 150
KATZ                 210
OUT OF DATA IN 80
```

8.

```
10   PRINT  "SUM OF POSITIVE NUMBERS"
20   SUM=0
30   INPUT  "TYPE A NUMBER OR -1 TO STOP";NUM
40   WHILE NUM<>-1
50      SUM=SUM+NUM
60      INPUT  "TYPE A NUMBER OR -1 TO STOP";NUM
70   WEND
80   PRINT  "SUM=";SUM
90   END
```

9.

```
1  5  14  30  55
```

12. (a)

```
X EQUALS 1
```

(b) 1 and so on *indefinitely*.
2
3
4
.
.
.

17. (a)

```
10   INPUT  "TYPE A POSITIVE INTEGER";NUM
20   IF NUM MOD 2=0 THEN PRINT NUM;"IS EVEN"
                   ELSE PRINT NUM;"IS ODD"
30   END
```

Chapter 10 Exercises

2. The computer will never reach the new line 85. Line 60 of the loop body causes it to branch to line number 90 after the flag is read. In structured programs, we never use GOTO or IF-THEN (line number) to exit from the loop body.

Chapter 11 Exercises

1.

```
10    DATA 4,7,6,2,8,6,6,9,1,8
20    SIXES=0
30    EIGHTS=0
40    FOR J=1 TO 10
50      READ NUM
60        IF NUM=6 THEN SIXES=SIXES+1
70        IF NUM=8 THEN EIGHTS=EIGHTS+1
80    NEXT J
90    PRINT SIXES;"SIXES"
100   PRINT EIGHTS;"EIGHTS"
110   END
```

3.

```
10    PRINCIPAL=200
20    RATE=.05
30    YRS=0
40    WHILE PRINCIPAL*(1+RATE)^YRS<=400
50      YRS=YRS+1
60    WEND
70    PRINT "OVER $400 IN YEAR";YRS
80    PRINT "BALANCE OF $";PRINCIPAL*(1+RATE)^YRS
90    END
```

12. BREAK IN 40

13. (a) Use a WHILE loop. Here is the pseudo-code

Before COUNT=0 : PRODUCT=1 : SUM=0
Prime the pump with READ X

During WHILE not flag
  COUNT=COUNT+1
  PRODUCT=PRODUCT*X
  SUM=SUM+X
  READ new X
WEND

After Print results

Chapter 12 Exercises

1.

```
10    INPUT "TEST SCORE";SCORE
20    IF SCORE>=85 THEN GRADE$="GOOD"
30    IF SCORE>=75 AND SCORE<85THEN GRADE$="FAIR"
40    IF SCORE<75 THEN GRADE$="POOR"
50    PRINT "GRADE: ";GRADE$
60    END
```

6.
```
PICK TWO NUMBERS? 5,9
  5 LESS THAN 9
  5 EQUALS 9
```

11. (b)
```
10  INPUT "ENTER AGE, YEARS WORKED";A,W
20  IF A>=65 THEN 40 ELSE 70
30  REM THEN
40    PRINT "MAY RETIRE"
50    GOTO 80
60  REM ELSE
70    IF A>=59 AND W>=20 THEN PRINT "MAY RETIRE"
                         ELSE PRINT "MAY NOT RETIRE"
80  END
```

14. (a) The printout would be

```
DOOR 1. YOU WON A COLOR TV
```

(b) Line 15 should be

15 IF DOOR<1 OR DOOR>3 THEN PRINT "INVALID ENTRY" : GOTO 100

Chapter 13 Exercises

1. (a)
```
 *
  *
   *
    *
     *
```

(b)
```
HELLO
A
        23
```

3. (a)
```
3.52
4.92
7.00
```

(b)
```
10  F$="##    ###"
20  FOR NUM=3 TO 10
30    PRINT USING F$;NUM,NUM*NUM
40  NEXT NUM
50  END
```

Chapter 14 Exercises

2.
```
10   DATA  8,5,7,3,9,4,6
20   READ MIN
30   FOR K=2 TO 7
40      READ X
50       IF X<MIN THEN MIN=X
60   NEXT K
70   PRINT MIN
80   END
```

3. 8,14, and 19.

4.
```
10   DATA  14,28,19,32,29,30,-1
20   READ X
30   MAX=X
40   WHILE X<>-1
50      IF X>MAX THEN MAX=X
60      READ X
70   WEND
80   PRINT MAX
90   END
```

Note that lines 20 and 30 could also have been

```
20   READ MAX
30   X=MAX
```

Chapter 15 Exercises

5.
```
10    DATA 3,6,4,2,8,9,7,3,6,5,9,5
20    COUNT=0
30    FOR J=1 TO 6
40       READ A,B
50       PRINT "WHAT IS";A;"X";B
60       INPUT YOUR.ANS
70       IF YOUR.ANS=A*B THEN PRINT "   YOU ARE CORRECT" : COUNT=
                                                          COUNT+1
                       ELSE PRINT "   SORRY. THE ANSWER IS";A*B
80    NEXT J
90    PRINT "**** YOUR SCORE WAS";COUNT;"CORRECT ****"
100   END
```

7. You cannot use a variable (STATE$ in the example) in an INPUT prompt.

Chapter 16 Exercises

1. (a)

```
1    25
2    49
3    81
```

(b)

```
HELLO
3
```

3. (a) The printout will be

```
MENU OF CHOICES
        1)      FOR DEPOSIT
        2)      FOR WITHDRAWAL
        3)      FOR BALANCE INFORMATION
TYPE YOUR SELECTION? 5
---IT WAS A PLEASURE SERVING YOU---
```

4.

```
100  PRINT "MENU  :  WHAT INFORMATION DO YOU NEED?"
110  PRINT "   1)   LIST STUDENTS WITH INPUT MAJOR"
120  PRINT "   2)   LIST STUDENTS WITH SCORE OVER 89"
130  INPUT "TYPE CHOICE 1 OR 2";SEL
140  ON SEL GOSUB 300,400
150  END
160  '
170  '
300  REM MAJOR
310  INPUT "TYPE FIRST FOUR LETTERS OF MAJOR";MAJ$
320  FOR J=1 TO 6
330    READ NAM$,SUBJ$,GRADE
340    IF SUBJ$=MAJ$ THEN PRINT NAM$
350  NEXT J
360  RETURN
370  '
400  REM SCORE>89
410  FOR J=1 TO 6
420    READ NAM$,SUBJ$,GRADE
430    IF GRADE>89 THEN PRINT NAM$
440  NEXT J
450  RETURN
```

8. (a)

```
CHOOSE YOUR VACATION PLAN
TYPE 1 FOR ECONOMY, 2 FOR DELUXE? 1
HOTEL: HOW MANY NIGHTS? 5
CAR RENTAL: HOW MANY DAYS? 4
ECONOMY VACATION
HOTEL ROOM $ 200
CAR RENTAL $ 60
ROOM SERVICE $ 0
TOTAL BILL $ 260
IT WAS A PLEASURE SERVING YOU.
```

(b)

```
CHOOSE YOUR VACATION
TYPE 1 FOR ECONOMY, 2 FOR DELUXE? 2
HOTEL: HOW MANY NIGHTS? 5
CAR RENTAL: HOW MANY DAYS? 3
CAR: TYPE M FOR MERCEDES, J FOR JAGUAR? M
DO YOU WISH BREAKFAST IN ROOM, Y OR N? Y
DELUXE VACATION
HOTEL ROOM $ 400
CAR RENTAL $ 270
ROOM SERVICE $ 50
TOTAL BILL $ 720
IT WAS A PLEASURE SERVING YOU.
```

Chapter 17 Exercises

1.
```
10    DATA "SNOW","A","BOND","B","FOSTER","C"
20    DATA "HALL","B","JONES","A","XYZ","XYZ"
30    COUNT=0
40    READ NAM$,GRADE$
50    WHILE NAM$<>"XYZ"
60      IF GRADE$="A" THEN PRINT NAM$ : COUNT=COUNT+1
70      READ NAM$,GRADE$
80    WEND
90    PRINT COUNT;"GOT AN A"
100   END
```

4. As soon as the last name in the DATA group matches, the computer exits from the WHILE loop. Therefore, the first name of only the first-occurring match of last names will be printed. For example, if "JOHN","SMITH" comes before "ED","SMITH" and "PETER","SMITH" in the DATA list, then only JOHN will be printed.

6. If WANT$ is not on the DATA list, NAM$ will eventually become the flag "XYZ". The printout would be

```
XYZ NOT ON LIST
```

Chapter 18 Exercises

2.
```
10    RANDOMIZE
20    SEVENS=0
30    FOR ROLL=1 TO 100
40      DIE1=INT(6*RND)+1
50      DIE2=INT(6*RND)+1
60      SUM=DIE1+DIE2
70      IF SUM=7 THEN SEVENS=SEVENS+1
80    NEXT ROLL
90    PRINT "SEVEN WAS ROLLED";SEVENS;"TIMES"
100   END
```

6. (a) 2 (b) 5

7. (a) [2,3,4,5,6,7,8,9] (b) INT(5*RND)+4

8. The given expression has an equal probability (namely, 1 in 11) of generating any of the numbers in the list. However, when rolling a pair of dice, there is a "bell curve" distribution rather than an equal (linear) distribution. This means that the numbers towards the center of the list have a greater probability than at either end. For example, there is only a 1 in 18 probability of rolling a 3, and the same probability for an 11, but there is a 1 in 6 chance of rolling a 7.

15.
```
10   RANDOMIZE
20   HITS=0
30   FOR AT.BATS=1 TO 26
40      IF RND<.312 THEN HITS=HITS+1
50   NEXT AT.BATS
60   PRINT "SMITH GOT";HITS;"HITS"
70   END
```

Chapter 19 Exercises

1. (a)
```
2    2
2    4
2    6
HI
3    3
3    6
3    9
HI
4    4
4    8
4    12
HI
```

(b)
```
7
```

(c)
```
3
```

5.
```
10    FOR LINE=1 TO 3
20       SUM=0
30       READ NUM
40       WHILE NUM<>-1
50          SUM=SUM+NUM
60          READ NUM
70       WEND
80       PRINT "LINE";LINE;"SUM=";SUM
90    NEXT LINE
100   DATA 5,8,24,17,19,14,-1
110   DATA 3,22,15,-1
120   DATA 10,18,14,5,18,-1
130   END
```

6.

STUDENT	AVERAGE
1	80
2	170
3	248

14.

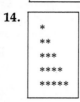

```
*
**
***
****
*****
```

Chapter 20 Exercises

1. When you wish to access an element numbered higher than 10.

2.
```
70   IF VOTE = 1 THEN A = A + 1
72   IF VOTE = 2 THEN B = B + 1
74   IF VOTE = 3 THEN C = C + 1
```

7. Line 20 should be

```
20   PRINT "BETWEEN";(10*K)+1;"AND";(10*K)+10
```

8. *Hint:* To determine the appropriate interval for a grade X, use the formula $Y = X \backslash 10$.

14. (a) 89

(b)
```
10    DIM F(25)
20    F(1)=1
30    F(2)=1
40    FOR K=3 TO 25
50       F(K)=F(K-2)+F(K-1)
60    NEXT K
70    FOR K=1 TO 25
80       PRINT F(K);
90    NEXT K
100   END
```

Chapter 21 Exercises

1. (a)
```
10   DATA "TOM","DICK","HARRY","JACK","JILL"
20   FOR K=1 TO 5
30      READ NAM$(K)
40   NEXT K
50   N=INT(5*RND)+1
60   PRINT NAM$(N)
70   END
```

4.
```
10   DATA  "SUNDAY",85,"MONDAY",78,"TUESDAY",87,"WEDNESDAY",90
20   DATA  "THURSDAY",72,"FRIDAY",65,"SATURDAY",74
30   SUM=0
40   FOR K=1 TO 7
50     READ DAY$(K),TEMP(K)
60     SUM=SUM+TEMP(K)
70   NEXT K
80   AVG=SUM/7
90   PRINT "AVERAGE TEMPERATURE: ";AVG
100  FOR K=1 TO 7
110    IF TEMP(K)>AVG THEN PRINT DAY$(K)
120  NEXT K
130  PRINT "WERE ABOVE AVERAGE"
140  END
```

6. (a) JACK OF DIAMONDS **(b)** EIGHT OF CLUBS **(c)** SIX OF SPADES

7. It sets the value of the appropriate element in the array A to −1.

Chapter 22 Exercises

1.
```
10   DATA  "HARRY","DAN","LOU","AL","JEAN","BABS"
20   DATA  "ALF","AARON","FLAG"
30   READ NAM$
40   WHILE NAM$<>"FLAG"
50     IF MID$(NAM$,2,1)="A" THEN PRINT NAM$
60     READ NAM$
70   WEND
80   END
```

3.
```
10   DATA  "HENRY HIGGINS"
20   READ NAM$
30   J=1
40   WHILE MID$(NAM$,J,1)<>" "
50     J=J+1
60   WEND
70   BLANKPOS=J
80   LAST$=MID$(NAM$,BLANKPOS+1)
90   FIRST$=LEFT$(NAM$,BLANKPOS-1)
100  PRINT LAST$;", ";FIRST$
110  END
```

Note: Lines 30 through 70 could be replaced by
30 BLANKPOS = INSTR(NAM," ")

10. (a) JOE*****

17.

```
┌─────────┐
│  D  R   │
│  7  0   │
└─────────┘
```

18. R

Chapter 23 Exercises

1. 5   8   3   9   4   10

11. (a) One example would be
   8   7   1   2   3   4   5   6

(b) Since it would perform one pass after the numbers were already sorted, the bubble sort program would actually perform 3 passes.

Chapter 24 Exercises

1. (a)

FIRST = 1, LAST = 11
FIRST = 1, LAST = 5
FIRST = 4, LAST = 5

Then 52 is located.

(b)

FIRST = 1, LAST = 11
FIRST = 1, LAST = 5
FIRST = 4, LAST = 5
FIRST = 5, LAST = 5
FIRST = 5, LAST = 4

53 is not on the list.

2. (a)

FIRST = 1, LAST = 16
FIRST = 1, LAST = 7
FIRST = 5, LAST = 7
FIRST = 7, LAST = 7

Then 38 is located.

Chapter 25 Exercises

1. (a) DIM A(2,5),B(2),C(3,3)

(b) row, column

(c) FOR ROW = 1 TO 5

2. (a)

```
1
```

(b)

```
11
22
```

(c)

```
4  7
```

3.

```
8
9
10
```

4. (a)

```
10   DATA  3,1,5,8,2,0,0,4,9,11,2,9
20   DIM A(3,4)
30   FOR ROW=1 TO 3
40      FOR COL=1 TO 4
50         READ A(ROW,COL)
60      NEXT COL
70   NEXT ROW
```

(b)

```
80    PRINT "ROW","SUM OF ENTRIES"
90    FOR ROW=1 TO 3
100      SUM=0
110      FOR COL=1 TO 4
120         SUM=SUM+A(ROW,COL)
130      NEXT COL
140      PRINT ROW,SUM
150   NEXT ROW
160   END
```

Chapter 26 Exercises

1. **(a)** Since the "I" stands for Input, the statement will be used to retrieve information.

   (b) Since the "O" stands for Output, the statement will be used to create a file.

2. **(a)** The # symbol is missing before the 1.

   (b) The correct statement is simply CLOSE #1

8.
```
10  OPEN "I",#1,"ROSTER"
20  COUNT=0
30  WHILE NOT EOF(1)
40    INPUT #1,N$,G1,G2
50    COUNT=COUNT+1
60  WEND
70  CLOSE #1
80  PRINT "FILE CONTAINS";COUNT;"RECORDS"
90  END
```

11.
```
10   OPEN "I",#1,"ROSTERA"
20   OPEN "O",#3,"ROSTERC"
30   WHILE NOT EOF(1)
40     INPUT #1,A$
50     OPEN "I",#2,"ROSTERB"
60     WHILE NOT EOF(2)
70       INPUT #2,B$
80       IF A$=B$ THEN WRITE #3,A$
90     WEND
100    CLOSE #2
110  WEND
120  CLOSE #1
130  CLOSE #3
140  END
```

Chapter 27 Exercises

1. (a)

$$LSET\ PRICE\$ = MKS\$(P)$$
$$LSET\ NUM\$ = MKI\$(N)$$

(b)

$$P = CVS(PRICE\$)$$
$$N = CVI(NUM\$)$$

2. (a) MKI$(NUMREC)
   (b) 2

3.
```
10  OPEN "R",#1,"ROSTER",12
20  FIELD #1,8 AS PERSON$,4 AS YEAR$
30  FOR REC=1 TO 3
40    GET #1,REC
50    PRINT PERSON$,CVS(YEAR$)
60  NEXT REC
70  CLOSE #1
80  END
```

4. (a)

```
10    OPEN "R",#1,"EMPLOY",15
20    FIELD #1,2 AS NUMREC$
30    FIELD #1,7 AS PERSON$,4 AS YRHIRED$,4 AS PAYRATE$
40    FOR REC=2 TO 7
50       READ NAM$,YR,RATE
60       LSET PERSON$=NAM$
70       LSET YRHIRED$=MKS$(YR)
80       LSET PAYRATE$=MKS$(RATE)
90       PUT #1,REC
100   NEXT REC
110   LSET NUMREC$=MKI$(6)
120   PUT #1,1
130   CLOSE #1
140   DATA "SMITH",1980,6.00,"COHN",1982,6.50
150   DATA "BOTZ",1979,5.00,"CANE",1985,4.00
160   DATA "PARKER",1983,7.00,"LUPO",1980,7.00
170   END
```

(b)

```
10    OPEN "R",#1,"EMPLOY",15
20    FIELD #1,2 AS NUMREC$
30    FIELD #1,7 AS PERSON$,4 AS YRHIRED$,4 AS PAYRATE$
40    GET #1,1
50    PRINT "EMPLOYEES HIRED BEFORE 1983"
60    FOR REC=2 TO CVI(NUMREC$)+1
70       GET #1,REC
80       IF CVS(YRHIRED$)<1983 THEN PRINT PERSON$
90    NEXT REC
100   CLOSE #1
110   END
```

Chapter 28 Exercises

1. Positions 7, 5, and 3.

2. Position 4 will have desirability value of 3. Therefore, the value of V(4) will be 3.

3. Insert the following lines in the Moving-at-Random program:

```
141   IF HUM>=COMP-2 AND HUM<COMP THEN 150
142   PRINT "HUMAN LOSES. ILLEGAL MOVE"
143   GO TO 220
```

Note: For the GET SMART program, make sure you don't update the desirability values for games won by illegal moves.

Index

ABS( ) function, 310
Absolute value, 310
Addition, 2
Algorithm, 13
AND operator, 54
Animation, 296–298, 303–307
APPEND, 265
Arrays
  one-dimensional, 195–205
  one-dimensional string, 210–217
  parallel, 211–212
  two-dimensional, 244–246
Artificial intelligence, xvi, 286–288
ASC( ) function, 225
ASCII code, 224
Assignment statement, 2, 4, 69.
  Also see LET statement
AUTO command, 18
Average, 95
  grades above class average, 204

Backslash \, 45
BASIC
  acronym, xi
  expression, 1, 41–47
  line numbering, 2, 17, 19
Binary chopping, 320
Binary search, 238–243
Binomial coefficients, 322
Blank PRINT statement, 66
Boolean variable (mock), 168–169, 234
Booting up, xiv
Bubble sort, 231–235

Calculus program, 326
Card-dealing programs, 212–215
Central Processing Unit (CPU), xii

CHR$( ) function, 225
CLOSE statements
  random file, 273
  sequential file, 259
Coding–decoding, 227, 229, 334
Coin flipping, 173–174, 176, 189
Colon, 58
COLOR, 291, 300
Commas in PRINT statements, 63, 64
Compound interest, 113, 312
Computed GOTO, 127
Computer-assisted instruction, 152
Concatenation operator, 222–223
Control statements, 49, 51, 127, 158
Control variable, 70
Convert functions
  CVD( ), 274
  CVI( ), 274
  CVS( ), 274
CPU, xii
CTRL/C, 18, 97
CTRL/J, 52

Data file, 259–283
Data pointer, 83
DATA statement, 2, 3, 83
Debugging, 6, 117–119
Decimal point alignment, 133
DEF FN, 311
DELETE command, 19, 27, 29
Dice rolling, 176–178, 181
DIM statement
  one-dimensional, 198
  two-dimensional, 224–246
Diskettes, xi
Divisibility, 45, 105
Division symbol, 5

Dollar sign, 9, 134–136, 210. *Also
  see* String variables
Drunkard's walk, 319
Dummy variable, 212

E, 43
Echo LPRINT statements, 36
Editing
  IBM, 25–27
  MBASIC, 27–30
Efficiency
  searching, 242
  sorting, 235
ELSE, 51
END statement, 2
EOF function, 261–262, 275
Erasing a line, 19
Error messages, 21–22, 198
Errors, 21–23, 81, 96
Euclidean algorithm, 316
Execute, 17
EXP( ) function, 310
Exponentiation, 41, 310

Factorial, 88
Fibonacci numbers, 209
Fields of a file, 272–276
Files
  random access, 271–283
  sequential, 259–270
Flag, 93, 95
FOR-NEXT, 69–90
  nested, 186–191
Format variable, 134
Functions
  built in, 310
  user defined, 311

366